PAUL: AN APOSTLE'S JOURNEY

PAUL

An Apostle's Journey

Douglas A. Campbell

WILLIAM B. EERDMANS PUBLISHING COMPANY

GRAND RAPIDS, MICHIGAN

Wm. B. Eerdmans Publishing Co.
2140 Oak Industrial Drive NE, Grand Rapids, Michigan 49505
www.eerdmans.com

ISBN 978-0-8028-7347-7

Library of Congress Cataloging-in-Publication Data

Names: Campbell, Douglas A. (Douglas Atchison), 1961- author.
Title: Paul : an Apostle's journey / Douglas A. Campbell.
Description: Grand Rapids : Eerdmans Publishing Co., 2018. | Includes
    bibliographical references and index.
Identifiers: LCCN 2017029709 | ISBN 9780802873477 (pbk. : alk. paper)
Subjects: LCSH: Paul, the Apostle, Saint.
Classification: LCC BS2506.3 .C365 2018 | DDC 225.9/2 [B] —dc23
    LC record available at https://lccn.loc.gov/2017029709

To Dorothy Leigh Campbell, nee Atchison (1937–)
and Graeme Douglas Campbell (1931–)
From whom I have received so much

Contents

CONTENTS

Preface

This book is designed to introduce the apostle Paul to a group of students or adult learners who haven't had much exposure to the dense scholarly conversation about him. The material it provides should supplement a series of lectures and studies of key passages in his letters nicely. If this proves to be the case, however, may I suggest interleaving some field trips into the standard classroom or Sunday school experience? In my teaching I emphasize two especially. The students in my "Life and Thought of Paul" class are strongly encouraged to go on a prison visit. We also travel to the site of a large local former slave plantation, Stagville. There we read out the Household Codes (see chapter six) in the luxurious owner's house and then again in the slave quarters. The impact of these embodied pedagogical exercises is hard to overstate. They have proved so valuable I would recommend as many as you can organize—perhaps to a morgue, a hospital, a synagogue, and/or a workshop where people are laboring hard with their hands. These are other key locations for Paul's instruction and for the circumstances that elicited his letters. An evening meal together is a good idea as well, preferably with a letter read out at the end of it by candlelight. I suspect that this sort of course will prove unforgettable to its participants, and (perhaps more importantly) it will shape them in tangibly Pauline ways.

Acknowledgments

Michael Thomson lured me into a restaurant during the Society of Biblical Literature conference in San Diego and I emerged having agreed to do something, although the exact details at the time were a little blurry. It turned out to be this book and I thank him for prevailing upon me. I have needed to provide people with an accessible overview of Paul, and he was quite right to see this and to press me to just do it.

All of the staff at Eerdmans have, as usual, been friendly, supportive, and professional, for which I am grateful, as has the indefatigable and indefatigably cheerful Judith Heyhoe, our in-house editor at Duke. And I am also deeply grateful to the professional, efficient, and delightfully happy staff at the National Humanities Center, where I spent a wonderful year on sabbatical.

I want to thank my "focus group." They helped me to find the right way to talk with people who have not been shaped by a seminary experience. There is an uncanny resemblance here to members of my family: Rupert, Georgia, Graeme, and Leigh.

Finally, I am grateful in ways that words can barely express to my best friend, my life partner, and my soulmate, Rachel. Nothing happens without her, and so much happens because of her. She is truly "lovely in form and beautiful," not to mention talented, supportive, insightful, faithful, and—most important of all—a great deal of fun.

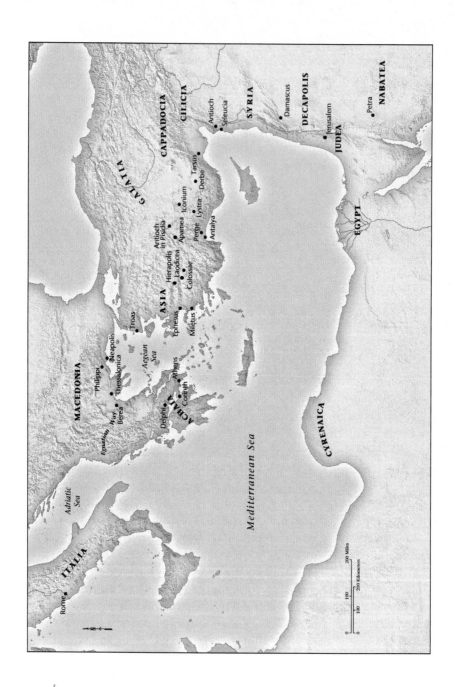

200 mi´

Introduction

Paul's influence

The apostle Paul is the most influential political philosopher in the USA today, and arguably in the rest of the world as well, and this surely makes him one of the most important figures in human history. He is not a contemporary philosopher, but he still exerts an unprecedented influence on current American culture and politics—far more than any modern figure, whether we are talking about someone like John Locke, who greatly influenced the Constitution, or a figure like David Brooks, who writes in the *New York Times* and is read by 1.3 million people every day. This is quite an achievement when we consider that Paul lived two thousand years ago and left a literary legacy of just a dozen letters or so (and one of them is very short). It is nevertheless this tiny literary legacy that drives his influence.

Thirteen letters gathered together in the New Testament bear Paul's name and comprise about 25 percent of that scriptural collection.[1] But he exerts an influence out of all proportion to this percentage. Of all the writers in the New Testament, Paul addresses churches directly and provides clear instructions about the significance of what Jesus did. Consequently he tends to be the go-to person for most modern Christian preachers, and especially for those who are Protestants of some sort who make up about one quarter of the current worldwide Christian population. The rest of the New Testament, and even of the Bible as a whole, is then frequently read in his terms, through Paul's spectacles we might say. And the Bible has had an enormous impact on modern American culture, and on Christian and post-Christian countries elsewhere, and still does—a Pauline Bible.

A third of the world's population—almost 2.2 billion people—is in some sense Christian; there are fewer and fewer Christians in European and post-European countries but more and more everywhere else. When these adherents go to church they will most likely hear a short passage written by Paul that they will have expounded to them as Scripture. Many of these listeners will try to understand this ancient paragraph, to reflect upon it, and to apply it, believing that God is speaking through it. It may be the basis for their prayers, meditations, exhortations, corrections, teaching, thanksgiving, and praise. The most zealous of these church attenders will read and ponder texts written by Paul every day. Few writers in the entire human race, if any, have had this influence. It should be no surprise to learn then that the interpretation of Paul is deeply and even bitterly contested.

He wrote a long time ago, not very much that he wrote has been preserved, and what he says is enormously important. These three factors create a situation ripe for interpretative conflict. We want Paul to say certain things, irrespective of whether he actually said them, because the stakes for him doing this are so high. If Paul says it, in some sense God says it. Did he support capital punishment? Was he anti-gay? Did he care about abortion? Did he believe in low tax rates? Many of these questions seldom if ever crossed the busy missionary's mind, but we need him to say something about them, and different people want him to say different things.

The interpretation of Paul is consequently one of the most important tasks for the Christian in the world today as well as being one of the most debated and confused. I myself would go so far as to suggest that the real Paul has been largely buried under later arguments and conflicts about how to read him. His presentation today—and certainly in the US—frequently derives more from the culture and politics of the person reading him than from Paul himself, which is why I am writing this book.

We badly need to recover the real Paul. We don't do this by pretending that we don't have reasons for reading him or positions that we want him to endorse. We all do, and I am no exception. I am deeply invested in what he says. But we recover his authentic voice by being honest about our reasons and positions, and assessing carefully, with the help of others, whether they are distorting the evidence that he has left behind for us. So I will try to do just this. And the best way to do this is by telling his story.

Storytelling

Paul led a very interesting life. He traveled a lot, got into numerous confrontations, jams, and controversies, and met and converted a lot of people. We have letters from him to about fifteen churches, eleven of which he personally founded, and this was no mean feat within the deeply hostile ancient pagan world. God worked mightily through him at times, while Paul probably felt utterly abandoned by God at others. He spent many years at the end of his life in prison, probably deeply frustrated. But it is only as we tell this story in detail that we will uncover the things that Paul thought about God and Jesus, and about missionary and church work, which is to say, his theology. This is because Paul learned all these things during this activity. They are intertwined together. We can't understand his thinking unless we grasp it within all the other activity that was shaping it (and this is really the case for everyone). As we investigate this synthesis of thought and action we will find out more about what sort of person Paul was, which is important as well. What Paul thought, what he did, and what sort of person he was, are, as for all people, tightly bound up with one another. All these things can only be gathered together by a story, so a story we will tell.[2]

But as soon as we realize that this is the right form for our description, we are faced with an initial problem. What materials are we going to use to tell this story? We must ask a historian's question about our sources that we will investigate carefully to work out what Paul was doing at any given moment. What are the sources for Paul and are they reliable?

Luke has his own interests

START The sources

There's an interesting little trap here that many people fall into.

There are two sources for Paul's life that are clearly way ahead of any others in importance: (1) his authentic letters; and (2) the book of Acts.

The book of Acts is interesting. It was probably written by the same person who authored the Gospel of Luke. Acts doesn't concentrate exclusively on Paul, so it is not a *bios* or ancient biography of Paul in the way that the Gospels are ancient biographies of Jesus, but Paul does dominate the book. Only Peter rivals Paul's importance, and Peter receives considerably less airtime than Paul does. So we do find a reasonably complete story of Paul in Acts ready-made for us. It stretches from just before his conversion through to a final dramatic voyage to Rome, after which the reader is meant to infer that he was executed.

Alongside Acts, however, we have letters from Paul's own hand. These don't tell us an integrated story in the way that Acts does. Only one letter supplies anything close to a long narrative sequence and that is clearly crafted to fit into a particular argument (Gal. 1:10–2:14). All the letters appear within Paul's story as against outlining it. So it is very tempting to start with the book of Acts—and it does appear in the Bible so it must be true, right?—and slot the letters into that story where they seem to fit best. *But it would be completely wrong to do so.*

Imagine that a nuclear holocaust has taken place and human history has been largely obliterated. A billion years from now scientists and scholars from Alpha Centauri come to earth to undertake research. One of the lucky travelers in the research team is a historian of US presidents. She wants to write a dissertation on the presidency of George W. Bush. In the ash heap of what was the White House she is fortunate enough to find two pieces of evidence: an old copy of a book titled *Bush: My Time Working with the Greatest President Ever* written by his close friend and advisor Karl Rove; and an old flash-drive with 500 emails from Bush to his advisors discussing various political events and what to do about them. How does she proceed?

Does she read the book and then try to fit the evidence of the emails into it, discarding messages when they don't seem to fit with that narrative? The book speaks constantly of Bush's strength and decisiveness as a leader, but the emails reveal a slightly petulant figure who often didn't know what to do. Or does she begin with the emails, squeezing as much information about Bush's life and thought out of them, and then turn to the book to assess its contributions, partly controlling those contributions with the information that she has already gathered from Bush himself? The latter obviously. The book is part history and part propaganda, but the letters come straight from the horse's mouth. The letters must control the spin that is present in Rove's book.

Somewhat strangely, most people get things the wrong way around in the case of Paul. They use Acts first, as an overarching frame for his life, slotting in the letters where they can, and sometimes discarding them when they can't. This is all clearly a big mistake.

We don't know very much about Acts. It is an anonymous work that later tradition ascribes to Luke without much reason for doing so. We don't know who wrote it, when it was written, or, most important of all, why. It might be a wonderful piece of historical work, carefully investigated and meticulously crafted. Or it might be the equivalent of an ancient novel, written in large measure to entertain, filled with fables and exaggerations and anecdotes. There's nothing wrong with the Bible containing entertaining and somewhat fanciful stories; think of Esther or Jonah, or the framing stories of Job and Ecclesiastes, or the delightful tale of Tobit included in Catholic Bibles. Readers just need to recognize what is going on and read accordingly. But is Acts like this? Or does it lie somewhere between these two poles? We just don't know.

Conversely, the letters are not easy, but they are firsthand. They attest directly to the events that were unfolding all around Paul as he wrote them, and often quite unselfconsciously. Paul wasn't trying to write history, so for much of the time they provide disinterested historical evidence. Paul gives us information about his life when he is not even aware that this is what he is doing. They are priceless sources.

We ought to begin reconstructing Paul's life from his letters then, and use this information to control the information supplied by Acts.[3] With an initial biographical framework in place—a basic story—drawn from the letters we will be able to undertake an accurate assessment of the veracity of Acts. Does its information about Paul measure up with what Paul himself said happened, or not? If it does, how does it help us? FOCUS —HOLY SPIRIT

Cutting a long story short, I judge that the individual stories in Acts—what we might call its "episodic" veracity—are 99 percent accurate. The order of those stories, however—its "sequential" veracity—is not strictly historical or chronological. The material is arranged in strips or panels and positioned partly to suggest important overarching themes or truths about the early church, much as the Gospels do as they arrange their stories about Jesus. The author wants his readers to understand that the church was based on an important partnership between Peter and Paul, but that authorization flowed from Peter to Paul, so Peter's activities as a missionary are positioned before most of Paul's in the story. It was more likely the other way around—Paul going on far-flung missionary work before Peter did. A few other similar things are going on.[4]

The author's arrangement of the key characters in the story is carefully worked out so that they constantly travel to Jerusalem, and they meet and authorize one another, again, from Peter and the rest of the Twelve onward. This allows a chain of eyewitnesses to extend through the book from the first apostles, who traveled around with Jesus, down through Paul, who was a controversial early Christian leader, to the author himself at the end of the book. Yet all these characters constantly loop back to the original church in the mother city of Jerusalem. The result of this careful plotting is a multiplication of Paul's journeys to Jerusalem during his ministry. Paul himself only speaks in his letters of three visits to Jerusalem but the careful reader of Acts will see that it has him traveling there five times.

ITS THE CHURCH
MOTHER
ITS THE LENS

IT'S THE TOUCHSTONE

My judgment is that the author of Acts knew exactly what was going on and knew that Paul went to Jerusalem on just three important journeys. He supplies a great deal of information about three visits, while the echoes of these visits that come up twice in other places in the story occupy a mere one and a half verses. To avoid getting tripped up by them in strict historical terms, we must conflate these brief statements into the major events they echo, and continue to presuppose just three action-packed visits by Paul back to Jerusalem during his ministry.[5] So we will have only three Jerusalem visits in the story of Paul that follows.

Once we have made this adjustment, I can find only one other place where the author of Acts presents the situation inaccurately in strict historical terms. He seems to want Paul to arrive in Athens and then to be tried as Socrates was, in heroic solitude, alone. This wasn't the case. Paul went to Athens as he usually did, with his mission team, which at the time, as he tells us himself, comprised Silas and Timothy.[6] This subtle modification of events by the author is a clear and well-motivated move intended to highlight the scandalous and shortsighted nature of Paul's coming trial and execution. Paul, like Socrates, was a good and wise person who was tried and executed foolishly and unjustly.

With this small additional adjustment I judge pretty much everything else the author of Acts says to be on the money—not always in strict order in terms of the overarching story, but the events and incidents are accurate in and of themselves. Acts is highly accurate for an ancient historian's work. In fact, I think that this is only explicable with the realization that for much of the time the author was there, as from time to time the narrative suggests.[7] But what does this story look like now that we have broken with the strict sequence that the book of Acts suggests and that many of us know so well?

Dates, times, and places

We don't know a lot about much of Paul's life—his early childhood years, his Jewish training, the middle part of his Christian ministry, and his long final imprisonment and trial—but we do know a lot about two periods. These two periods are like two spotlights shining on an otherwise dark stage.

The first begins just before his call on the road to Damascus and extends through the first eight years or so of his missionary work. I calculate that this period ran from 34 to 41 CE, so this biographical spotlight is broader but a little dimmer than the one that follows. We know quite a bit about what Paul was doing during this time, first when Tiberius was the emperor of Rome, then the infamous Gaius, better known as Caligula,[8] and finally Claudius. During this period Paul, as usual, did a lot of journeying, from Damascus, through Syrian Antioch, all the way to Greece.

For the next seven years we don't know so much about what Paul was doing. We just have fragments of information like 2 Corinthians 11:23–27, which speaks of various struggles arising from the challenges of traveling in the ancient world, and from trying to gain a hearing in its paranoid and xenophobic cities. Times have obviously been tough, but we have no evidence that Paul achieved anything significant during this period.

Paul starts coming back into view later in 49 CE. Things come into sharper focus in 50; then we know a lot about 51, which I call his year of crisis. This level of detail continues into the spring of 52 and then the details fall off very rapidly, so this is where our second spotlight starts to fade out. It is rather smaller than our first one—that is, shorter in time—but brighter, extending from early 49 through the spring of 52 CE for three important years. During this period we don't see Paul traveling to new places very much. But it does begin with him traveling through a part of modern-day Turkey that he hadn't been in before as he heads to Ephesus, an important city on the east coast of the Aegean Sea. At the end of this period, in the spring of 52 CE, he heads back to Jerusalem in an anxious frame of mind.

We only have information from Acts from this point onward but we can still see things happening for the next five years or so, hence from 52 through 56 CE. Paul travels to Jerusalem and is arrested and imprisoned, eventually traveling to Rome. But after Acts ends its story around 56 we have very little to go on, and it seems most likely that Paul was executed soon after.

In short, Paul's story has these two zones of illumination followed by the lingering details found in Acts concerning his final travels under guard, all of which we could recast in more dramatic terms as scenes in a play or drama.

An opera

As I write this, the rap opera *Hamilton* is on everyone's lips, so imagine an opera unfolding about Paul (which a student did suggest to me once that we should co-write together). It is arranged in two acts (so clearly I have given this proposal some thought).

The key protagonist bursts onto the stage mature and not a little angry in act 1. He is hunting down the blasphemous members of the Jesus movement. But a dramatic conversion takes place, and then eight years of revolutionary missionary work unfold, extending from just near the Jesus movement's headquarters, in Jerusalem, to the distant pagan land of Greece. By the end of this period our hero has succeeded in creating and nurturing a chain of little communities as far as the ancient metropolis of Corinth—the Las Vegas of the ancient world. He has battled ancient pagan culture, along with occasional opposition from local Jews, and has managed to create and to establish small Christian communities in half a dozen pagan towns and cities—a great achievement.

His success now stalls for a bit. Our hero works hard for many years in other regions but achieves very little. Then, suddenly, after an interval of about eight years, things take off again. Mass conversions even take place in the city of Ephesus. But in the midst of these new successes, further challenges arrive. Our hero is repeatedly detained and imprisoned. Charlatans and competitors begin to infiltrate his communities and to challenge his teachings. One of his largest and most important churches to the west, in Corinth, begins to fracture around other leaders and a host of challenging issues—as usual, many involving sex. But our hero fights back. He writes letters furiously, travels, sends delegates, and even escapes a riot, finally ending up in the spring of 52 CE in Corinth, exhausted, but with everything under control. The curtain falls on act 1.

Act 2, like act 1, opens in dramatic circumstances. There is a sudden new twist in the plot—enemies! The pause in Corinth turns out to be a mere lull in an ongoing battle. Lethal opponents arrive in and around Corinth, attacking Paul and his teachings. They drag him before the local governor asking for the death sentence! To understand where they come from, however, we have to flash back three years to a series of bitter disputes that took place in Syrian Antioch and Jerusalem between Paul and his supporters, and certain nameless Jewish Pharisees. These prestigious new converts insist that all of Jesus's followers should become Jews and obey the Torah. This attacks Paul's communities at their very heart! His movement will be wiped out if they succeed.

Again, our hero fights back. He writes letters, stands his ground in court, and prepares to travel to Jerusalem to confront the problem at its source. He even finds the presence of mind to pen one of the most famous texts in human history, his letter to the Romans. This letter—unbeknownst to him, his last will and testament—states in closing that he is journeying back to Jerusalem, hopeful that his conflict with the other Christian leaders living there can be resolved satisfactorily. The arrival of a very large sum of money to give to the Jerusalem poor might make the necessary accommodations rather easier as well. Following this visit our hero says that he wants to travel to strategic new evangelistic pastures like Rome itself, and then beyond Rome to Spain. But these dreams are stillborn. A dramatic and tragic story plays out instead.

Our hero travels to Jerusalem and a riot breaks out around him. He is arrested and imprisoned. This marks the beginning of four years of incarceration and trials interspersed by a horrific sea voyage to Rome. After a long imprisonment in Rome, our hero is summarily tried, unfairly condemned, and executed, at which moment our story—our opera—comes to a close, except to note that the letters our hero dashed off in the midst of all his labors and troubles lived on long after him as one of the most important literary legacies in human history.

Before we plunge into this story in detail, one further feature of its telling is worth noting.

Discoveries

We are interested in what Paul thought about things. What he thought was bound up tightly with all the other ways he acted, but by the end of this book we do want to be able to give a brief account of Paul's "gospel." Gospel is Paul's shorthand for what he thought God was up to when God sent Jesus to enter our human situation to save us in some sense. A host of critical questions circles around this basic claim, and Paul supplied a lot of important answers to them. He was a very smart guy, as well as an early and a particularly significant one. Consequently, Paul was on much more than a geographical journey in his ministry. He was on a theological journey as well. He learned things as he went along. Different situations and diverse people forced him to think things through, doubtless something he did with much prayer and a great deal of searching of the Scriptures in the local synagogues. We will note carefully the lessons Paul learned at each stage of his work. We can detect these lessons accumulating, step by step, as he worked his way around the cities dotting the coast of the Mediterranean Sea. So we will know, by the end of this journey, how to plant and to nurture a Christian community, Paul-style, and how to defend it.

PART 1

CHAPTER ONE

Conversion

When Paul was Saul

Paul tells us very little about his life prior to his call. He says that he was a Jew descended from the tribe of Benjamin. He writes in Greek but he also knows Hebrew, the language of Judea, the Jews' homeland, and of most of their Scriptures. He belonged to a particular sect within Judaism known for its precision vis-à-vis God's Scriptures, the Pharisees. Perhaps think here of Catholics who have become Jesuits. The book of Acts adds some details to this.[1]

Paul grew up in the city of Tarsus on the Cilician plains. These lie on the southern coast of present-day Turkey where it wraps around the northeastern corner of the Mediterranean Sea. Paul would have received the equivalent of his primary and secondary education from the small Jewish community living there, and from the city's Greek system when he went to the local "gymnasium." The Greek secondary schools of the ancient world were known as "gymnasia," and we still speak of "gyms" today because the Greek education included a lot of physical training and competition. Paul then went off to college in Jerusalem to do a degree in Pharisaism, perhaps following in his father's footsteps. He was known at this time by his Jewish name, Saul. The original Saul, Israel's first king, was the tribe of Benjamin's most important biblical representative, although things didn't work out so well for him.

Acts says that Paul was a Roman citizen, so he must have had a Roman name too. Roman names had three parts: a forename chosen from a very limited list of candidates like Marcus or Lucius; a family name, which was preferably as prestigious as possible; and a "cognomen," which was really just

13

a nickname added so that all the people bearing the name Marcus and Lucius could be distinguished from one another. The full name of the person we know as Cicero, for example, was Marcus Tullius Cicero. Marcus was his first name, Tullius his not-so-prestigious family name, and Cicero his cognomen. In Latin it means "chickpea," so one of the Roman Republic's most famous rhetors and statesmen was known everywhere as Chickpea. "Paulus" means "small" in Latin—or, a little more poetically, "humble"—so it was almost certainly Paul's cognomen. He would have been known everywhere in non-Jewish circles as "Tiny."

But how did Paul get to be a Roman citizen? A lot of people wanted to be Roman citizens. The Roman empire was basically a vast political and economic octopus spreading out from a huge head that was the city of Rome, and membership had its privileges. Wealthy people would try to buy their way into the city's citizenship, and legionaries received citizenship after serving in the army for twenty-five years. However, Roman citizens were primarily people who had been born in the city of Rome or who had descended from the same. The simplest explanation for Paul's citizenship is that he was descended from Jews who had been enslaved and sent to Rome and then received citizenship there after they had been set free, as was customary. The great Roman general Pompey, Julius Caesar's contemporary, had enslaved tens of thousands of Jews when he annexed Galilee and Judea in 65 BCE and taken many of them to Rome. Paul could easily have been a descendant of the survivors of some of these unfortunate Jews.

We don't know when Paul was born, but it is entirely possible that his great-great-grandfather and grandmother had been born to Jews deported to Rome by Pompey. His family had left Rome at some point, probably to travel back to Judea, but had settled down on the way in Tarsus, perhaps for business reasons.[2]

So Paul came from Tarsus but had a Roman ID card in his back pocket, something that would come in handy. He does not seem to have been especially wealthy because he tells us that he worked with his hands. Acts uses the unusual word *schēnopoios* to describe his trade. We don't know exactly what this refers to. Literally it denotes a "scene-maker." Scenes were canvas screens stretched and painted to be used as backdrops for plays. But it is hard to envision a Pharisee painting scenery for pagan plays for a living. It is more likely that he was a canvas worker, which this word could describe at a pinch. Mediterranean cities get very hot. Shops and stadiums in Paul's day used canvas awnings to provide shelter from the sun, as well as from the occasional cloudburst. It is possible to see a magnificent set of canvas awnings extending into the sky when Maximus (a.k.a. Russell Crowe) arrives in Rome for the first time and looks up and sees the colosseum in the film *Gladiator* (2000, dir. Ridley Scott). Paul probably stitched canvas awnings for a living when he had to, carrying his tools around with him in a small pouch—an awl, a knife, thread, and some thick metal needles. To ancient eyes he wouldn't have looked like much. The small but hugely influential upper class despised people who had to work with their hands for a living because they looked like slaves. Artisans like Paul were very low down in the pecking order.

One final detail in Paul's background is important. He was "zealous" in a way that not all Pharisees were. Zealots were Jews who were prepared to kill for God, and our newspapers are sadly studded with the same phenomenon even today. Something about the early followers of Jesus offended Paul to the point that he placed them in a category that needed to be wiped out.[3]

History would have been largely uninterested in Paul, however, except for the strange event that now took place. Paul was converted to the very movement that he was trying to exterminate.

Conversion

Acts tells the story of Paul's conversion with the author's typical knack for drama.[4] Paul was "breathing out hostility," persecuting any adherents of the dangerous new messianic sect that he could find. He had been conducting the ancient equivalent of police sweeps in Jerusalem and the surrounding region of Judea, and we shouldn't sugarcoat this: Paul was the leader of a death squad. Such was his zeal, he wanted to pursue these deviants wherever they had fled, even to foreign cities.

At some point in 34 CE he started out for Damascus to hunt down any fugitives there that he could find.[5] But God had other ideas. Paul tells us that he was stopped short en route to Damascus by a revelation of God's Son (Gal. 1:15–16). Acts provides the further details that he was literally flattened by this, struck blind by a light beaming from heaven. A voice spoke to him: "Saul, Saul, why do you persecute me?" "Who are you, Lord?" Paul asks, not unreasonably. "I am Jesus, whom you are persecuting" comes the reply.

An astonishing amount of information is packed into this short exchange, and we can see it informing almost everything that Paul later wrote and did.

Jesus is God

About twenty years after this moment, in a letter written to his bickering converts in Corinth, Paul has a long discussion about whether food that has been slaughtered in a pagan temple and so offered to its gods could be eaten by Christians (1 Cor. 8). Pagan priests were the butchers of the ancient world. They partly funded their expensive temples by being given live animals to sacrifice by rich donors. They would take a cut to eat themselves and then sell the rest of the meat secondhand out the back of the temple in a meat market. The proceeds funded the temple. Meat was a luxury product, so this made a lot of money when rich donors were doing their civic duty. Some Corinthian Christians, influenced by Judaism, thought that meat bought in this way should be avoided because eating it would be an act of idolatry. After all, it had been part of a pagan worship ritual. Others, however, were quite happy to socialize with their pagan friends who were feasting on this meat. Conflict ensued.

Navigating this conflict in chapter 8 in the letter, Paul begins by talking about who the real God is. He says in verse 6:

> For us there is but one God, the Father,
> from whom all things came and for whom we live;
> and there is but one Lord, Jesus Christ,
> through whom all things came and through whom we live.

We can see immediately that Paul is not saying anything very different here from what he first heard on the road to Damascus about the Lord Jesus. But if any Jews who had not converted to Jesus were around when this statement was read out in Corinth, their jaws would have hit the floor. Paul is quoting one of the most treasured of all Jewish texts, Deuteronomy 6:4, which was used by many Jews as their main confession of faith. They prayed it every day. "Hear O Israel: the Lord our God, the Lord, is one." It goes on to say in verse 5, "Love the Lord your God with all your heart and with all your soul and with all your strength." But Paul has inserted Jesus directly into this statement about God, distinguishing between him and his "Father," although maintaining the oneness or unity of God. Extraordinary.

Both the Father and Jesus are confessed as creating, which was an activity that the Jewish Scriptures attributed solidly and consistently to God alone. To make matters worse, the sacred name for God, which was so holy that Jews did not even speak it but hid it behind the word "Lord," is being attached here to Jesus. So clearly Jesus *is* God. But Paul is not splitting God into one God and then another Lord, Jesus, who is also a God. There is one God and one Lord, who are on some level the same thing. The conclusion is inescapable that Paul is stating here—quite calmly, and apparently in a way that all the Corinthians were fully comfortable with—that the one God who cannot be imaged and who made the heavens and the earth includes Jesus within his identity. Two figures are visible here within the one God, and a third will be added shortly.

[handwritten note: he's a Jewish Christian living in a Greco-Roman world]

God reveals God

Earlier on in 1 Corinthians, in chapter 2, Paul spends a bit of time talking about how the Corinthians worked all this out. Grasping the truth about Jesus doesn't depend on the manner in which it is presented, he argues. The information that we have just described wasn't introduced to the Corinthians by an elegant rhetorical display but by someone who looked more like a shaking bedraggled vagabond. In contemporary terms, then, it could be the subject of a stunning feature-length film, a gripping novel, a newspaper editorial, a conversation, a blog, a tweet, a badly written child's essay, a boring lecture, or a conversation. It doesn't matter. The claims being made are only understood to be true when the Spirit reveals them to be so. "God has revealed [his secret] to us by his Spirit," Paul observes. Hence "we have received the Spirit who is from God that we may understand what God has freely given us" (1 Cor. 2:10, 12, although the whole chapter is relevant).[6]

It seems then that the Corinthians didn't work all this out for themselves. They responded to the promptings of God by way of his Spirit. It was this revelation in their hearts and minds that introduced certainty about the truth of the information they were hearing by way of Paul's unimpressive words. Because of this deep work of conviction, the human messenger doesn't matter so much, Paul says, and a highly stylish messenger might even detract from the information's truth because she or he would draw our attention away from the Spirit who is doing the important underlying work.

We can now see two revelations working together whenever God is being revealed and understood. There is Jesus, and there is the Spirit. These two figures operate like the two hands of God gathering people up and bringing them back to the Father. Presumably this is what happened to Paul near Damascus as well. He was touched by both the Lord Jesus and by God's Spirit.

These claims can frustrate modern historians who like to build pictures of people out of the factors that shaped them as children and young adults—their families, early childhood homes, cultures, and so on—and explain their subsequent behavior in the light of those influences. What happened to Paul earlier on that made him convert in this astonishing way? But this assumes that the most important factors in history are things that take place within history, where we can see them—things like sociological and psychological factors. This would miss the point of what Paul tells us. He says that the most important factors in history come from outside of it, from God. He goes out of his way in his longest account of this event, in his letter to Galatians, to empha-size that whatever his background was, whatever the preceding factors, they didn't matter that much. He was a learned Jew, he says in Galatians 1:14, and so dedicated, he says in the previous verse, that he was persecuting religious deviants.[7] But he was heading in the completely wrong direction and God changed him by breaking into his life, the chapter continues. It was a surprise, a shock, a sudden about-face. Conventional historical analysis couldn't predict this and can't explain it. It can only be explained by divine revelation—and this applies just as much to Christians today. Christians believe that Jesus is Lord (God), because God has revealed this to us through God's Spirit.

God is both three and one

We have just seen that three people are working together within the one God: the Father, the Lord Jesus, whom Paul sometimes calls the Son, and the Spirit (2 Cor. 13:13).

The Spirit was well known already within Judaism.

There was a sense in which Jews always understood that God was "out there," far above them and above the earth, creating and sustaining it. The clos-est that they could get to God generally was through their temple where, after elaborate purification rituals, certain designated people could carefully and oc-casionally enter God's presence, which hovered over the ark of the covenant. Any mistakes and, like the final scene in the first Indiana Jones movie, *Raiders of the Lost Ark* (1981, dir. Steven Spielberg), you died! However, sometimes God showed up in other places very close by as well. Prophets received a "measure" of the Spirit, and the Spirit would come upon people like Moses, Samson, and even Saul. This Spirit gave life, healed, directed, spoke, and empowered. Jews knew well then of God's presence with them, close by, which they would speak of in Hebrew as God's "breath" (*ruach*), rendered in Greek translations as "spirit" (*pneuma*). With Jesus revealed to us as Lord we can grasp even more deeply what is going on here.

The Father and his Son Jesus are people, and so the Spirit is best un-derstood as a person too. Later Christian thinkers pulled these revelations about God together into an all-important position or "doctrine" we know as the Trinity.[8] God is one, but made up of three persons: the Father, the Son, and the Holy Spirit. This claim stands at the heart of the confessions that all Christians recite, confess, and affirm to the present day.[9] But we know from Paul's conversion near Damascus that this is not just a definitive account of who God is. It is a definitive account of how we know God, indicating that this knowledge does not rest on our own efforts or insights, which is just as well. As Job said some time ago, where would we go to find God (Job 23:3, 8–9; see also 28:12–22)? The creeds affirm that God reveals the truth about God, reaching all the way down to us in our humanity in Jesus, and to our hearts and minds with his Spirit. This might seem obvious, but it is incredibly important. We must remember with crystal clarity that God is in charge of how we know about God, and of the definition of what God is really like, and we must hang on to these truths through life and death.[10]

What we learn next

Most introductions to Paul would describe Paul's background and then build to the story of his conversion. I am doing the opposite here. I don't want to understand his conversion in the light of his background. I want to understand his background in the light of his conversion. Fortunately, Paul thinks about it this way as well. In a telling passage written to his converts in the ancient city of Philippi, he speaks of the extraordinary reevaluation that the arrival of Christ imposed on his life.

> If someone else thinks they have reasons to put confidence in the flesh, I have more: circumcised on the eighth day, of the people of Israel, of the tribe of Benjamin, a Hebrew of Hebrews; in regard to the law, a Pharisee; as for zeal, persecuting the church; as for righteousness based on the law, faultless.
>
> But whatever were gains to me I now consider loss for the sake of Christ. What is more, I consider everything a loss because of the surpassing worth of knowing Christ Jesus my Lord, for whose sake I have lost all things. I consider them garbage, that I may gain Christ and be found in him.... (Phil. 3:4b–9a, NIV)

Looking back on his past, Paul asserts confidently that in any competition in terms of Jewish markers and practices he would win. In the Olympic games of Judaism Paul is an uncontested champion. He was circumcised correctly, on the eighth day, and is of impeccable ancestry, being descended from the tribe of Benjamin. He speaks the right language, Hebrew, and such is his zeal for God's Scriptures he belongs to a group that practices stringent application and accountability, the Pharisees, and militantly persecutes those who step outside the appropriate boundaries of God's people. But now, in the light of Christ, looking back on this previous life, he counts everything that previously seemed to be a gain as a loss. In comparison to Christ these things are not absolutely negative in and of themselves but, just so we don't miss the point, in relation to Christ he says that these badges of pride and gold medal activities are tantamount to excrement (Greek *skybala*). (The translators of our Bibles are generally a little more polite here than Paul was in the original.) From a gold medal to what the Irish lyrically call shyte. That's a big reevaluation.

If we grasp just how dramatic the shift in Paul's thinking was as he looked back on his previous life in the light of Christ, largely inverting its valuation from outstanding to odious, we need to extend this process to any aspect of Paul's past. Whatever he thought the issues facing humanity, Judaism, or him individually were before his dramatic confrontation with Christ on the road to Damascus, it is his view now that matters. The view looking back, illuminated by Christ, is the correct view. But what does this actually look like?

From this moment, we tell the story of Paul roughly in the way that addicts recount the stories of their recoveries. These are stories that also only make complete sense when their tellers look backwards on their past, and they are stories that pivot on a definitive revelation—the step from full addiction to being clean, with its attendant clarity.[11]

Let us suppose that I have just made it through a successful rehab program. Supported by a generous and honest community, a local meeting of Alcoholics Anonymous, I have beaten my habit—although, as experienced AA members would say, only for now. One of the most striking features of my recovery is my new ability to tell a truthful story about my past struggles.

I now begin my story confessionally, with the acknowledgment that I am at present free, although I can see that in and of myself I am an addict. Then I recount my tragic former biography in these terms—how I fought a long battle with drugs, say, with heroin. I describe how heroin effectively controlled me, leading to deeply destructive and tragic activity. Because of the constant need to find money to buy a hit, I damaged all my close relationships, lying to and stealing from those I loved. Fortunately, because of the twelve-step program, the support and penetrating honesty of my buddy and my group, and a long period of time with my mind free of the abusive substance itself, I am seeking to rebuild the trust within the important relationships I have damaged. I am beginning to see things clearly, as they really took place.

But I did not tell this story prior to entering rehab, when I was in the grip of my habit. Then I spoke very differently.

I never said at that time, in the full throes of addiction, that I was an addict, out of control, and enslaved. I said the very opposite. "I am in control of my drug-taking and doing just what I want." Then I would add, "In fact I'm having the best time of my life. No one is getting badly hurt by my behavior. It's just harmless fun. And I can give it up any time I want to. I'm not like those addicts over there."

With a mind clarified by rehab and free from the distortions of the drug itself, I see that this narrative is utterly delusional. In many respects it is the opposite of the truth, while its very dishonesty masks the deeply destructive activity that is going on in tandem with its callous legitimations. It is a false account of my former life—although narrated from within the midst of that life. And Christians are all in the same basic position as this substance abuser.

We can look back with minds being clarified by the Spirit and tell a more honest story about our previous activity. We confess now the center of our lives and the key point of our developing clarity, Jesus, and our commitment to letting his clarity penetrate more deeply into our distorted and twisted minds, showing us, among other things, how destructive and broken we are. We can now see, in his light, where our constant collaboration with sin has led to destructive behavior.

There is something in this whole dynamic that is very reminiscent of Augustine. Although he converted to Christianity in 386 CE at the age of thirty-one, it was only later on, from 397, that we see the development of a deep sense of his own sinfulness. Then, around 400 CE, fourteen years after his conversion, he wrote one of the most famous accounts of Christian sinfulness ever penned, *The Confessions*. My best friend from my teenage years, while training to be a banker, and a new Christian at the time like me, told me that this book captured his own spiritual struggles exactly. This sense of personal incapacity continued into Augustine's later reflections when he trenchantly opposed the naïve optimism of Pelagius concerning the ability of sinful humans to behave well in and of themselves and affirmed instead the centrality and totality of grace.

What we see here is the clarification that Augustine experienced as his mind was cleansed, and the resulting need to redescribe the events that led up to his conversion and ministry—to provide an explicitly retrospective but far more accurate account of his past, of his conversion, and of his underlying nature. Any account of our past must be undertaken in this confessional mode. Looking back, in the light of Christ, we confess our previous actions to be sinful, and generally know rather better than we did before just what to confess. But the first Augustinian Christian was Paul, and I suspect that he came face-to-face with his sin very early on in his Christian career.[12]

Paul is refreshingly honest about his mistakes. Prior to the revelation of Christ to him on the road to Damascus, Paul was a deeply devout servant of God but, as we already know, he understood that as a readiness to kill the followers of Jesus. But the revelation of God in the person of Jesus revealed in the same moment the utter, total, and complete misdirection of his zeal. Instead of accelerating ahead of the pious crowd, winning the race for Jewish virtue, Paul was deeply and profoundly mistaken about God, God's nature, and God's purposes—so much so that he was zealously opposing God, fighting against the very God he thought that he was serving. From this event onward, Paul's story changes dramatically, including his account of his past. The zealous Pharisee is a zealous misdirected Pharisee.

This must have been a humbling moment, and I doubt that Paul ever forgot the way that his own zeal had misled him. He now realized that in and of himself he had nothing to offer God and was in fact deeply twisted in his understanding of his Lord. The God revealed in Jesus Christ judged his activity and exposed its corruption. The result was a Paul who speaks very much like a recovering substance abuser. He was able to look back on his previous life with a mind clarified by this revelation and see where his previous activity, which looked entirely reasonable if not praiseworthy at the time, was profoundly distorted. Moreover, the story he now tells retrospectively, after the fact, is the correct one. It is the story clarified by the gift of truth in Jesus. "Whatever I previously considered gain or advantageous, I now consider, in the light of Christ and in comparison to him, loss. Indeed, compared with the surpassing wonder of Christ I consider everything as mere excrement!" (Phil. 3:6–7).

Every story that we tell about what precedes the arrival of Jesus up to that arrival needs to be told in this way. Moreover, we need to cleave to this practice faithfully because of the subtle traps that lurk here for the unwary. We Christians must learn to craft our stories backward, and in a confessional mode, like the testimony of the addict emerging from addiction. This is how the mature Augustine spoke, and how Paul himself learned to speak several centuries before him. We must, as Paul himself put it, bring every thought captive to Christ (2 Cor. 10:5b).

A purpose-driven life

We have already seen that Galatians 1:13–16 is a key text for understanding Paul. It speaks to us clearly about the importance of revelation for understanding who Jesus was, and consequently for understanding God. It now adds one further detail to our developing story.

> When God, who set me apart from my mother's womb and called
> me by his grace,
> was pleased to reveal his Son in me
> so that I might preach him among the pagan nations,
> my immediate response was not to consult any human being.
> I did not go up to Jerusalem to see those who were apostles before I
> was,
> but I went into Arabia. . . . (Gal. 1:15–17, NIV modified)

This text tells us that on the road to Damascus Paul was given a job to do. God set him apart from his mother's womb to proclaim the good news about Jesus to the pagan nations—quite a job for a dedicated Jew. So Paul's encounter with Jesus on the road to Damascus was not just a revelation and a conversion; it was a commissioning. Moreover, the job he was assigned involved a constituency, and a rather unexpected one. A group of people is in view: the pagans.

Readers of Paul sometimes think that when he said that he went into "Arabia" in Galatians 1:17 he was going into a long period of desert retreat while he thought about what had just happened to him. But Arabia was a name given in Paul's day to the regions that lay to the south of Damascus down the King's Highway, which was the age-old road that ran through this area on the way from Babylon to Egypt. Arabia contained a group of Hellenistic cities known as the Decapolis—"the ten cities" (although there were actually more than ten)—and the kingdom of Nabataea, whose capital was in the magnificent fastness of Petra. (Indiana Jones finished his last crusade there.) It was an area filled with cities and packed with pagans, so when Paul says that he immediately went to Arabia, it's pretty likely that he was doing what God had told him to do. He was taking the good news of Jesus to the pagan nations. The pagans in the Decapolis and Nabataea were the most accessible pagans he had.[13]

There was clearly something special about what Paul was appointed by God to do. He was an apostle. Apostles are basically missionaries. They take the good news of Jesus cross-culturally, and there are many challenges in this job that they must be especially gifted and skilled to navigate. I don't think we

23

are all called to be apostles. But we are all called. This means we all have a job to do and that job will most likely involve a constituency.

The famous little tract "The Four Spiritual Laws" begins: "God loves you and has a wonderful plan for your life."[14] This is exactly right. A recent Christian bestseller that has sold thirty million copies is titled *The Purpose Driven Life*.[15] God is all about purpose, and purpose specifically for us. We have all been set apart from our mother's womb for something. But what Paul's statement in Galatians 1 tells us is that these purposes will be bound up with a constituency. We will be sent in some sense to people, and those people might not be the ones we expect.

Questions

› What is the most likely explanation for Paul's Roman citizenship?

› What does Paul tell us he was like when he was a Jew called Saul?

› Why is it significant that Paul and the other early followers of Jesus called him "Lord"?

› How did these early followers learn that he was Lord?

› What is the one-word summary for this process?

› What does the doctrine of the Trinity tell us about this process and about God?

› How does talking about this event as a call and a commission help us to understand Paul's life—and our own?

› Why do we understand our past best as we look back on it?

› How did Paul probably learn this important lesson?

› What is an apostle?

CHAPTER TWO

Breakthrough

The early years

After his conversion Paul began to travel up and down the King's Highway. He went from Damascus down southward to what is present-day Jordan and back trying to make converts from among the pagans as God had instructed him to. However, he seems to have been trying at this time to attract pagans who were already drawn to Judaism—an interesting group of people the book of Acts calls "God-fearers," although this is probably better translated "God-worshipers," meaning by this phrase "worshipers of the one true God [and not the disgusting pagan idols]."[1] The God-worshipers attended synagogue and socialized with Jews, so they were the most accessible group of pagans for Paul, the zealous messianic Jew, to approach. I'm not sure he had much success with this strategy, however, although he certainly irritated a lot of people.

The first source of irritation was the God he was proclaiming. We learned in the previous chapter that Paul was quite unashamed of declaring that Jesus was Lord, and proclaimed him in terms drawn from the heart of Jewish theology, Deuteronomy 6:4. So Jesus was God. The Holy Spirit was invoked a great deal as well. This resulted in a startlingly early anticipation of later Trinitarian doctrine. God was three-in-one: God the Father, as Paul called him, God the Son, and God the Holy Spirit. Doubtless a lot of Jews in the areas in which Paul was preaching found this highly offensive. It is hard to get your head around the idea that a God comprising three persons is still one. It is even harder to accept that this God has chosen to become a person without ceasing to be God—not so hard for pagans, perhaps, who had lots of gods and a lot of interactions between them and mortals, but hard for Jews who believed in a creator God who utterly transcended creation.

But Paul was irritating Jews in another way. Not only was he proclaiming a complicated if not blasphemous God who was absurdly involved in his own creation. Paul was proclaiming that pagans could become followers of this God and thereby inherit a place in the Age to Come. What?!

Jews had taken quite a beating from history throughout their existence, and especially in the last several hundred years. They had been conquered and sent into exile in the 500s BCE. Seventy years later they had returned to a rather paltry existence in Judea. They had then been conquered by a further succession of great pagan empires. How do you maintain that your God rules heaven and earth when his people are being repeatedly pulverized? In the obvious trial of strength playing out on the plains of history, the Jewish God was not doing well. He had been beaten down by the Assyrians, the Babylonians, the Persians, the Macedonians in several different versions, and lastly by the Romans.

Jews responded to this challenge with hope.

They believed that a great day would come when their God would suddenly unveil himself as the ruler of heaven and earth, re-creating the earth, ruling it directly, and lifting up his people into prominence and prosperity. The Jews would triumph. At the same moment, their enemies would be destroyed. It would be a day of payback! The Jewish dead would be resurrected—well, the good Jews. Families would be reunited. Jerusalem would become the center of the earth. The teachings of the Torah would be universally loved and obeyed.

This vision of the future made sense of the present struggles of Jews. They just had to wait for God to show up and then they would enter an entirely new situation. Some Jews would even undergo astonishing trials to resist renouncing this future hope, secure in the knowledge that their death was not final and neither was the victory of their persecutors.[2] And along came Paul, telling everyone that pagans could convert to Jesus en masse and get entry into the Age to Come as well.

If nice neighbors came and patiently inquired if they could become Jews, most Jews didn't turn them away. But Paul was out there begging any pagan who would listen to convert willy-nilly, so he wasn't just accepting the occasional pagan as a proselyte. Foreigners to the USA can go through an arduous process and obtain a green card and then eventually become a US citizen—a process I, a New Zealander, have still not managed to complete as I write these words after fourteen years living in North Carolina. But some advocates want an amnesty for everyone who walks over the border, north or south, or who enters by air or sea and overstays. Paul was throwing the green card process under the bus. He was proclaiming an amnesty.

Wow. The special privileges of the Jewish nation quashed again. Not only was present history a struggle, but a horde of despised, unclean, bullying pagans were being admitted into the playground of the future. We can practically hear Paul's offended compatriots crying "Jews for Heaven and Heaven for the Jews" as they flogged him in their synagogues, expelled him from their communities, and eventually planned to take him out for good. Paul, for his part, seems to have persevered for two years or so after his conversion in this difficult work. We pick up his trail in the second half of 36 CE.

Escape!

Paul was working for these early years in the Decapolis and Nabataea, which are mainly in present-day Jordan, and he was ruffling a lot of feathers while he did so. Then he had to run for his life. We will spend a bit of time unraveling the historical situation surrounding this event because this will enable us to pinpoint it exactly and we then end up with an incredibly precious thing—a date.

The governor of Damascus, a "chief" or "sheikh" (in the Greek, *ethnarch*) responsible to King Aretas IV of Nabataea, was guarding the city's seven gates to try to catch Paul. But Paul evaded capture by being lowered in a basket from a window high up in one of the city's walls and slipping away. When I visited Damascus I could see little cranes on the houses perched on top of the city walls. These saved their operators a long walk. It was easy to imagine Paul being lowered in one of these contraptions at night and stealing away. Paul tells us about this incident to emphasize his ingenuity. Homer wrote an entire book about Odysseus's similar tricks and escapades—the *Odyssey*—as the great Greek hero struggled from the siege of Troy back to his home on the island of Cephalonia. In similar terms, Paul might not have looked like much, but the powerful governor of Damascus was outwitted by his Odysseus-like cunning.

Paul's escape helps his modern readers unexpectedly because it dates his movements precisely. The only time that King Aretas IV could have had enough control over Damascus to appoint his own governor there, one of his tribal chiefs (we don't know his name), was in late 36 CE. Aretas was the king of Nabataea, which was in present-day Jordan, and Damascus was in present-day Syria, way to the northern end of the independent alliance of cities that was the Decapolis. How did Aretas manage to get control of Damascus to the point he could appoint his own governor there—and collect taxes?

We know from the Jewish historian Josephus that Aretas had a brief war with a local Jewish ruler at this time, Herod Antipas, besting him in a battle near the Sea of Galilee. Herod Antipas is known to most of us as the man who executed John the Baptist at the behest of his vindictive wife, Herodias (see Mark 6:14–29). A lot of local Jews who revered John the Baptist thought that this defeat at the hands of Aretas was Herod's comeuppance for this horrific act. Aretas's victory opened up all the territory north of Nabataea to Aretas's control. After the battle he could annex the rich prize that was Damascus, which had been controlled for a time by his predecessor, Aretas III. While this was good luck for—or good planning by—Aretas IV, it was bad luck for Paul.

Paul had previously been safe from any Jews he had antagonized in Nabataea, and there were a lot of Jews living there at this time. He could, in effect, flee over state lines. If angry Jews wanted to catch and discipline him, he was safe as soon as he reached his home city of Damascus, which was an independent city. But when it fell under King Aretas's control, his enemies in Nabataea could reach him, and presumably they did it in the usual way, by bribing an official to do what they wanted. The new governor of Damascus, an appointee of Aretas, duly used his forces to try to catch Paul, "locking up the city" (i.e., guarding its walls and gates), but the cunning former zealot eluded him.[3]

Fortunately for us, the window for this strange little incident is narrow. Aretas won his great victory around the fall of 36 CE, and then in the spring of 37 the emperor Tiberius died. The new emperor, Gaius, gifted all the territory around Damascus to one of his great friends—his gambling and drinking buddy Herod Agrippa. Consequently Aretas had to relinquish his grip on his newly acquired territory or face off with three Roman legions stationed in Syria. He made the smart choice and sent his troops home, which means that Paul couldn't escape from King Aretas's governor of Damascus after early 37 CE. Aretas no longer controlled the city then. He had to have fled before this, and we will soon have reason to believe that it was in the fall of the previous year.[4]

This all gives us the most solid date we ever get from Paul's own writings, and one of the most solid in all of the New Testament: Paul's flight from Damascus in late 36 CE. We will hang a lot on this date. Using the time intervals and events Paul supplies in Galatians 1 we can now calculate that he converted in mid-34 CE. We already know that he spent the next two years or so evangelizing up and down the King's Highway in the Decapolis and Nabataea before his escape from Damascus in late 36. Galatians tells us that he visited Jerusalem for an important meeting in late 49 CE,[5] "thirteen plus years later," writing his letter to the Galatians shortly thereafter, and these data give us the big frame on which we will hang all the other events in Paul's life. But where did Paul flee to after his escape? The entire area was now too dangerous for him to visit. He did what any self-respecting convert to Jesus would do. He went to Jerusalem to visit with Jesus's original disciples, a visit we now know with some confidence took place in late 36 CE. This was the first of two visits to Jerusalem that Paul tells us in Galatians that he made, although they were separated by quite a stretch of time. The first was in 36 CE, and the second much later, in 49.

The dog that didn't bark in the night

Paul only spent a fortnight in Jerusalem. This seems a little odd until we remember that the arrival back in Jerusalem of a former death squad leader would have been pretty awkward. Many of the Jesus movement's members must have been scared of him while some would have doubted his sincerity. Was he winkling out more Jesus followers by going undercover? His former Jewish colleagues must have regarded him with loathing as a turncoat. To make matters worse, Jewish communities in Nabataea had a price on his head. Small wonder that he spent only fourteen days with Peter and James and didn't see any of the other leaders of the early church. (They might have been away doing missionary work at the time in any case.) Paul quickly headed away to his home region of Cilicia, and to the neighboring area of northern Syria. But we need to notice something important here before we follow him. In fact, we need to notice something important that did not happen.

As we just noted from Galatians 1, thirteen years after this first visit Paul returned to Jerusalem for a second time as an apostle in 49 CE, and a very important meeting took place—the first great church council. The leadership of the early church gathered to consider whether converts to their movement from paganism needed to observe all the Jewish commandments. They concluded, as church meetings often do, with an affirmation of coexistence—of live-and-let-live—that we will explore in more detail later on in chapter ten. The courage of this *modus vivendi* should not be downplayed. A group of Jews had agreed that converts to their movement from the disgusting pagans did not need to become Jews, so they basically ratified the most radical missionary proposal of all time. We will explore the rationale for this remarkable decision carefully in due course. The key thing to note for now is that this momentous discussion, with all its politicking and disputes and decisions, did *not* come up during Paul's first visit to Jerusalem. How can this be?

The best explanation for this strange absence is that this radical approach to pagan mission did not yet exist. Did Paul just fail to mention that he was doing something unbelievably radical? Did the Jerusalem leaders not notice that his converts were still acting like pagans? These explanations seem highly implausible. The absence of Paul's radical missionary approach at the time is the best account for why the Jerusalem dog didn't bark. There was nothing to bark at. Something happened later on that elicited this remarkable missionary approach, which the critical meeting in Jerusalem then processed many years afterward, and we don't have to wait long to find out what that was.[6]

Antics at Antioch

Fairly soon after this Paul ended up in Antioch—Antakya in modern-day Turkey. "The" Antioch, that is, the original and most important of more than a dozen cities of that name, was the former capital of the Seleucid empire. It was positioned strategically on the Orontes River in northern Syria, near the Mediterranean coast, and was the third most important city in the Roman empire after Alexandria and Rome.[7] It was large, vibrantly multicultural, somewhat disaster-prone, yet thriving. It had a big Jewish community, including some followers of the new Jesus movement. We don't know much about them, including their names. These anonymous disciples had converted to Jesus while visiting Jerusalem on a festival pilgrimage. There were as many as three of these opportunities a year. But something strange took place after they got back to Antioch. We don't know exactly what happened, but I think it was basically the following scenario, although to grasp it fully we will need to sketch out some of the basic activities that characterized ancient cities.

Greek cities were a buzz of hospitality. People constantly entertained one another, banqueting together, whether for political reasons or for sheer amusement. But Jews didn't socialize with pagan cultures as freely as most pagans did, and consequently they developed a reputation for being anti-social and even misanthropic. They avoided images of gods, which studded pagan houses, and only ate meat and wine that had been prepared in a ritually pure way, as the book of Leviticus dictated. They had strict sexual mores and married internally to their communities. They ran their lives on an entirely different schedule, resting every seventh day and observing ancient Judean agricultural festivals. So they were completely out of step with their pagan neighbors who worked seven days a week but took festival days off in honor of pagan deities, festivals that could run for a week or more. When the pagans were working the Jews were often resting, and when the Jews were working the pagans were often partying. The Jews were different, although they were not cut off from pagan society altogether.

People are attracted to one another and tend to find various ingenious ways of navigating across social barriers. I once watched a modern documentary on a young Englishman's conversion to Judaism. This involved arduous Torah-learning, concerning things such as feasts, that was duly examined by the elders. He also had to get circumcised—and he did it to get the girl! I doubt that a lot of ancient social interaction was much different, and there is even an ancient Jewish book detailing a similar scenario, the romance of *Joseph and Aseneth*. Just so, some ancient pagans practiced a semi-Jewish lifestyle that allowed them to associate more freely with fully practicing Jews, whether to get the girl or simply to hang out with interesting Jews—"God-fearers." Male God-worshipers were not circumcised and so were not proper converts, but they had cleansed their houses of pagan idolatry and ate appropriately prepared food. They prayed to God, gave alms as Jews did, rested on the Sabbath, and could be important donors to Jewish communities.

Drawing this picture together, we can see that Jews socialized with one another within a city culture that was based on socializing. Jews could socialize under very limited circumstances with out-and-out pagans—or when they were being lax in their observances. However, they were quite happy to sit down and to eat and talk with God-worshipers, who didn't violate any key rules for associating.

The early followers of Jesus in Antioch, who were Jews, were presumably no different. But eating in the home of an early Jesus follower meant worshiping with them, and this changed things a bit. Jews met in local gathering places—synagogues—to worship and pray and to teach and to learn Torah. They had long integrated many of these practices into their homes as well, combining worship, meals, and prayers. The early followers of Jesus emphasized these activities as well but with modifications. Their central ritual, the Lord's Supper or Eucharist, took place during a meal. The bread for the meal was broken beforehand and shared out with the appropriate words of remembrance about Jesus. The cup of wine was drunk at the end and passed around in the same ritual way. The meal was then followed by the appropriate religious entertainment, as opposed to the usual pagan fare, and this seems to have meant worship in a style modern Christians would identify as Pentecostal or charismatic. When Paul describes one of these gatherings in Corinth he says that people brought songs to the meeting that they had composed. During the gathering they spoke in tongues, prophesied, and prayed for miracles, healings, and deliverance. Perhaps they had "quakers" and "shakers" as the Spirit came upon people who shook and fell to the floor in a way that is familiar from the great revivals in the US.

The scene is now set. God-worshipers seem to have been present for a meal in the home of an early Jesus follower in Antioch. Clearly there was nothing untoward here. But after the sharing of the cup, as the worship began to intensify, the evidence of the Spirit's activity seems to have spread from the front row to the back row of the meeting (so to speak). It was not just Jews who were expostulating and shaking as the Spirit rested upon them. It was God-worshipers as well. I doubt that these early worshipers noticed much that was odd about this. The sociological distance between Jews worshiping Jesus and God-worshipers worshiping Jesus is quite small—perhaps as minor as a snip of skin from a male's member. This activity would have looked pretty much the same. But Paul arrived in Antioch at some point and grasped that something significant was going on. The evidence of the Holy Spirit indwelling the non-Jewish or not-entirely-Jewish followers of Jesus was a massive theological challenge. God was saying something.[8]

The Spirit of God who had raised Jesus from the dead and would raise his Jewish followers was stating here that non-Jewish followers of Jesus would inherit the Age to Come as well. So far so good, although Paul probably already knew this. This situation at Antioch suggested, however, that they do so *without adopting all the practices of the Jews.* God had clearly accepted them just where they were—as uncircumcised God-worshipers, to focus on the men for a moment. But how could God be accepting pagans without making them Jews first? This would be like God accepting pagans today without asking them to join the church. What had just happened to Israel and to the central story of the Jewish Scriptures?! Yet this is what had plainly happened. Shocking. Incomprehensible—and clearly in some way part of the divine plan.

It was this impossible possibility that forced Paul to think through what was going on, and he was the right man for the job. He was unspeakably brilliant—a brain the size of a planet—but he was aware of his own shortcomings. He was deeply versed in Jewish tradition, but he was strongly committed to converting pagans to the new Jesus movement, people whom he had previously despised but had now begun to grow quite fond of, having spent some years evangelizing them. The result was a revolutionary account of God's activity on our behalf in Jesus that we now know as Paul's gospel. It is the basis for the church today, so we had better hope that he was right.

Christian ethics

The real challenge before Paul at Antioch is the explanation of Christian ethics. Both words here—"Christian" and "ethics"—are important.

Acts tells us, in a moment of supreme importance, that the Jesus followers at Antioch were called "Christians" (11:26). This name was given to them by the Romans—it comes originally from Latin—and means "members of the household of Christ." It was also a mean joke. *Christos* sounds like *Chrēstos*, especially to Romans who don't know Greek. *Chrēstos* means "useful" and was a common slave name. So the Romans were saying that the people in this new movement, unlike any sensible person's attachment to an aristocratic house, were attached to a shameful slave's household. Imagine today celebrating your descent from ancient cockroaches or rats. "I am Douglas Campbell, originally descended from the great Scottish cockroach Duncan." The fascinating thing about this act of mockery, however, is what it confirms about the new situation. A group of Jesus followers at Antioch needed a new name. Why? What was wrong with the old ones? Something very simple. The old names were Jewish and these new Jesus followers *no longer looked like Jews*. So the Romans, after investigating them to see if they posed a threat, and concluding that they were harmless dreamers, gave them a title they thought appropriately respectful. The arrival of this new name is a decisive piece of evidence—small but telling—that something strange happened in Antioch. Not all of Jesus's followers now looked like Jews. Some looked like Christians. But we haven't answered our pressing question yet, and to do so we need to turn to the second key term noted above—"ethics."

The word "ethic" comes from the ancient Greek *ethos* and refers to how one lives one's life. It denotes our activity and behavior. Rather sensibly, ancient Greek philosophers like Aristotle realized that everyone was making choices, acting, responding to situations, and behaving, all the time. Everyone has a way of life known as an *ethos*. So the important question is not whether one has an *ethos*. Everyone does. It is how to have a good one. This is the question of *ethics*. Is our ethos ethical, we might say? Is the way that I live good?

Jews, steeped in their history and traditions, understood their way of life, gifted by God, to be *the* ethos. Ethics is Jewish! Anyone converting to their God should obviously follow the traditional Jewish ways that had been laid down in the books of Moses. Men should be circumcised, everyone must purge their house of idols, meat must be drained of blood before it can be eaten, people must marry Jews and not sleep around, they must recite and try to obey the Ten Commandments, and so on. But Paul is now faced with the awkward fact at Antioch that God seems to be saying another ethos is possible. What can make sense of this?![9]

This all has something to do with resurrection.[10]

Paul's most extensive discussion of this question—the question, technically, of what grounds a Christian ethos independently of a Jewish ethic based on Torah-observance—is found in Romans chapters 5–8.[11] In chapter 6 Paul talks a lot about baptism, which was the entry ritual for converts, and he speaks of the transition that converts undergo from their pagan life to discipleship following Jesus. New converts to the Jesus movement stripped off their own clothes, were immersed naked in water, and then probably received a gift from the community of fresh new clothes. Most people in the ancient world possessed only one set of clothes, and for poor people these quickly became dirty and ragged, so this gift of new clothes was an important practical marker of a new identity.

In Romans 6, however, Paul interprets this ritual of immersion and cleansing followed by reclothing—the obvious meaning of a bath in water—in terms of death and resurrection in Jesus (and he treats the Eucharist in the same way in another letter).[12] Converts die and are buried with Jesus as they dip under the water. They are raised with Jesus as they stand up and receive their new clothing. Moreover, this is not just symbolic. Something quite concrete is going on. "Understand that you yourselves are, on the one hand, dead to sin, and on the other hand, alive to God in Christ Jesus," he concludes (6:11).

It is hard to make complete sense of all this without the involvement of the Spirit. But as we read on in Romans 5–8 we encounter a thicket of references to the work of the Spirit at the start of chapter 8, while there is a subtle signal of these coming references at the start of this whole sweep of discussion in 5:5. The Spirit is the presence of God, his "breath," which gives life (see Gen. 2:7).[13] Through the Spirit "God makes alive the dead and calls that which is not into existence" (Rom. 4:17), gifting converts with a completely new mentality—with a resurrected mind. "We have the mind of Christ," Paul says in 1 Corinthians 2:16. Moreover, "the mind of the Spirit is life and peace," displacing the corruption and conflict of one's old mind, Paul says in Romans 8:6. Because of this gift, Jesus followers are guaranteed a complete resurrection on the Day of Judgment. "If the Spirit of the one who raised Jesus from the dead lives in you, the one who raised Christ Jesus from the dead will also make your mortal bodies alive—by means of his Spirit dwelling within you" (Rom. 8:11).

Paul's position has some tricky implications that we will have to grapple with in due course.[14] But for now let's work with what he is saying directly. Has Paul explained what happened at Antioch, when pagan

converts who had not fully adopted a Jewish ethic were touched by the
Holy Spirit and thereby designated as acceptable? He has done so if the
new reality that the resurrected converts live out of lies beyond many of
the structures that characterize the present age—and this is what he often
claims. Paul's most famous such assertion is Galatians 3:28, which is best
read along with its two preceding verses. This text has rightly been called
the Pauline Magna Carta.

> All of you who are in Christ Jesus are, by means of that fidelity,[15] sons
>   of God.
> For you have been immersed into Christ;
> you have been clothed with Christ.
> There is no Jew or pagan, no slave or free, no "male and female."
> All of you who are in Christ Jesus are one and the same. (vv. 26–28)

Those who have been immersed and reclothed are something new, Paul
says here. They are "sons of God" and not characterized by ethnicity (Jew or
Greek/pagan), social status (slave or free), or gender (male or female).[16] These
claims confirm our earlier suspicions that something quite concrete happens to
converts and that this new state lies beyond existing visible categories like race,
class, and even biology. Incidentally, this tells us that we shouldn't understand
being a "son of God" as a strong claim about gender; it is metaphorical. Paul
makes much the same claim in 2 Corinthians 5:17.

> If someone is in Christ, he is a new creation.
> The old has departed. Behold, he has become quite new.

And he concludes his letter to the Galatians with the same claim in 6:15:

> Neither circumcision nor uncircumcision is anything
> but a new creation.

Hopefully we can now see Paul's explanation of what happened at Antioch emerging into view. He saw very clearly that Jesus's resurrection is a
victory over death and has effected his entrance into heaven and therefore,
in a sense, into the Age to Come. This means that life in the Age to Come
must transcend our mortality. This means in turn that it must leave behind
almost all of our present structures and forms, which frequently are bound
up with death. Our means of reproduction, for example, is a way of ensuring

life in spite of death. The Bible is pretty clear about this. Adam "knows" Eve and calls her "life" after the fall, and the difficulty of this imperfect arrangement is acknowledged in the pain and struggle of childbirth. Fortunately, in the Age to Come it will be redundant. But this means that our biology, our gender, will be redundant. Our bodies will be very different. This is why celibacy reflects the Age to Come more than marriage. It follows that food will be transcended as well—stomachs will be as redundant as sexual organs—so the Jewish rules about food don't need to be taken too seriously. This is why Paul can say,

> The Kingdom of God is not a matter of eating and drinking
> but of deliverance and peace and joy through the Holy Spirit.
> (Rom. 14:17)

Class, too, will be irrelevant because we just won't be arranged in these ways anymore, working for one another, or not, while even race will be left behind. The lands where people live, their dress and language and customs, and even their bodies—all the things that combine to create an ethnic group or a race—will be transcended by new spaces and bodies.

These claims raise a lot of questions. But if we grant for the moment that Paul is latching onto something true and real, they do make sense of why converts to the Lord Jesus from paganism did not need to take up a Jewish ethic. The customs comprising that ethic were rooted in the structures of the present age—food, drink, clothing, land, marriage, and so on. Jews had specific customs and habits here. But converts to Jesus have died and been resurrected into a new age altogether. They are living not so much in Judaism as in the fulfillment of Judaism; they live not as Jews but as the people the Jews are waiting to become. They get direct access to the Age to Come where these former things no longer matter and, as we have already noted, the glories of this Age make all the structures and practices of the present age look like dung. It is that much better.

Why hitch up a donkey to an unsprung wooden cart and drive for three months across the US from the east coast to the west when you can step onto a Dreamliner and be there in five hours, having had a lovely meal of steak, washed down with red wine, amused all the time by the latest British sitcom? Why attach leeches to a child's leg in the hope that she can be cured of cancer when a program of radiation treatment at the local hospital has 100 percent success rate for this particular form? This is how Paul views things. Living out of the Age to Come instead of the present Age? No contest!

> But whatever was to my gain—these things—I consider a loss for the
>   sake of Christ.
> Moreover, I consider everything to be a loss for the sake of the
>   surpassing wonderfulness of knowing Christ Jesus my Lord,
> for the sake of whom everything has become a loss,
> and I consider them excrement so that I might gain Christ and be
>   found in him! (Phil. 3:7–9a)

But clearly questions do arise and we need to try to answer them. The first and most obvious challenge arises when we just look around us and see that the world of mortality and death, and of sin, is far from gone. There is so much ongoing dreadfulness that the claim that people who have converted to Christianity possess a resurrected mind of peace, life, and joy, just seems fanciful. It is make-believe.

This seems like a fair point. Can we handle it?

I think so.

A musical reality

Paul thinks that converts basically live in two worlds at the same time. They still live in the world that he calls "the Flesh," and Paul spends most of his letters battling fleshly actions by his converts. We see this world beckoning his readers in Romans chapter 7. But they also live in the new age, the age of the Spirit. We see the transition to this world being laid out in Romans 6 and the dynamics of this world being articulated in Romans 8.

The world of the Flesh is plainly accessible through the senses. You can just see it, not to mention touch, hear, smell, and sometimes even taste it. The spiritual world is revealed by the Spirit and is only accessible to those attuned to that dimension. Paul "knows" and "believes" it is there. However, this is the world that ultimately matters because it is the world of life. It will last. So Paul counsels the Corinthians at one point, "fix your eyes on what is not visible, not on what is visible, because the visible is temporary, but the invisible is permanent" (2 Cor. 4:18).

If we question the basic plausibility of this situation, doubting the presence of a resurrected mind in Christians on the grounds of the ongoing existence of a horrible world of Flesh, I suspect that part of our problem is being caused by the metaphors that modern western people tend to use when they try to understand how two different dimensions or things fit together.

People shaped by modern culture tend to think about entities as occupying discrete and mutually exclusive spaces. Rather like oil and water in a bottle, we expect different things to separate out from one another and to occupy different layers when they are introduced to one another. Things don't mix together.[17] Moreover, we seem to be biased toward visual metaphors. When we think of accessing reality we imagine looking at it with our eyes and then we see things that are, again, mutually exclusive. We see tables sitting next to chairs and on carpets and they don't move through one another. The world is full of prepositions! We even think about people this way, a problem we will have to correct shortly. If we insert these convictions into Paul's claims about the world of the Spirit being present with the world of the Flesh, then we will find his claim nonsensical. The fact that the world of the Flesh is present means that the world of the Spirit cannot be here. They can't coexist. It is one or the other and the Flesh is definitely still here, so the Spirit is by definition excluded. Either it is somewhere else—perhaps in the distant future—or it doesn't exist.

But these difficulties can be resolved if we switch metaphors. Let's think about this situation sonically, using music, with our ears, instead of optically, visually, and with our eyes. Reality is musical. This will enable us to think about things in ways that are both more accurate and not necessarily mutually exclusive.[18]

Imagine that I have just heard this challenge from a smart student in a classroom: "How can even part of us be resurrected in the Spirit, with one foot in the Age to Come, when we are so obviously still caught up in the world of the Flesh?" Instead of responding with some elaborate argument about false Newtonian dualisms or some such, I click on a link and start to play a song by Zao through the classroom's loudspeakers. I crank up the volume a bit. "Praise the War Machine" floods the seminar space—the music (with due apologies to death metal rock music) of the Flesh. "We shall destroy the earth. Rebuild it. None shall inherit it." Then, while Zao is in full voice, I take my iPhone and flick to Bach's *Air on a G String* and begin to play it—quite softly. I can just catch the delicate resonances of the strings as they move through their interlacements of pizzicato and bowing—the music of heaven (at least, for those who love Bach). Then I begin to slowly turn down the volume on Zao.

As the death metal fades—perhaps we catch "Carry us off in your claws"—Bach's music begins to become audible. I turn down Zao's music still further and turn up Bach a little more. The *Air* can now be heard easily all over the room and begins to dominate Zao, although the pulse of the death metal can just be heard in the background. Then I explain the metaphor to my doubting but intrigued students.

There is nowhere in the room that lacks the music of both pieces. Every single part of the space that we occupy together is touched by Zao and by Bach at any given moment. Both pieces of music were fully present, within and alongside one another, and yet completely distinct from one another. Moreover, even when the volume of one piece was so high that the other was drowned out, we knew that the music was still there. Both pieces were present, but we couldn't hear one because our senses were dominated by the other arrangement.

Just so, Paul's suggestion that we live in two dimensions simultaneously makes sense when it is conceptualized sonically and musically. The music of the Flesh might dominate, but this does not in any way prevent the music of the Spirit from being fully present and accessible. Both arrangements occupy exactly the same space in all their fullness. Christians live with the music of the world and the music of heaven playing in the same location all the time. So if the presence of the music of heaven is doubted, the volume on the music of the world might be turned up too high. If it is turned down the Spirit's music might emerge—a gentle, delicate music present there all along that we were just unable to hear. The problem was not the music itself then, but our inability to hear and our lack of attention. Hence the real question for our doubter might actually be—as it has always been—"Where do I go to hear God?"[19]

In short, the resurrected mind of the Spirit can coexist quietly in, behind, and within the jarring music of the Flesh. So to affirm the presence of the resurrected mind is by no means to deny the ongoing presence of the Flesh, of sin, and of death. Paul's basic claim that converts to Christ possess the resurrected mind of Christ remains plausible as long as we remember that reality is musical.

The next issue that arises is quite practical. Paul has a new theology, a new account of Christian behavior, and consequently has a new missionary approach as well. Just as his converts no longer have to act like Jews, he no longer needs to find his converts hanging around with Jews. He is not limited to the synagogues or to Jewish hosts anymore, and given how they were frequently reacting to him this was probably a good thing. Nor does Paul himself have to respect Jewish practices quite so much. If he is called to do so he can sit lightly to the Jewish rules guiding his eating and resting and visiting. The result of this is flexibility. Paul can enter social spaces that he couldn't previously. He can boldly go where no Jew has gone before. And this is just what he did.

Questions

- Why did Jews react negatively to Paul's mission in the first years after his conversion?

- (You can skip these questions if you are not interested in chronology: When did Paul escape from a governor of Damascus appointed by Aretas IV, King of Nabataea? How do we know this? What other important dates can we immediately calculate from this fixed point, creating a frame for Paul's life? Something important did *not* happen when Paul visited Jerusalem for the first time as an apostle. What was it? And what does this suggest?)

- The disciples were first called Christians in Antioch. What does this tell us?

- What situation probably led Paul to think in a new way about the conversion of pagans?

- Where does Paul lay out Christian ethics in full?

- What are some of Paul's most famous summary texts for his radical gospel?

- What is the basic rationale underlying Paul's understanding of Christian ethics?

- How does this explain how Christians following Jesus do not need to convert to Judaism?

- If someone says the claim that Christians now possess the resurrected mind of Christ is fanciful and silly, how might we respond to them? (How might we respond if we say this to ourselves?)

CHAPTER THREE

Networking

Journeys

One of the most telling moments for me in the book of Acts is the command given by the Holy Spirit in 13:2. Acts 13:1 states that the important community at Antioch was busy serving the Lord and fasting. Acts gives some details about its leaders, whom it calls prophets and teachers. A delightful diversity is evident within their broadly Jewish identity: Barnabas was a Jew from the island of Cyprus who had a priestly lineage; Simeon was nicknamed "Black" and came from Africa; Lucius, who came from Cyrene, which is modern-day Libya, had a Roman forename, so he was a Roman citizen like Paul; a companion raised with Herod Antipas called Manaen was a Jewish aristocrat; and Paul. All of this sounds a bit like a bad joke: "A priest, an African, a Roman, an aristocrat, and a Pharisee all walked into a pub. The priest said to the African . . ." But in 13:2 the Holy Spirit issues an explicit command: "Set apart Barnabas and Saul for me for the work that I have called them to." So the priest and the Pharisee turned around and went out the door as they had been commanded, leaving the African, the Roman, and the aristocrat behind.

Paul had already traveled a fair bit by now. He had been based for over two years in Damascus, traveling mainly in a north-south direction up and down the King's Highway. Just recently he had been forced to flee from the entire region, however, so, after a short visit to Jerusalem en route, he had arrived in northern Syria, setting up a new base camp at Antioch. What did he do next, after this firm command to work with Barnabas?

The mission team went to Cyprus first, which was Barnabas's home territory. The two missionaries landed and tried their luck in Salamis. Rather typically, they soon got into trouble. Paul quickly found himself at the other end of the island, in the ancient city of Paphos, arraigned before the governor, an aristocrat called Quintus Sergius Paulus. (Sergius and Paulus are both aristocratic Roman family names; we don't know his nickname.) Paul now got into what ancient people would have viewed as a contest of magical powers. A Jewish magician employed by the governor was trying to hex Paul to discredit his powers and his message. But Paul blasted him with "the evil eye," striking him blind, and the governor was deeply impressed. Clearly hoping to avoid the same fate, he did the intelligent thing and became a Christian (see Acts 13:5–12).

This is noteworthy because the governors of provinces run by the senate, which included Cyprus, were drawn from the uppermost echelons of Roman society. Sergius Paulus had to have previously been a "praetor," an office to which just ten high-ranking and extremely wealthy senators were elected every year. It was as if Paul had just converted a former member of the US president's cabinet, now on diplomatic duty.

Following this notable conversion the mission team went north. They docked at a river port in what is now southern Turkey, Perge, which today is a beautiful ruin being absorbed into the outer suburbs of the resort town of Antalya. These communities both lie on the southern plain of Pamphylia famous for its orange groves and beaches. From here Paul struck up into the mountainous central plateau, evangelizing the ancient city of Pisidian Antioch—today, another nice ruin, although rather colder and more windswept than Perge. Acts has him preaching a long sermon in the synagogue there. Pisidian Antioch was a Roman colony founded by the Emperor Augustus. It was one of several colonies planted along a new Roman road that looped up from the port of Antalya and through the central part of modern-day Turkey—the Via Sebaste or "Imperial Road." There it stitched together the southern part of the Roman province of Galatia.

Scholars have been puzzled by this itinerary until quite recently. Why would Paul travel northward in this obviously motivated way, landing specifically at Perge ultimately to arrive at the obscure town of Pisidian Antioch, close by modern-day Yalvaç, which—no disrespect intended—is still obscure? The recent excavations of Pisidian Antioch have yielded a fascinating answer.

A series of inscriptions have been found there. Inscriptions were a bit like the advertisements of the ancient world although the analogy is not exact; they doubled as political campaign slogans and civic acknowledgments of key donors. They placed the names of important people up in lights. The inscriptions in Pisidian Antioch reveal that one of the dominant families in the little town was the Sergi Pauli. They were enormously wealthy, largely because of sheep.

Sheep-owners were the oil barons of the ancient world. Ancient society lacked waterproof materials. There were no oilskins or umbrellas. When it rained most people got wet, which was not just inconvenient; it was a health hazard. However, wool garments provided warmth in the cold and, due to the lanolin in the fiber, they were an effective barrier against the wet. Even when wet, wool retains 86 percent of its capacity to insulate, which is why sailors have traditionally worn thick woolen jumpers. They keep the shipwrecked warm and alive. It is a remarkable fiber. As a result, it was enormously prized. But it was also expensive.

There were not many areas suitable for pasturing sheep. Warm fertile land was farmed intensively, so only more marginal territory was suitable for sheep-raising, although it had to have good grass. The highest parts of central Turkey were ideal for sheep-farming, and Pisidian Antioch was an excellent local base for the processing of wool and the oversight of operations by wealthy local owners like the Sergi Pauli. They were wool billionaires then. We learn from all this that Paul had been sent by his wealthy and important convert on Cyprus, the governor Quintus Sergius Paulus, up to spread the good news to the rest of his extended family, who lived in Pisidian Antioch.

Following his efforts in Pisidian Antioch, Acts describes how Paul went to other communities along the new Roman road—to Iconium, which is modern-day Konya, and then Lystra. Paul was stoned in Lystra but survived. He seems to have crawled off to an unimportant local town called Derbe, where he recovered. He then returned the way he had come, through Lystra, Iconium/Konya, Pisidian Antioch, and Perge, until he broke away from his original travel route. He preached in the busy port of Antalya—still there in the middle of its modern urban sprawl—and caught a boat back home to Antioch in Syria by way of its Mediterranean port, Seleucia.

The team had been traveling and evangelizing from the spring of 37 CE to the fall of 38—eighteen months of hard work. It was time to debrief and to regroup back at home base. But the break didn't last long. There was too much work to do. As the team prepared to head out in the spring of 39, however, there was some unresolved fallout from the first mission.

John Mark had left the mission team after it landed at Perge. We don't know why. He seems to have wanted to rejoin the team for its next adventure, but Paul didn't trust him. Barnabas did, and advocated strongly for him, and the two leaders ended up having a major falling out and splitting up. Barnabas went off to check on Cyprus, accompanied by John Mark, and Paul headed off to check on the congregations along the Via Sebaste, in present-day Turkey, with a new co-leader, Silas. These relationships were eventually patched up; John Mark shows up in Paul's team later. Meanwhile, something curious happened after Paul had visited Pisidian Antioch.

It was time to explore new territory. The obvious places to go lay either to the north—the fertile coastal plains along the northern coast of present-day Turkey, whether beside the Sea of Marmara, ancient Bithynia, or beside the Black Sea, ancient Pontus—or to the west, along the shores of the Aegean, where some of the largest and richest cities in the empire lay: Ephesus, Smyrna, and Pergamum. There were potential converts there aplenty. But Paul ended up deviating to the coast of the Aegean not far from where ancient Troy lay, arriving at the massive Roman port of Troas. From there he made a beeline for the start of the Roman communication network in Macedonia and Greece. The Via Egnatia or "Egnatian Road," a massive east-west stone highway connecting the Aegean with the Adriatic, touched the Mediterranean at its eastern end at the port of Neapolis, which is now the beautiful resort town of Kavalla. From Neapolis travelers on the road climbed up over the coastal hills and down onto the flat Macedonian plain beyond, reaching the town of Philippi, before turning westward and stretching out for the key cities on the way to the Adriatic, and ultimately, to Rome. But Paul stopped in Philippi.

Philippi was a mini-Rome founded by military veterans from the Roman civil wars. The site still boasts a magnificent forum, as well as parts of the Egnatian Way, rutted with centuries of travel. Paul succeeded in founding a congregation there. But in order to appreciate just what he achieved we need to learn a few things from some sociologists.

Network theory

My eyes were opened to the following aspects of Paul's missionary work through the research of sociologist Rodney Stark and his colleagues into the beginnings of new religious movements in the USA. In a salutary sentence Stark says, "In the early 1960s John Lofland and I were the first social scientists to actually go out and watch people convert to a new religious movement."[1] They followed a missionary from Korea, Ms. Young Oon Kim, who was trying to convert people in San Francisco to the Unification Church, better known as the Moonies. Later on they studied conversions to the Church of Jesus Christ of the Latter Day Saints (LDS), that is, to the Mormons. What they found, in defiance of all the theorizing, was that conversions took place informally through preexisting relationships of friends or family as friendships formed there. All the formal attempts at conversion by Ms. Kim—public meetings, pamphlets, press releases, and so on—yielded no converts at all. But her community did come into being and grow, through the young housewife she first lodged with. A group of three neighboring housewives and friends converted at this time, followed by their husbands, and then some relatives who visited from Oregon.

The study of conversions to the LDS community yielded the same results. In fact the LDS statistics are particularly compelling. The LDS community gives an enormous amount of time and talent to formal evangelism. Its leaders devote two years to this practice full-time. Who has not met LDS missionaries many times knocking on the front door? But the actual conversions from these efforts are next to negligible: about one in a thousand (0.1 percent). The impressive growth rate of the community—about 4 percent annually—is achieved almost entirely through the conversions of relatives and close friends. An astonishing 50 percent of these contacts are converted after a period of around three years of general informal contact.

This sociological lens helped me to see the same phenomenon playing out on the pages of Paul's letters. Many know this approach as "friendship evangelism," although it needs to be appreciated that these friendships are not random. They form within preexisting networks.

Paul's letters are studded with comments, instructions, and greetings from people he knew well, who were often accompanying him, or perhaps hosting him, but who were not Jews, and so had been converted by him at some point. A large circle of supporters and co-workers is evident almost everywhere he went, composed of people who were basically just his personal friends.[2] These were not merely friendships, however. As I often put it, they were strange friendships.

Paul seems, like Ms. Kim in San Francisco, to have formed close relationships with people who were very unlike him in many respects. Ms. Kim was a conservative single Korean, but she traveled to the heart of US decadence, San Francisco in the 1960s, and made friends with young English-speaking housewives. Similarly, Paul, despite being a mature Jewish scholar living in Jerusalem in the shadow of his religion's all-important temple, traveled far from his home to convert low-status artisans, teenagers, women, and slaves from among the disgusting pagans. In order for these types of friendship to take hold, the befriender had to break through various barriers of gender, class, race, location, and language, to name just a few of the challenges. How did these strange friendships even form?

Often they began in unexpected places where the befriender had been prepared to travel but had thereby encountered someone very different, whom they then managed to form a deep and genuine personal bond with. One of my favorite examples of this process is the conversion of Lydia, which was so strategic for the formation of the congregation in Philippi (Acts 16:13–15).

Lydia

Lydia was a female business owner in Philippi, involved, Acts tells us (16:14), with the ancient purple dye industry. She was originally from Thyatira, so she was probably involved with the ersatz toga business.

Roman citizens had a carefully coded public profile. They wore a distinctive, white, very expensive Roman garment, the toga, which was often marked with purple to denote their status. Children, magistrates, and senators wore togas marked with purple bands of various widths, the toga praetexta, while emperors, curule magistrates at important public occasions, and consuls wore the completely purple and comprehensively embroidered toga picta (so an emperor was "born to the purple"). The city of Philippi was "a little Rome" and so aped the garments and codes of its mother city—and many people simply liked purple cloth. But it faced a problem. Purple dye was enormously expensive.

The genuine article, Tyrian purple or porphyry, was obtained by crushing the purpura rock snails found in the eastern Mediterranean, although in particular abundance near Tyre, hence the name. But it took perhaps twelve thousand snails to produce 1.4 grams of dye sufficient to stain the hem of one robe. So Tyrian purple cost a small fortune—it would have been cheaper to sprinkle a toga with gold dust—and we can see immediately that even striped Roman togas signified enormous wealth. They were key ancient items of conspicuous consumption and this is why the Romans wore them. So what were the rather poorer, provincial Philippians to do?

They did what many Roman imitators did and obtained a cheaper substitute, which was derived from a madder plant known as Erythrodanon or "dyer's red." It was found in many ancient locations including in the regions of Phrygia and Lydia. The product was nowhere near as good as Tyrian purple, but neither was it anywhere near as expensive. It seems that Lydia was involved in this business—the ancient guild of the purple-dyers or *purpurarii*.

However, her name also suggests that she was a slave. Slaves were frequently named by their owners after their places of origin since their original barbarian names would have been both unpronounceable and inappropriate. She came from the ancient territory of Lydia, which in modern terms is in western Turkey. Her behavior in Acts suggests that she was a freed slave who ran her own business. She probably worked hard with her hands in this despised manual labor. Acts also states that she was a Jewish sympathizer or God-worshiper.

Paul met Lydia in a Jewish meeting place because of her Jewish sympathies. But she was technically a pagan. Despite her relative independence, she was a low-status person. She was a foreigner, a freed slave who continued to work with her hands, and a woman. Yet he converted her and then accepted her hospitality. Twenty years later he begged two important women in the local Christian community at Philippi to get on with one another, Euodia and Syntyche—he begged, and did not command (Phil. 4:2). It is quite likely that one of these was Lydia, here using her preferred name, not her slave name.

This was a strange friendship. The place where Paul and Lydia first met is not entirely unexpected, although a riverbank in Philippi is a long way from a temple in Jerusalem. This encounter led to a friendship that led in turn to a Christian community in Philippi that would live on for a very long time. Polycarp wrote a letter to it around 150 CE. But the conversion of Lydia is significant for one further reason.

Missionary snakes and ladders

Shortly after this Paul traveled down the magnificent Roman highway that is still partly visible today in northern Greece, the Egnatian Way. He arrived in Thessalonica, the capital of the province of Macedonia and the Aegean Sea's key northern port, and succeeded in starting a Christian community. It had a rocky start. There was strong local opposition from both Jews and pagans, and Paul and his fellow missionaries were forced out of the city, leaving the young Thessalonian Christians exposed to their local antagonists. However, because of this premature departure we now possess two letters from Paul written to sustain the community in these difficult days. These are doubly fascinating because they are so early. They were written around 40 CE, so a good ten years before his other letters. They are in fact the earliest documents in the New Testament by some margin.

These letters tell us that Paul converted the Thessalonians by working alongside them in manual labor. In one of my favorite verses, 1 Thessalonians 2:9, Paul writes:

Remember, brothers, our toil and labor;
while we worked night and day so that we would not burden any of
    you,
we proclaimed the good news about God to you.

You only showed up unannounced to stay in an ancient city if you had a death wish. Life in the ancient world was proverbially nasty, brutish, and short. There was no social welfare and little sympathy for outsiders. Similarly, you did not show up in an ancient city and practice a trade. There were local organizations that protected the precarious lives of handworkers, and there needed to be opportunities to work—shops, contracts, materials, and so on. Without an introduction, starvation and exposure were the probable outcomes for poor single traveling handworkers. It is highly likely then that Paul had an introduction to certain artisans in Thessalonica, asking them to welcome him and to provide him with work. It was this work opportunity that opened up in turn into the friendships that formed the Christian community. Moreover, this opportunity almost certainly came from Lydia's contacts as an artisan with the handworking communities in this city neighboring hers, and from any other businesspeople in the Philippian congregation. Paul's work in Thessalonica was made possible by his friendships in Philippi, although there is also a twist.

In Thessalonica Paul was connecting again with potential converts through a network. But he was also shifting between overlapping networks to increase opportunities for friendships. We could call this "missionary snakes and ladders" since he shifted from one network to an intersecting one when he got the chance in the way that a lucky throw puts our counter on a square with a ladder that lifts us up to an entirely new level on the board. If a convert was part of two or more networks, Paul could access a whole new world of potential friends and converts.

Paul contacted Lydia in a Jewish way. She was a God-worshiper whom he encountered at a Jewish meeting place. However, his mission continued down the Via Egnatia through a network of artisans. Lydia knew and dealt with artisans as a businessperson and handworker. So she was the key contact, positioned within two important networks, which allowed Paul to segue from Jews and God-worshipers to handworkers. Once we notice this practice of missionary snakes and ladders we can see it in Paul's earlier evangelism as well.

Paul and Barnabas traveled from Antioch to Salamis on Cyprus, Barnabas's homeland. This was a family network within a broader Jewish network. Sergius Paulus's conversion is unusual because it was so dramatic and sudden—a direct work of the Holy Spirit. But once that conversion had been made, Paul traveled to Pisidian Antioch exploring his family network, although this time of an out-and-out pagan family. And Paul's later letter to the Galatians suggests that more than just family members converted in Pisidian Antioch. Whole households turned to Jesus (see Gal. 6:10). Households in the ancient world, especially wealthy ones, contained more than immediate families. They were full of relatives, friends, retainers, and slaves. The household of a wealthy upper-class Roman also anchored a network of clients spreading out from their immediate area to other dependent households in their cities and to their country estates—their patronage network. Clearly Paul worked all these contacts in Pisidian Antioch and as they extended down the Via Sebaste. He could travel and be supported as far as letters of introduction from the Sergi Pauli had influence, although they could not guarantee his safety in other cities.

We can see clearly now how Paul was operating.

He was open to what we have called strange friendships. He was inclusive. God had sent him to the pagans he had previously despised, but he had gotten to know them now for several years and found that many of them were really quite nice people. God loved them and had a wonderful plan for their lives.

Paul was also highly motivated. He was prepared to travel. This meant covering geographical distances. But it meant traveling across social distances as well. He was prepared to hang out in unexpected places, and he couldn't do this—or couldn't do it as easily and constantly—before the breakthrough in Antioch, when he was observing Jewish practices vigilantly. Jews cannot eat and drink with people all the time, and they have scheduling clashes, while various pagan social spaces are downright problematic. Jews don't want to be too exposed to pagan idols, or to corpses, thereby incurring corpse impurity, or to eat food with blood in it. Paul's new flexibility with respect to food, drink, and timetabling meant he could access new social spaces without these impediments. Unexpected places offered strange new friendships, and these friendships could be with anyone, whether someone of high status like Sergius Paulus, or of low status, like Lydia. No one was too important or too unimportant to talk to and to befriend.

Another way of accessing new networks is also apparent in these events. Sometimes the Holy Spirit miraculously cracked open new networks in unexpected ways. Paul had no idea when he sailed to Cyprus that he would be dragged before the governor and then led to strike his deceptive sorcerer blind. But this is what happened. The Spirit thereby opened up this aristocratic Roman's familial and patronage networks suddenly and directly. What people sometimes refer to as "the first missionary journey" in the book of Acts, which looped from Cyprus up through central Turkey and back, derived almost entirely from this dramatic event and Paul's subsequent movement through the new set of networks it accessed. Paul had to be prepared to travel to Cyprus, obviously, and to stand trial before the governor, for all this to happen. The miracle by the Spirit—here a curiously stern one—still had to take place at the critical moment. But Paul speaks frequently in his letters about how his preaching of the good news about Jesus was accompanied by signs and wonders, so this was clearly not unprecedented.

With networks accessed in this way, through strange friendships in unexpected places and/or dramatic conversions, Paul worked through them. He probed for conversions, traveling at the recommendation and possibly also under the protection of the people within the network whom he had already converted. But he did not just mine a given network. He jumped from network to network by making converts who were positioned within different networks—missionary snakes and ladders.

Lydia was operating on the periphery of the Jewish community in Philippi. Once she had been converted, Paul had access to her contacts among local and more distant businesspeople and handworkers, Jewish and non-Jewish. Local veterans, whom Paul might have met through his imprisonment in Philippi (Acts 16:23–34), would have been networked with artisans too. After Cyprus in Galatia he worked through pagan family connections, then patronage connections, trying all the while to open up any Jewish networks that he could. So four primary networks are detectable at this moment in Paul's missionary work: familial, Jewish, artisanal, and patronal. His skill in jumping from one network to the other and back again was a key factor in his success in establishing communities in various cities around the Mediterranean coastlands at this time, and I suspect that this approach still works.

Being open and inclusive; being prepared to travel flexibly, not just to foreign countries, but to unexpected social spaces and thereby sometimes make strange friendships; being prepared to value anyone, high or low; working through any resulting networks, but being open to working off at an oblique angle through new networks overlapping with the present one; and being open to the unexpected openings, and closures, by the Holy Spirit—all these practices in combination add up to a formidably effective missionary approach, although it is not yet complete. We turn now to consider an important question that arises from all this activity.

Questions

› Acts 13–14 describes what many people refer to as Paul's "first missionary journey." Where did the mission team go? What significant conversion took place on Cyprus? Why did the team end up traveling in a rather odd, northerly direction from Paphos on Cyprus to Pisidian Antioch in what is today central Turkey?

› Paul made an important conversion in Philippi. Who was it? How would you characterize this relationship? Why was it so significant?

› When did Paul preach to the Thessalonians? How did he meet them in the first place?

› How does it appear that Paul usually met people in order to convert them? What missionary principle seems to be operating here? Why was he able to be so socially flexible?

› What is "missionary snakes and ladders"?

CHAPTER FOUR

Alongsiders

The situation

We have been tracing out Paul's missionary work in some detail to learn about how he skillfully accessed new networks to make conversions. He explored family, Jewish, handworker, and patronage networks from Antioch right across to Macedonia. Now he turned south into Greece, where we will learn some critical additional things about his missionary methods. He wasn't just about networks. We have briefly mentioned already how the team had to flee Thessalonica prematurely. We pick up Paul's trail in Athens, which is directly to the south of Thessalonica. From Athens Paul wrote two letters to the struggling Thessalonians in fairly quick succession.

Paul's two letters to the Thessalonians can get a little overshadowed by the big letters that Paul later wrote—Romans, 1 and 2 Corinthians, and his fiery short letter to the Galatians that was so beloved by Luther. But we need to appreciate how extraordinary it is that we possess these two documents from 40 CE. This movement's founder, Jesus, was executed by the Romans in Jerusalem in 30 CE. Just ten years later his advocates were in Greece and Macedonia.

Jesus was a poor handworker from Galilee who traveled through rural villages and seldom left the tiny Jewish territories around the river Jordan. His followers were now a new religious movement working through the cities of the Roman empire, and they were almost at Rome, and we have two documents from this era. Amazing. Priceless. But someone might ask how we know that they are from this early period since not everyone thinks that this is the case.

The date

I provide the full details of this dating in my technical treatment of Paul's life, *Framing Paul*.[1] Suffice it for now to say that the tumultuous events of 39–41 CE are to my mind stamped quite clearly on 2 Thessalonians.

Paul writes that letter partly to allay the fears of the Thessalonians that Jesus's return has already taken place and that they have been left behind. Some nasty neighbor has tried to deceive them by suggesting this, and they seem to have taken the bait. They have communicated with Paul in a panic. Paul responds with a timetable concerning the end-times, pointing out that certain things need to happen before Jesus can return, and they haven't, so he hasn't—a fairly simple argument. But the events in this timetable help us in a way that Paul would not have anticipated. They map onto broader events unfolding at the time that allow us to date this letter fairly precisely.

Paul says that before Jesus returns a man of lawlessness, a "son of perdition," will first have to be seated in God's temple proving that he is a god, arrogating himself over everything that is called "God" or "august" (i.e., consecrated as divine). A great apostasy will then take place accompanied by all sorts of false wonders worked by Satan. Jesus will overthrow this dreadful figure at his glorious coming. But since none of these things have happened yet, Jesus has not returned and the Thessalonians have not been left behind—although this is all close. We are in a period of "delay" (2 Thess. 2:1–12).

These events resonate with an awful episode that took place during the short reign of Gaius, who ruled from March 37 through January 41 CE. Gaius was the son of a Roman war hero, Germanicus, who, as his name suggests, had conquered parts of the feared Germans' homeland on the northern Roman frontier. So Gaius's accession was greeted with great acclaim and this meant with emperor worship, something strongly resisted by the Jews, who would not worship images and would not worship other gods besides their own Lord. Gaius was not a stable war hero, however; he was a sociopathic narcissist, which is why he was soon assassinated by the Praetorian legion at Rome. But he would still do some damage before that happened.

He was infuriated by the Jews' resistance to his cult and decided to have an enormous statue of himself installed in the Jewish temple. This statue was not just a portrait. It was to be worshiped—an act of horrendous desecration that sent Jews everywhere into a complete frenzy. The plan was hatched in late 39 CE and went through a number of stages and delays, but it was only halted permanently by Gaius's assassination in January of 41.

This plan seems to lie behind Paul's fairly specific description in 2 Thessalonians 2 of the fateful events that must precede Jesus's second coming. The statue of Gaius, which would contain his genius or spirit and be installed in the Jerusalem temple, was a seated figure. We know this because the famous statue of Zeus in the temple at Olympia—one of the seven wonders of the world—was an enormous figure of the god seated on his throne, and Gaius's statues were modeled on this one. He fancied himself as a bit of a Zeus. This sounds very like the "man of perdition seating himself in God's temple in Jerusalem and exalting himself above everything properly called 'God' or 'august,'" bearing in mind too that the first emperors of Rome were called Caesar Augustus. Moreover, no other historical events match Paul's description remotely closely.[2] So 2 Thessalonians, and 1 Thessalonians by implication, were written during this tumultuous time, when the plan was in full swing but not yet completed. This all points to 40 CE, an extraordinarily early date to have sources about this new religious movement. But we come now to the practical missionary questions. What do these letters tell us about Paul's approach that we don't already know?

They add some further key elements to our growing understanding of how Paul converted people.

What are our intentions?

A subtle trap lurks here for the unwary.

Christians often fail to get in touch with the shocking message that can lie at the heart of evangelism: "I am here to change you, and I'm going to change you so that you become like me." There are some obvious dangers here once we think about all this. If we approach people in this way, we are not treating them as people. We are not respecting them. We are treating them as part of our own program, like an objective and a statistic, and this is self-centered as well as disrespectful. An obnoxious smell of superiority is apparent. Further, we are judging people as fundamentally inadequate. We are okay, of course. Missionary work conducted in this spirit is a well-intentioned but self-centered power-play.

It is true that Christians do want to convert people to their own position, as Paul did. There will be judgment on non-Christian behavior as well. Change of a certain sort can be expected. But if we lead with this agenda and only this, we lapse into this somewhat unattractive missionary imperialism. We must, rather, place these concerns within the correct broader framework, and that begins with the reorientation of our intentions.

As we have just seen, if we approach people in terms of our own agenda we inevitably frame them disrespectfully. They become part of our project, and we are caught up in self-centered behaviors. We can avoid this instrumentalizing of potential converts—a making of them into something like an instrument or tool that then does something for us—only by approaching them for their own sakes and hence not as potential converts at all. We must value our initial relationships with people for what they are and not in terms of what we want out of them. This means that we must want to become their friends. Moreover, it must be a friendship with no strings attached. We must seek out relationships because we are interested in and value other people for who they are, right where they are. Conversions would be nice, but they are not our main agenda. We hope and pray for the best for our new friends, but that is not our principal motivation for relating to them. In this way and only in this way do we avoid colonizing people as we convert them.

There is a simple way to test if this is what we are doing.

Will we initiate and stay in relationship with someone if they never become a Christian? If the answer is yes, then we are conducting our relationship in the right spirit. If the answer is no, then we are lapsing at some point into one or more of the power-plays just described.

A former teacher of mine who had lived for many years in Israel as a Christian was once asked this question by a Jewish friend: "Will you love me even if I never become a Christian?" The answer was, "of course," and this is the right answer. But while it slides glibly off the tongue, it is a costly act in practice. Yet it is the only approach that maintains integrity in any relationship with a person we are getting to know who is not overtly following Jesus.

The importance of friendship is one reason why I have emphasized strange friendship within Paul's missionary practice so strongly in what has preceded up to this point and, in particular, his relationship with Lydia. But 1 Thessalonians offers further evidence of the way Paul related. There is plenty of evidence that Paul loved the Thessalonians, grounding their relationship in a deep friendship. Deep friendships are relationships of love.

He gives thanks for them and prays for them continually (1:2–3; see also 5:17–18), naming their virtues of affection, endurance, and hope. He and his co-workers originally labored among them with their hands "night and day" when the community was founded because its people "had become beloved to us" (2:8). The missionaries were as gentle as a mother suckling her own infants (2:7); and they encouraged, comforted, and exhorted them like a father his children (2:11–12). Paul has been so concerned for their welfare since he left the city that he has sent Timothy back on what was possibly a dangerous mission to report about them (3:1–5). On Timothy's return with the good news concerning their loyalty and longing he is so overjoyed that he triples the number of thanksgiving sections he normally supplies in letters, writing three instead of the usual one (3:6–10; see also 1:2–10 and 2:13).

The language used here is the language of intimate parental relationships in a healthy, loving family, intertwined with emotions of deep attachment—joy, relief, affection, longing, and loyalty. The practices of commitment are evident: a humble hard-working arrival (that we will talk more about shortly); constant thought and prayer and contact, including letter-writing; and an ongoing endurance and loyalty, salted with hope. Insofar as we can work these things out from this distance, Paul seems to have loved the Thessalonians and they seem to have loved him. We are justified, then, in calling them friends. Paul even says as much as he encourages them to love one another with a brotherly love (Greek *philadelphia*).

When we love people we often want to help them—to meet their needs. As Jesus once said, what parents do not want to give their children good things (Luke 11:11–13)? But if we allow this attitude to underlie our evangelism we might slip into another trap.

How much capital do we have?

If missionaries arrive with a great deal of capital, whether straightforward material wealth or what economists call capital (that is, money and property), or large accumulations of what sociologists call social capital (things like education and social connections), their relationships with their potential friends and converts can be distorted in significant ways, and from both ends of the situation.

Missionaries arriving with a lot of capital are tempted to view their potential friends as people in need—as people who are poor. Similarly, their potential friends, viewing the riches of their visitors, are tempted to view them as potential donors and patrons. The result is a patron-client relationship and not a relationship of equality and of authentic friendship.

The framing of potential friends in terms of need is destructive, whether that is done by the patron or the client. A patron who frames a friend in terms of need risks imposing a set of deficiencies on that person from outside, thereby misreading the situation and disempowering the ostensibly needy person who should really be allowed some part in the conversation concerning what they require. But people who spy a wealthy donor and act accordingly risk doing the same things in reverse. They define themselves in terms of need, sliding perilously close to a self-definition as a victim, and define their wealthy friends primarily as resources and not as people desiring a relationship of equality. They view their friends as ATM machines, and not as people.

These dangers should not be underestimated. As James Scott has shown, centuries of social hierarchy have equipped disempowered groups with techniques for dissembling and subtly subverting those above them who have power and resources. Lying, parodying, stealing, cajoling, avoiding, loitering, and mocking are entirely understandable ways of resisting the powerful and exploitative.[3] But they are deadly to any healthy relationship, which ultimately needs to unfold between equals. Moreover, once they are in play, these corrosive dynamics are next to impossible to erase. A relationship that begins in this fashion tends to stay there.

The church today is especially aware of this dilemma. The modern missionary movement was launched by Christians from Europe and the USA, areas that were the cradle of the industrial revolution, which in turn catapulted these regions to enormous accumulations of capital and to global dominance. Consequently, missionaries sent out from these regions to evangelize other parts of the world arrived with vast amounts of capital, in material, political, and cultural terms. The result was frequently a pernicious colonial dynamic. Converts were framed in terms of need and were victimized and infantilized. Missionaries were framed in terms of provision and identified with European mores—often described as quintessentially white values. Authentic relationships were distorted and difficult. What are we to do? Can Paul help us here?

In fact he can. Although he was not materially rich, Paul was rich in cultural capital. He was highly educated, well connected back in his homeland, and a leader. He was accustomed to organizing, pronouncing, and formulating and directing policy. So he was a wealthy person compared with the despised handworkers who occupied one of the lowest echelons in the ancient city and had no such training, connections, or confidence. But what did he do?

It is highly significant that Paul arrived in Thessalonica looking like the people he was hoping to befriend and to convert. He adopted the persona of a handworker and worked alongside the humble Thessalonians. We have already noted 1 Thessalonians 2:9, but its importance cannot be overstated:

> Brothers, remember our labor and our work.
> We proclaimed the good news from God to you
> while we worked, night and day,
> so that we would not burden some of you.

We need to let the full implications of this statement sink in. Paul, a former member of the Jewish ruling council no less, whose learning was legendary, arrived in Thessalonica and worked away like a humble craftsperson. He would have looked like one as well, wearing a single set of clothes, carrying a few tools, dirty and bedraggled from his journey, and with little to no money in his belt. He could have showed up and asked for free meals and lodging. He could have insisted that his former hosts send him on in the manner to which he was accustomed, possibly in a rented carriage. A professional like him could demand to be paid a speaking fee. His rivals did. But he didn't. He abandoned his cultural capital, lowering himself to the place where the Thessalonians lived, and became like one of them, so they could become like him (see Gal. 4:12). And this is just what we would expect. In another highly significant passage Paul says exactly the same thing about Jesus.

> Christ Jesus . . . being in the form of God,
> did not consider equality with God something to be used to his own
>   advantage;
> rather, he emptied himself
> by taking the form of a servant,
> being made in human likeness.
> And being found in appearance as a man,
> he humbled himself
> by becoming obedient to death—
> even death on a cross! (Phil. 2:6–8, NIV modified)

This passage is one of the first treatments of what theologians would later call the incarnation, and it is a wonderful thing. God chose to become a human being like us in order to encounter us and to relate to us, ultimately to save us. There is no greater lowering than this. In its light we can see that Paul's lowering of himself to the social level of the Thessalonians is a distant imitation of this principal act of identification by God. What Jesus did for us Paul copies in the midst of his potential friends and converts—and thereby solves the riddle we just posed.

We avoid framing potential friends as victims and ourselves as patrons by entering their situations where they are, not from above, but alongside them. We must set aside our material and social capital. If we possess it there will be opportunities to reintroduce it later on, but this is not and cannot be the right place for that. Rather, by following in the self-sacrificial footsteps of Jesus we can avoid the problems of initiating a relationship from a superior position. We travel to where our potential converts are in order to befriend them, ultimately with the expectation that they may or may not convert. We travel wherever we need to, whether across actual territory or into new social spaces. And when we arrive we set aside any privileges we might have and enter alongside our potential friends, as equals, as Jesus came alongside us. It is all so simple, and so difficult.[4]

In sum: we have gleaned two further critical lessons about Paul's missionary approach from Thessalonica. (1) We have learned about the importance of beginning a missionary relationship with friendship, avoiding the problem of treating people as potential converts and thereby instrumentalizing them, disrespecting them, and judging them. (2) We have learned about the importance of trying to abandon our cultural capital and to enter into friendships with people who are supposedly lower down the social ladder than ourselves, and then relate from a place alongside them, as equals. (This is a very difficult posture to achieve authentically, without a degree of pretense or patronizing.)[5] Moreover, these two practices should reinforce one another. If we genuinely desire friendship with someone we won't initially want to change them, or to intimidate them, or to frame them as needy and then begin to sort out their problems. If these lessons have been learned—or, at least, we have learned that we need to learn them because they are so difficult in practice—we can press on with Paul's story.

Friendships have now been formed in Thessalonica—as they have in Antioch, Paphos, Pisidian Antioch, Philippi, Berea, and Athens—without violating people's dignity or lapsing into a patron-client relationship, and some of these friends have converted. Little clusters of friends of Paul can now be found dotted through all these cities. What happens next? We pose here, that is, the whole question of what "church" is all about.

Questions

› Why do we suspect that 1 and 2 Thessalonians were written very early, in the 40s CE?

› Why does this early date make these letters so remarkable?

› In what two ways do we risk colonizing people when we convert them?

› What attitude and approach help us to avoid this danger?

› What key text that Paul wrote about Jesus helps us to understand the basis of this approach?

› What key text suggests that Paul practiced what he preached?

CHAPTER FIVE

Life Together

The Father and Son

In order to work out what church is all about, we have to consider more deeply what sort of God we are involved with. Some stunning insights await us here, both about God and about ourselves. We have already grasped that our God is triune or three-in-one; hence we have spoken quite a bit already about the Trinity. Now we need to press into this three-ness.

Our God is personal. He is so personal that he is composed of three persons; hence speaking of God as a single "he" isn't really right at all. We should speak about a "they." This truth takes us to the brink of a momentous discovery. We are about to find out what a person is. If we can work out what exactly these persons composing God are like, we will know what we are like as well, since we have been made in this image. We humans are admittedly rather dim copies of the divine persons, damaged and inferior, but we are still in some sense the same. We are persons too, made in the image of the personal God. But what are the divine persons like? What are their key features? In order to discover the answer to this question we will need to investigate some of Paul's key terms for God.

Paul often calls one person in the Trinity "the Father." He doesn't call Jesus "the Son" nearly as often—he prefers to speak of him as "Christ" and "Lord"—but the designation comes up at strategic points, confirming that it is implicit in every statement concerning God the Father.[1] At the beginning of both 1 and 2 Thessalonians Paul declares the involvement of his Thessalonian converts with this God and speaks—as he does in every other letter—of the grace and peace that come from them.

60

[From] Paul and Silvanus and Timothy,
to the Thessalonians assembled before God our Father and the Lord
    Jesus Christ.
Grace to you and peace from God our Father and from the Lord Jesus
    Christ.

We learn something quite stunning about God from all this, and consequently about ourselves. It is apparent here that both God "the Father" and God "the Son" are defined primarily by their relationships with one another. The Father is not the Father without the Son, and the Son is not the Son without the Father. These relationships name the most important things about them as persons (and the same applies to the Spirit, as well). We learn from this that persons are fundamentally *relational*, and the same truth must apply to us. We are relational. Moreover, we *are* our relationships. Like God the Father and God the Son, our relationships are the key to our personhood—to what we are. We are literally constituted by our relationships with other people. As a result of this, people are what we might call "extrinsic." We exist "outside of ourselves."

Many people today think that a person is something deep and internal and individual. We are who we are deep down inside, in our hearts or minds or spirits. To understand ourselves we must journey within. But we aren't and we shouldn't. These things are important. Without them we can't function as people. But they are just a sort of platform that we need in order to get on with the really important activities that define who we are as people—our relationships with other people.

We need to let this insight sink down into our bones. We are our relationships.

I am fortunate to enjoy a very happy marriage, and it is quite clear to me that I am who I am in large measure because of my relationship with my spouse, Rachel. She is part of my personhood, quite literally. Where I go she goes and where she goes I go. Because she lives I live, and as she lives I live. If she dies part of me dies. Similarly, my two children, Emile and Grace, are part of who I am. They are not important; they are essential (however frustrating that might be at times, whether for me or for them!). I will never not be the parent of Emile and Grace. Never. They define me.

We see the significance of relationships in Paul's life as well. Paul was a celibate, so he doesn't refer to a spouse or children to speak of his identity in these terms. He speaks of his deep connections with friends within his mission teams and communities, whom he uses familial terms to describe. They are his "brothers"—and this whether they are male or female. We have already seen how loving and intimate his relationship with the Thessalonians is. He longs for them; he worries about them; he is proud of them; he encourages and admonishes and instructs them as parents their children. But we can see now just how closely Paul and the Thessalonians are bound up with one another. Paul is constituted as a person in large measure by these relationships, as they are by him. He is what he is as a person by way of these relationships, and they are who they are now in relation to him.

With this realization we are ready to take another important step and to grasp what church is all about.

Church as relational

We have just learned that God is personal and to be personal is to be relational. It stands to reason then that this God would reach out to create other persons to relate to. This is not a need or a lack on God's part. It is a surfeit or overflow of the generosity of God. The personal God gives of himself. The richly and happily interpersonal God wants to share this life with others and so calls us into existence to live in communion with him. This is God's great plan for everything—for the entire cosmos—in place before the foundation of the world.

> For those whom he foreknew
> he also predestined to be conformed to the image of his Son,
> in order that he might be the firstborn of many "brothers." (Rom. 8:29)

Unfortunately, something has clearly gone wrong. Our communion with God and with one another has been sadly and deeply disrupted. But this does not alter God's desire to commune with us or derail his plan. It simply necessitates an intervention by him to draw us back from our fractured wandering into that communion again, something that God accomplishes for us in person, in Jesus. But Jesus did not come only to solve this problem. He did this, but he did so much more. God's plan has always been positive and it has always been communal, so Jesus effected this plan too. He drew us back into the community we were designed and destined for, and we know what this looks like underneath it all. He drew us back to full personhood, which means into full, authentic, healthy relationality—and that's basically it! So simple, so profound, and so enjoyable. God is in the business of drawing us all into communion with him. When that communion has been disrupted he restores it—patiently, gently, and inexorably. When that communion is reestablished he nurtures and deepens it, which means enhancing its relationships. And this is what church is all about. Of course we constantly forget this—we take our eye off the ball—or avoid it and wander off deliberately, because it is so difficult. But church is meant to be at bottom an entering into and living within the loving relationality of God.

One marker of how much we have grasped this—or how much we have missed it—is how we visualize church. Visual metaphors must be used with caution, but they have their place. Do we think about church visually in the terms we have just laid out? Or do we think about it rather differently, and thereby fundamentally distort what we are involved with?

Many of us probably think about church as a walled compound like a fortified city or castle. This sort of church is a bounded entity with a space inside it and a great barrier between Christians and non-Christians—a wall. This leads to endless discussions about what non-Christians have to do to get through the wall—presumably through a gate by saying the right password—and what exactly the wall consists of. Church is a gated community. The relationality and personhood of those both inside and outside the wall are neglected.

Alternatively, Christians are all independent entities that gather together consensually to affirm the basis of their gathering. They are like a bag of marbles. They get collected together into the bag for church on Sunday, and then get thrown out of the bag to cannon around for the rest of the week with all the other marbles in the world. (Perhaps they regather in a small bag on Wednesday nights for home group.) Here again the terms of the gathering are to the fore, and the nature of the interactions between the marbles is secondary.

It is fine to think spatially if it is done appropriately, but these metaphors do not just operate in terms of space; they think about church and people *as* spaces, and this is misleading. If people are fundamentally relational then they must be visualized in terms of relationships and so as webs or networks. People are a mass of lines and connections, and communities are a lacework of relationships that criss and cross. Churches (and societies) are a bit like the internet! What matters, moreover, is the tenor of these relationships. How are they functioning? Are they healthy, authentic, genuine, good, and happy? Or are they inauthentic, distorted, and even toxic? Church is all about making the transition from the negatives to the positives. Although it might seem significantly different from our usual visualizations and conceptions, church is something very simple. It is a relational network that is supposed to function well. But a key question is now emerging into view.

What exactly is the right tenor of a godly relationship? How is a good relationship supposed to function? What does a good network of people actually look like?

Strictly speaking, this is not a new question. We are returning here to the question of ethics that we broached when we discussed Paul's breakthrough in Antioch. There, however, we described its flexibility. Here we are emphasizing a new angle.

To answer this question, we must turn once again to God.

The greatest commandment

In Romans 5:6 Paul points out a simple but stunning truth.

> God demonstrates his own love for us in this:
> while we were still sinners, Christ died for us.

Our God is a Father who has sent his only Son to die for a recalcitrant and hostile humanity, and this means that he loves us. And the Son loves us. And the Spirit loves us. It makes no sense otherwise. This God was prepared to pay the ultimate sacrifice to reach out to us when we were ungodly, unyielding, and uncaring. The Father and the Spirit were prepared to sacrifice their beloved Son for us; the Son was prepared to die for us; and this while we didn't give a damn. This God must be loving all the way across and all the way down.

I like the song whose chorus goes, "God never lets up, never lets go, never gives up on me."[2] We need to sing this chorus all day and every day until this revelation into what God is like sinks all the way down into our bones. (If you don't like choruses, find some equivalent.)

Paul himself is well aware that this depth of love is difficult to grasp. So he prays in Ephesians 3:14–19 that God will gift to us, by his Spirit, the capacity to begin to understand this.

> For this reason I kneel before the Father,
> from whom all fatherhood in heaven and on earth derives its name;[3]
> I pray that out of his glorious riches
> he may strengthen you with power, through his Spirit, in your inner
>   being,
> so that Christ may dwell in your hearts through believing;
> and I pray that you,

being rooted and established in love,
may have power, together with all the saints,
to grasp how wide and long and high and deep is the love of Christ,
and to know this love that surpasses all knowledge,
that you may be filled to the measure of all the fullness of God.

It was this sort of God, loving all the way down, who could forgive Paul for attacking the followers of his Son and draw him back, appointing him to be a key leader in his new movement going forward. "I know you hate me and deeply misunderstand me, Saul, but I love you and have a wonderful plan for your life." It is this sort of God who draws us all to him now and shapes us as we respond to this invitation. This places the ultimate but entirely appropriate challenge before us.

We are called to be communities that love one another. Healthy relationality is constituted by love. Good relationality is loving. Bad relationality is activity that disrupts and hinders love. On the deepest ethical level it's as simple as this, although we will need to develop things a little more if we want to be practical about how all this works out on the ground.

The virtues

People established within relationships of love will act in certain specific ways in different situations, and we need to describe some of these in more detail. I sometimes call these "dynamics," since they are detailed characteristics of and activities by a basic underlying relationship. Ancient thinkers called them "virtues."

A loving person will trust God, and other people where this is warranted. They need not be naïve, but neither should they be needlessly cynical or suspicious. In part this trust will be oriented toward the future. There will be an expectation of promises fulfilled and good things over the horizon—an attitude of hope. To live as love and within love is to be happy, although to be happy in a deep and profound way, not in a superficial fizzy one. We can speak here of joy. It is also to be fundamentally at peace with God and the cosmos, and to work for peace where people are disrupting and sabotaging this. Love is restorative. People who love respond in particular ways to those who are misbehaving or struggling. They are patient and kind. They are giving when this is needful, and they are generous with their time and resources. They are not violent or coercive, actions that violate loving relationality at a very fundamental level. Conversely, they are gentle and self-controlled. All of this activity—what we might call love in action—constitutes goodness. We see Paul thinking in these terms in his letter to the Galatians:

> the fruit of the Spirit is
> love, joy, peace, patience, kindness, generosity,
> faithfulness, gentleness, and self-control. (Gal. 5:22–23)

But someone might ask me, is this really what church is all about? Is church basically ethical? Is it focused on how we behave and relate to one another? Is this it?

If we turn to the earliest Christian community we know about from Paul, the Thessalonians, the short answer is "yes, it is."

The Thessalonians

The bulk of Paul's two communications with the Thessalonians is devoted to matters of relationality—to ethics. Moreover, a fundamentally loving ethic is in view.

Paul spends a lot of time in his first letter affirming and reinforcing his attitude of love toward the Thessalonians (1 Thess. 1:1–3:13, so the first three chapters of the letter). He wants them to stay loyal both to him and to the God whom his gospel proclaims. His specific emphasis here is on love as trust and on trust over time under duress, which is best rendered faithfulness. This is a constant motif (1:3, 8; 2:13–16; 3:2–10; 5:8). These relationships are mediated through his co-workers as well. Timothy and Silas greet the church, co-write the letter, co-bless the recipients, and pray together for them. Timothy has also visited them, possibly in quite risky circumstances, thereby modeling Paul's commitment. Underneath all this anxious longing, commitment, and affirmation, we detect the love Paul has for his fledgling converts. But in addition to this basic set of relationships Paul works on the relationality of the Thessalonians with one another.

They are not to upset one another through sexually predatory behavior, a standard cause of community upset (1 Thess. 4:3–8).[4] Rather, they are to love one another with a "brotherly love" (4:9–10). They are to trust God that the dead will be raised, an act of hope (4:13–18). They are not to grieve at the rupture of their personal relationships by death but trust that these will be restored. They are to reject the partying culture of ancient society with its frequent substance abuse, being self-controlled (5:4–11). In closing, they are to love and therefore respect their leaders, be peaceful, be encouraging to one another (4:18; 5:14), and be patient and kind, renouncing vengefulness.

There is almost nothing in this letter that is not ethical and relational. It is church, ethics, and relationality all the way through, all the way down, all the time. Further, this relationality is primarily loving, issuing forth in more specific situations as trust, loyalty, hope, and so on. Our theological inferences are confirmed here then by the evidence in Paul. But a little more should still be said.

We have talked about the nature of the relationality in view, emphasizing its fundamentally loving tenor. We also need to work out how this should be organized. Churches are often very preoccupied with organizational questions. They tend to come up a lot. We need to ask, how is a relationally oriented community of love best arranged?

Organizing relationally

As Aristotle said some time ago, the goal of ethics is also the means. What he meant was that the goal of our activity—here right living—is approached through right living. This seems obvious at first glance, but actually it isn't. What he is claiming—along with most of the ancient moral tradition that Paul stood within, but not our modern traditions—is that ethics has to be learned, and, further, that it is best learned in community. Putting things succinctly, communality is learned communally. But Aristotle was a pagan philosopher. Was he right? Careful theological reflection suggests that—suitably tweaked—he was.

God chose to come to us and to restore us in person as a human being. The Son became a person we know concretely as Jesus, who called his followers to come after him. This is where God met humanity. The Spirit continues to invite humanity to meet God in this place and in this way, anointing human followers and successors of Jesus in the way that the Spirit anointed Jesus himself. So the Thessalonians met God through Paul and his friends and co-workers (2:13). God's engagement with us is embodied and personal and is automatically communal. God meets us within people and through people. (God is not reducible to people, but they mediate him, assisted by the Spirit.) The best way to make sense of this is to grasp that persons are not relational in a static manner in the sense that this is what they are and they stay this way, fixed in place like a wire basket. Relationships transform people. They are dynamic and in constant movement.

The astonishing degree to which people relate to and emotionally resonate with one another has been confirmed recently in a longitudinal study in the USA. Originally a mapping exercise investigating heart disease, exhaustive data were collated for a population of 5,209 people living in Framingham, Massachusetts, from 1948. The data were so detailed that they allowed social psychologists to map the emotional well-being of many of the participants as well. They found that people were remarkably sensitive to one another's emotional states. An increase in happiness within one person would radiate out through three degrees of separation, losing 10 percent of its intensity at each step. A significant 40 percent increase in one person's happiness would consequently increase the happiness of someone who was a friend of a friend of their friend by 10 percent. Needless to say, the distant friend of a friend of a friend had no idea what had just happened three relational steps away from her, and may not even have known the original happy person at all. Yet that person's well-being was measurably and significantly changed by the original happy person and by their community and its networks of relationships.

People are incredibly sensitive to one another. They respond to minute shifts in emotion, often without even registering the fact consciously. These responses then radiate through their relational networks to four degrees of separation and beyond. Aristotle's insight consequently seems well confirmed, both by theological warrant and by the evidence of social psychology, that people change in relation to one another, communally. To teach people to relate lovingly, then, we must construct a loving community and live in it, copying its most loving members.

When we consider this quickly, it seems incredibly obvious. When we press on it harder, however, it is anything but.

Most of our pedagogies are not set up imitatively, and this might explain why most of them are so ineffective at transforming people's actual relationality and relating. Protestants have long placed their faith in the transforming power of the preached word. They are frequently surprised at how little the communication of information about the Bible and from its texts—however eloquently and passionately done—changes the behavior of its churchgoing listeners. How unsurprising though. There is nothing to imitate here, or to copy. People cannot copy a preacher except by becoming a preacher, and that activity can leave a lot of other moral activity unaddressed. Writing a book will not change much either. It can help, but it can only be secondary to the main business of constructing healthy learning communities out of people that are influenced by people.

But if we suspect that a lot of the things we are currently doing in church are not very effective, what would be? How should a community that is aware of the importance of relationality, and of the need to teach through relationality, arrange itself?

We have already noted that the basic relationship is imitative. People copy people. But who copies whom? We come face-to-face here with the irreducibly elite nature of a learning community, and we shouldn't get too upset by this. Sociologists have long confirmed that all communities have elites. Every community has leaders and followers. There just aren't any alternatives to this. The $64,000 question is not, should we should have elites? but what sort of elites should we have? The answer for Christian communities is that we should have Christian leaders who are characterized by the relational qualities that we want everyone else to copy.

Appropriate churches will be arranged as learning communities with leaders and followers or disciples (sound familiar?). The leaders will have co-leaders, who may be well on the way to becoming the full package. We will pick up a number of threads from this brief summary later on. At Corinth in particular we will press much deeper into the authentic markers of Christian leadership and the mechanics of communal restoration. For now, however, we are limiting ourselves to the more loyal and placid Thessalonians. Does that community confirm the organizational insights that we have been inferring theologically and sociologically here?

Very much so.

Thessalonica again

If we had only Paul's letters to the Thessalonians and had to construct a picture of the early church from them, we would come up with an arrangement very like the one we have just articulated.

Paul is the leader, although he is supported by Silas and Timothy. He is primarily a moral teacher. He expects his Thessalonian converts to imitate him and his co-leaders. "You became imitators of us and of the Lord," he says at the start of the letter (1 Thess. 1:6). This imitation is expanded as Paul elaborates on what sort of person he is, which he does by elaborating on how he has been relating to them—praying for them, thanking God for them, being dedicated to them, being loyal and faithful, working hard for his own living, being gentle and caring, admonishing, encouraging, and longing to see them. We have also seen already how much relational instruction Paul gives them from a distance. His first letter is almost entirely devoted to ethics, and after the second has addressed the Thessalonians' worry that they have missed out on the second coming, ethics return. Paul is especially concerned that some Thessalonians are mooching. They are participating in the communal meal but are not contributing to it, being too lazy to work. What does he do? He commands them to follow the example of him, Silas, and Timothy, "working day and night, laboring, and toiling" (2 Thess. 3:8). This was a "model" (Greek *typos* or type) for them.

None of this should be too surprising. Paul had been trained as a Pharisee, and the Pharisees were an interesting instance of Jewish "hybridity." Judaism by Paul's time had been deeply influenced by Hellenistic culture (from the 300s BCE), including by its educational models and philosophical traditions. Things had blended together into an interesting new synthesis—into something hybrid. The Pharisees, who appeared in the second century BCE, are a Jewish version of a Greek philosophical circle.

They gathered around teachers to study the right way to live on the basis of their sacred texts, in the case of the Pharisees the Jewish Scriptures. They preserved the teachings of their preeminent teachers, in Paul's day by memory and orally. They copied their teachers, living like them and to a degree with them so that they could live like them. In particular, they met together for meals. They were concerned to practice scrupulous purity vis-à-vis these meals, but this was an ancient Greek setting for teaching and learning as well. The Greeks called them "symposia," meaning literally gatherings to drink together and to learn. Pharisees refused to teach for money, supporting themselves with a trade. This was evidence that their teaching was sincere. But in doing so they were reproducing the older position of the Greek philosophers that extended back to Socrates over against the more venal and arguably less trustworthy approach of the Sophists, who spoke and taught for money. Like the philosophers, the Pharisees met together in houses without idols or images, although Pharisees in Judea did venerate the temple. In the far-flung communities of the Diaspora, however, they did not frequent temples.

It is not surprising then to find that pagan commentators viewed both Jews and Christians as vulgar philosophers. The people were more uncouth than the average disciple of a philosopher, and their writings were rather less interesting and eloquent, but they looked fairly similar and behaved in much the same way. This is because the philosophers had stumbled upon a particularly appropriate way of learning and living that the Pharisees and the early Christians utilized in their own Jewish way: the imitation of a wise teacher within a community.

What is church all about then?

It is about relating, and about learning to relate together ethically, in a good way. This means gathering together and learning from one another, especially from the community's teachers, who are copied and imitated. Admittedly, this is a Christian development of the ancient Greek philosophical tradition. But it enjoys strong theological warrant. Jesus did this, and Paul and the Thessalonians continued the basic pattern, although in a distinctively flexible way since the guidance of the Holy Spirit at Antioch. However, in the light of what we have just said, this flexibility makes perfect sense. In a relational community the how is more important than the what—something the Pharisees sometimes failed to appreciate.

With these important realizations about the church in place, it is time to move on to the next scene in Paul's unfolding story.

The Corinthian mission

After his sojourn in Athens, from where he anxiously wrote his letters to the Thessalonians, Paul and the rest of the mission team headed south to Corinth. Corinth was a boomtown—the Las Vegas of Greece at the time. It was positioned by the isthmus joining the Peloponnese peninsula to the Greek mainland. Maritime traffic traveling east-west or west-east liked to transfer cargo from one ship to another there to avoid the dangerous and rather longer sailing route around the cliffs and rocks of the peninsula to the south. Smaller craft could be dragged across the isthmus on sleds (the grooves worn into the stone sledding route are still plainly evident today), and for every vessel Corinth took its cut. The city emphasized its stature by holding huge athletic games in honor of Poseidon every two years. These alternated with the other big quadrennial games at Delphi and Olympia. Money, travel, and big sporting events are always a rich combination.

Paul followed his usual pattern when he tried to plant a church in Corinth, but there were some notable differences in how things panned out there.

He lived as a handworker, trying to convert humble artisans, and he tried his luck in the local synagogue. Unusually, however, while he was doing this, he met some other early Jewish Christian missionaries who had just left Rome—Priscilla and Aquila. They were handworkers like him, although possibly at the level of running a business and so a rung or two up the social ladder from the average artisan. Paul seems to have formed a strong bond with them, and they worked together on Corinth's "street mission." In addition to this successful mission among the downtrodden and the down-and-out, Paul's outreach in the local synagogue at Corinth went atypically well, and his successes there included the well heeled. He converted a wealthy God-worshiper, Gaius Titius Justus, and was able to stay with him, next door to the synagogue. Other leading figures in the synagogue joined the church as well, notably, Crispus, an *archisynagogos* no less—that is, a wealthy community patron. But when did all this happen?

According to 2 Thessalonians 2, which bears the stamp of the Gaian crisis, Paul was in Athens in 40 CE. We can date the arrival of Priscilla and Aquila in Corinth to just when we would expect it, right after this, in 41 CE.

Acts says that the couple left Rome because of an imperial edict by the emperor Claudius (18:2). When Claudius came to the throne rather unexpectedly in early 41, the Jews were in a worldwide turmoil because of the horrendous desecration that Gaius was planning for their temple in Jerusalem. Claudius was a more sensible figure than Gaius and moved to take the situation in hand. He sent a long letter (and we still have a copy of this) to the massive Jewish community in Alexandria, offering the proverbial carrot and stick. Provided they calmed down he would not insist on any emperor worship, along with its offensive installation of images in their synagogues. If they didn't, he promised retribution. Claudius, as the Roman historian Dio Cassius informs us, dealt with the situation more firmly in Rome, which also contained a large Jewish community. There he was a little more restrictive, which is understandable; Rome was his capital. He enacted something the Romans frequently did when they got worried about a social movement. He banned them from meeting together. Technically, he removed the Jews' right to associate.[5]

This common Roman policy was based on the reasoning that if people couldn't get together then they couldn't plan political activity or gather a mob to have a riot. But this created a problem for pious Jews who could no longer do what they needed to do as Jews, namely, associate together on the Sabbath to read and study Scripture and to pray together. Synagogue life was shut down by this decree. What were they to do? Many did something impressively costly. They pulled up stakes and left the city, which is why Priscilla and Aquila, who were pious Jews, arrived in Corinth at roughly the same time as Paul, in 41 CE.

With these events, the first phase in Paul's life draws to a close. We have a fairly clear idea about what Paul was up to from just before his conversion through to now, about seven years later (34–42 CE).[6] However, we now lose sight of Paul and only pick up his trail again in 49, around seven years later. A great deal will happen between late 49 and early 52 CE, so there will be much for us to talk about, but for now Paul's story becomes rather dim and hard to determine. I call this period "the years of shadow." Almost everything we know about this time has to be inferred from short statements in his letters, and there isn't much to go on. But we do know some things.

The years of shadow

Paul lists a remarkable catalog of hardships in 2 Corinthians, which looks back on this period. He is comparing himself sarcastically with some rivals.

> I have worked much harder, been in prison more frequently, been flogged more severely [than my rivals], and been exposed to death again and again. Five times I received from the Jews the forty lashes minus one. Three times I was beaten with rods, once I was pelted with stones, three times I was shipwrecked, I spent a night and a day in the open sea. I have been constantly on the move. I have been in danger from rivers, in danger from bandits, in danger from my fellow Jews, in danger from Gentiles; in danger in the city, in danger in the country, in danger at sea; and in danger from false believers. I have labored and toiled and have often gone without sleep; I have known hunger and thirst and have often gone without food; I have been cold and naked. (2 Cor. 11:23–27)

This short text tells us that Paul has been traveling, which was always tough in the ancient world; that he has traveled a great deal by sea (three shipwrecks no less!); and that he has frequently been in trouble with the law (here at least for some of the time, the Romans). It seems fair to infer that Paul spent the years preceding this statement, which was written in 51 CE, traveling around the areas in the northeastern part of the Roman empire that he hadn't visited yet trying to plant churches, because there is another revealing comment at the end of his letter to the Romans in 15:19:

> . . . from Jerusalem all the way around to Illyricum,
> I have fully proclaimed the gospel of Christ.

Illyricum is a region lying on the eastern side of the Adriatic Sea toward its northern end. So it correlates with present-day Croatia. The book of Acts never has Paul anywhere near the Adriatic and only has Paul on a boat half a dozen times before he gets to Ephesus, where we will pick up his story again after these years and events. But Acts is interested in Paul's successes, and we have just documented a string of those. Working from a home base in Antioch, Paul managed to plant communities in the ancient Roman regions of Galatia (maybe four), Macedonia (three), and Greece (two). I suspect that Paul passes out of sight now in Acts because despite half a dozen years or so of hard labor—of brutal travel and frequent interrogation and imprisonment—he did not succeed in planting any more churches until 49 CE. This tells us something.

Paul's life was by no means a string of successes. It was frequently a long struggle with very little to show for it. But he persevered, and eventually good things did happen.

Questions

‣ Where do we find out what a person is?

‣ What is a person?

‣ What was God's plan for us, in place from before the foundation of the world? Can you name a key text in Paul that talks about this?

‣ What is the basic nature of Christian relating and relationality?

‣ How does love work itself out in specific situations?

‣ What word did ancient thinkers use to describe these relational dynamics?

‣ How are these dynamics best learned?

‣ How should communities be organized to foster this learning?

‣ When do we think that *we* have learned these things best? *Whom* have we learned them from?

‣ Who invented this approach to learning? So how did Paul learn about it?

‣ How was the mission in Corinth unusual, and unusually successful?

‣ Why were Priscilla and Aquila in Corinth?

‣ What happened during "the years of shadow" (42–49 CE)?

CHAPTER SIX

Insights in the Dark

The Lycus Valley mission

Seven years after he faded from view in 42 CE, Paul comes into focus again in 49. Despite working hard during this interval, he did not add any communities to the half dozen that he founded in his early years of work in Galatia, Macedonia, and Greece. In 49 CE he decided to try his luck in Ephesus, one of the three big coastal cities dominating the Roman province of Asia, which stretched up the western, Aegean coastline of present-day Turkey. This was an enormously rich province, one of the jewels in the Roman crown. However, his plan did not unfold smoothly.

Paul visited Ephesus in 49 CE, debating for several months in the synagogue, then had to leave, vowing to return when he could. He traveled back to Antioch, and then to Jerusalem for a critical meeting. However, it will be easiest to talk about that journey and its important negotiations later, in chapter ten. Suffice it to say that after this meeting in Jerusalem, Paul needed to deliver its decisions to his churches. So he traveled in early 50 CE from Jerusalem to Syrian Antioch, and then on to Galatia, which lay in the central part of present-day Turkey up near its mountainous central plateau. It was one of the first regions that he evangelized. After this he was free to head back to Ephesus to resume his missionary work there.

One of the routes from Pisidian Antioch, his key church in Galatia, to Ephesus, out on the Aegean coast, goes overland. It runs down from the central Turkish plateau westward into a sequence of interconnected river valleys that eventually lead out to the coast, and this is still the way someone in a car travels through this part of Turkey. (I have done it myself several times.) It wasn't the quickest route. But following this road would allow Paul to speak in pagan cities that he had not yet visited. So he made the obvious choice and headed westward on foot. Once he had crossed into the province of Asia, however, he was held up again. He was arrested in the strategic frontier town of Apamea and imprisoned there for several months.[1]

This sort of thing happened to Paul a lot. He caused enough upset wherever he went to draw the interest of the local officials. Officials did not like public disturbances. They would arrest Paul and detain him for questioning after any burst of unrest from offended Jews or pagans. Paul was normally able to talk his way out of trouble, although usually at the cost of having to leave the area. Typically, then, he was now locked up in Apamea after some local disturbance. But some interesting things happened to him during this particular imprisonment.

We can piece these events together because we possess three letters that he wrote at this time: to Philemon, a letter written rather unusually for Paul to an individual; to the Colossians living in the small town of Colossae just to the west, a group of converts that he made by proxy, through Epaphras; and to the "Ephesians," an unknown group of converts that needed to know Paul's entire vision of the gospel. I write "Ephesians" because this identification of the letter's recipients is unlikely. It appears only occasionally and in late manuscripts, while our earliest manuscripts leave this space blank. A more likely location for the letter's recipients was Laodicea, the town just down the road from Colossae that we also know from the book of Revelation (3:14–22). At the end of his letter to the Colossians Paul comments on the two letters he is currently sending, one to the Colossians and one to the Laodiceans. "Ephesians" and Colossians are very similar texts, so this identification makes sense.

This cluster of letters will deepen our understanding of Paul's mission considerably.

The strangest friendship

Paul wrote to Philemon for quite specific reasons.

In ancient Greco-Roman society, slaves could flee to people who had influence with their owners for help in a difficult situation. This was better than running away, which would put the fugitive outside any protection at all. Fugitive slaves could be mutilated or summarily executed on recapture. But there was a precedent for running to a patron and asking for help, and an unhappy slave called "Onesimus" had turned up at the Apamean prison and asked for Paul's help.

Owners generally renamed their slaves on purchase. They would not deign to learn a slave's own barbarian name, so they supplied impersonal numeral designations like "One" or "First" or a place-name derived from their place of purchase like "Ephesus." There are lots of slaves in the New Testament. "Second" travels around with Aristarchus (Acts 20:4). "Third" writes the letter to the Romans, while "Fourth" sends his greetings (Rom. 16:22–23). (This is very unusual by the way.) Onesimus means "useful" in Latin, so a slave known in these terms today might be called something like "Handy"—and he is miserable. Reading between the lines of the letter that originally accompanied Philemon, to the Colossian church as a whole, I think we can work out a bit more about what was going on.

In Colossians 3:11 Paul echoes his famous statement in Galatians 3:28 (although, strictly speaking, he hasn't written his letter to the Galatians yet):

> . . . be clothed with the new person
> who is being re-created in understanding,
> in accordance with the image of his creator,
> where there is no Greek or Jew, circumcision or uncircumcision,
> barbarian, Scythian, slave [or] free,
> but Christ is everything in every way.

Scholars have puzzled over Paul's use of "Scythian" here, which usually refers to the ferocious barbarian nomads who roamed the great Eurasian steppe to the north of the Black Sea. But this makes perfect sense. Slave-traders were basically pirates who raided ashore and kidnapped people to sell as slaves. Some would capture people from the shores of the Black Sea and sell them, often in Ephesus, as "Scythians," and sometimes slaves even received that name. Paul is hinting here, then, that Handy was originally a white barbarian captured to the north of the Black Sea—in modern terms, a white Ukrainian slave. Clues in the prescript of the letter to Philemon suggest that his master, Philemon, was a Phrygian. This was a barbarian lineage too, but an ancient race located in the Colossian area and long civilized by Greek customs. Two axes of tension are detectable, then, in the relationship between Philemon and Handy: one is a master and the other a slave; and one is a Phrygian and the other a Scythian—in modern terms, a Turk and a Ukrainian. Furthermore, as was common in deeply hierarchical and exploitative societies, Handy is dragging his feet. He is an unwilling, lazy worker and possibly given to a bit of pilfering as well. Beatings and the threat of reprisals have probably caused him to flee to Paul for help.

We come now to the critical moment.

The difference between Paul and Handy in social status was extreme. Paul was sufficiently high status in religious terms to have influence with Handy's master, Philemon. He was well educated and divinely empowered. He was the founder, at one remove, of the Colossian church. He was, at the least, a Christian micro-celebrity. Handy was a lazy and dishonest barbarian slave, the lowest of the low. The social contrast could hardly have been stronger. But the letter to Philemon suggests that Paul really loved Handy. The letter overflows with the terminology of affection. Handy is Paul's "child," "whom he has given birth to" while he is in prison. Handy is "his beloved brother." He is "his very heart," whom Paul wants desperately "to keep to help him in his current confinement." "He [Paul] will pay back anything owed." Moreover, Paul converted Handy during this visit. Philemon will receive him back no longer as a slave "but as a brother." Handy was "begotten while Paul was in chains" (Philem. 10–13, 18–19, 16, 10).

We might be suspicious at first that this strong language is a little over the top. It could be fake, or at least artificial. But it cannot be overstated how odd this level of affection is coming from a high-status person like Paul for a low-status person like Handy. I think that these phrases express just what they are saying—that Paul loved Handy. A useful point of comparison is afforded by a letter that Pliny the Younger wrote around the same time as Philemon and in similar circumstances.[2]

A slave has fled to Pliny for help with his master—the same situation that Paul deals with in writing to Philemon. However, the slave in question is seldom directly in view and is never mentioned by name. Pliny's contentions are generally superior and sometimes overtly bullying. All this is in stark contrast to Paul's tone and approach. Pliny's superiority and distance from the slave concerned would have been the norm. Paul's astonishing commitment and intimacy are the exception.

It seems then that Paul and Handy had become close friends, and this confirms that Paul was prepared to go anywhere to talk to anyone on the assumption that God valued everyone. It confirms in addition that Paul formed relationships of genuine affection with his potential converts. He loved them while he persuaded them. In short, Paul practiced what he preached, and what he preached and practiced was a Christian friendship that pushed through social barriers.

We now need to think more deeply about an important feature of Paul's life that we have encountered here in detail for the first time: imprisonment.

Prisons, and everything that goes with them

We usually fail to notice just how caught up with prisons Paul was for most of his life. We are looking now at a cluster of three letters he wrote during an imprisonment. His letter to the Philippians was also written from an imprisonment, taking the total number of letters in the New Testament that Paul wrote from prison to four out of ten—a full 40 percent! Clearly this uncomfortable location was a key context for his letter-writing.

Prisons are quite specific environments with a number of unique dynamics. I never noticed any of this until my wife became involved with one of our son's friends after he had done something terrible. As she walked alongside him during his pre-trial imprisonment, trial, and subsequent incarceration, I was drawn in with her in a supporting role and my eyes were opened. Spending time in courts and prisons in the US opens up new perspectives on the courts and prisons that Paul spent much of his time in. It is difficult to understand a prison until your body is inside one. Then a lot of things begin to clarify. The situation Paul was in was admittedly different from the situation of most people who are imprisoned in a modern western country today. But they are not so different that they don't relate to one another. When the state locks you up, for whatever reason, you are confined and under its coercive control. The basic experience doesn't change. However, there are differences too.

In Paul's day, law-enforcement as we know it did not exist. There was no police force and no general rule of law. The rulers of towns and cities wanted to preserve public order, and they acted to suppress any sort of disorder, seizing perceived troublemakers. Acts has a nice example of this when Paul is grabbed by Roman soldiers during a riot in the temple precincts in Jerusalem and then held and interrogated (21:27–36). The relevant officials would hold detainees in a secure environment until they were ready to interrogate them. There were no purpose-built prisons or prison cells, so a room had to be found, and usually this meant the least desirable one—a space such as an empty cistern or well—that was often dank and dark. Some legal codes of the time specify that prisoners should receive half an hour of exercise a day, rather as prisoners in a modern high-security segregation cell are allowed half an hour of daily exercise in a small cage open to the air and the sky. But, then as now, this was often overlooked, so prisoners spent long periods of time in one room together, perhaps crowded, probably very dark, in unsanitary conditions. They were environments characterized by darkness, lice, hard floors, damp, and stench. The rooms were not purpose-built and were not very secure. Security was maintained through something like an iron fetter or stocks. High-status prisoners might have been treated better, perhaps enjoying their own room or something like the house arrest that Acts speaks of for Paul in Rome (28:16). But ancient government was highly discretionary and often corrupt. Those people with status might be looked after; those with money probably were. But an official could throw anyone into a dark hole during detention, leave them there for a very long time until they could be bothered interviewing them, perhaps encouraging cooperation through flogging, holding them secure with harsh physical restraints, and ignoring their requests and the requests of their friends to support them. It was a lottery, and Paul doubtless knew its fickle probabilities well.

I won't go into all the new questions that these basic realizations raise here.[3] Nevertheless, three important features of prisons apparent in Paul's letters to the Colossians and to Philemon are worth highlighting.

1. *Celebration*. We often view prisons as places of deprivation and are drawn to characterize their occupants as victims (that is, if we do not think of convicted people as morally defective and dangerous). There is some truth in these insights and they need to be maintained. But if we begin here, we risk framing the imprisoned in a patronizing way when they are already being stripped of their dignity by their carceral environment. It is better to begin somewhat counterintuitively, by recognizing that prisons are also places of celebration and of opportunity.

Christians are already in prison. The church is already there. God is present. In my experience God loves showing up in prison, not within those who visit or guard as much as in those who are being visited and guarded. Paul's letter to the Colossians reminds us that God is present in prison primarily by way of those who are imprisoned, and here in the person of nothing less than an apostle. God is in prison with the prisoners. The church is already there, and the job of Christians on the outside is, first of all, to recognize this. Moreover, because God is there and Christians are there, the basic Christian truths can be celebrated and enacted in worship, teaching, prayer, and discipleship.

2. *Opportunity*. Two of Paul's letters from his Apamean imprisonment reveal that a congregation has been founded by proxy in Colossae. It met in the house of Archippus the veteran, and another congregation is meeting in the house of Nympha at the town of Hierapolis, which lay farther down the road. Epaphras, a slave, has somehow met Paul and his circle of friends while Paul is doing his time, has converted, and then has converted this network of households in these towns that were a few days' walk down the road. This is a classic instance of strange friendship in an unexpected place evolving into network conversions. This is also a major step forward in our understanding of

how Paul evangelized. We must now add a fifth web to our list of key networks. Paul works family, Jewish, patronage, handworker, and prison connections (and a link with veterans might now be detectable as well).

Paul has enhanced this small network by converting Handy, and he has tried to contribute to a more harmonious one by addressing his conflicted relationship with his master, Philemon. Paul's solution won't satisfy most of his modern western readers who are fortunate enough to live in a world where slavery has been massively delegitimized. However, it is worth noting that Paul is overtly countercultural in the moral pressure he places on those with power as he asks them to receive Handy back with respect and care. He draws the leader of the small community, Archippus, into the situation, commanding him to carry out his ministerial duties; he sends personal representatives; he sends a rhetorically powerful personal letter, which was to be read out in the presence of the rest of the congregation; and he promises to arrive shortly in person, with checkbook—and presumably rod—in hand to see if his new child in Christ is all right.[4]

We learn here, then, that prisons are seldom isolated experiences of removal as we might first suspect—a rather modern perception of a prison, and still an incorrect one. They are intensely social environments that allow a great deal of networking to take place (albeit, not always positive). Hence they are places of great opportunity for new friendships and community work. Moreover, these connections immediately spill out into the rest of their locales through the myriad relationships that flow to and away from incarcerated people. God is at work in prisons. They are hubs of unexpected activity.

3. *Support.* At the end of Colossians Paul sends greetings to his Colossian listeners from a group of friends: Aristarchus, Mark (yes, the same Mark that Paul dumped when he headed out from Syrian Antioch with Silas in 39 CE, obviously now back in the fold), Jesus/Justus, Epaphras, Luke, and Demas (4:10–18). A more abbreviated list can be found at the end of Philemon (v. 23). The lists are the same, with slight variations in order, but, in a curious moment, the roles of Aristarchus and Epaphras switch. In Colossians Aristarchus is a "fellow-POW" of Paul's, and in Philemon Epaphras is a "fellow-POW," not Aristarchus. What is going on?

Some scholars think this is a telltale mistake made by a forger while creating a letter to the "Colossians" in Paul's name, basing the details on Philemon, which is genuine. He makes a small slip with the final names here when most people are not paying attention, making the wrong person a fellow-prisoner.

I am not convinced by this explanation. More likely is a phenomenon that is well attested later on in church history as more and more Christians were sent to prison. But modern scholars who are not attuned to the practicalities of prison life might not think of this.

The officials detaining people in the ancient world had little interest in their welfare, and less accountability. They provided few if any resources—things like water, food, fresh clothing, bedding, and so on. Prisoners might hope for a daily cup of water and a slice of bread from their jailers and that was it, and they didn't always get even this. People in prison in Paul's day were primarily supported by their friends and family on the outside. But this was expected, and facilitated by bribes, and Christians developed a reputation for being involved with their imprisoned brothers and sisters to a positively irritating degree. Lucian, a cynical Roman writing in the second century CE, wrote the following about a Christian leader who had been imprisoned: "from the very break of day aged widows and orphan children could be seen waiting near the prison, while their officials even slept inside with him after bribing the guards. Then elaborate meals were brought in, and sacred books of theirs were read aloud, and excellent Peregrinus—for he still went by that name—was called by them 'the new Socrates.'"[5] In view of this practice, a likely explanation for the epithet "fellow-POW" switching between Aristarchus and Epaphras in Colossians and Philemon is that the two men are taking turns sitting with Paul through his incarceration and probably staying overnight, thereby sharing in its conditions.[6] When he wrote Colossians 4:10 Aristarchus was staying with him; when he wrote Philemon 23 Epaphras was.

We need to recall now that prisons are still places of pain. God and the church are there; they are places of unexpectedly rich opportunity. But they are also a crucible. They are designed to intimidate, immobilize, and degrade. Consequently, the smallest degree of support by those willing and determined enough to gain access to them is deeply significant. Paltry sums of money can contribute surprisingly large increases in well-being for people who are imprisoned. Even today small sums can buy stamps to send a letter, to change out a pair of worn sneakers, to replace a broken radio, to get a magazine subscription, or to buy some books. And they can pay for a visit to a doctor or a dentist, bearing in mind that an appointment might cost seven dollars, which is a week's wages in the upholstery shop if someone is lucky enough to have this coveted job.

Paul's letters speak subtly of the support he needed and received during his incarceration. We have just noted his companions. But another way in which Paul received support was help writing letters. It is doubtful that he took a small writing desk, a lamp and oil, rolls of papyrus, ink and ink pots, trimming knives, and pens into his detention room with him. These things all either had to be supplied to him by those visiting him or used by those who had visited him to write down outside what they had memorized while they were sitting with him in the dark.[7] If this was the case, they brought drafts of the developing letters back to Paul for his revision, and then for his final approval and signature.[8] Scholars sometimes forget what practical difficulties attend letter-writing in a prison. Martin Luther King's famous "Letter from Birmingham Jail" was smuggled out of his cell written on scraps of newspaper concealed in his visitors' shoes, and then written on his lawyer's legal pad while they were supposedly consulting. The final letter was edited together from these fragments and published not by King himself but by Rev. Wyatt Walker and Willie Pearl Mackey.[9] Philemon, Colossians, and Ephesians are Paul's "Letters from Apamean Jail," and they attest to the support he received from Christians outside while he was there. They also attest to how a little generosity can go a long way for people who are doing time. Without that support in Paul's day we would be missing a lot of the New Testament!

But we have yet to look in much detail at the third of these letters, Ephesians, and as we do so, another significant feature of prison settings will become apparent.

A manifesto

As King's programmatic "Letter from Birmingham Jail" suggests, Christian activists often pen their most resonant pieces from prisons.[10] This stands to reason. They are activists, and activists lead busy lives. They travel, talk, organize, agitate, meet, protest, and have time for very little else. When they are detained, however, a period of quiet space is literally forced upon them. Literate activists tend to do a lot of thinking at such times and, if it is made possible through outside support, writing. So figures like Martin Luther King and Paul were too busy to do a lot of reflective work while they were engaged in community founding and organizing. But they both spent a great deal of time in prisons and jails, which amounted to periods of enforced quietness, and it is there that we find them writing some of their most programmatic statements—what we might call their manifestos. The letter we know as Ephesians is Paul's manifesto and is inordinately important.

It is not that Paul wanted to sit down and write a manifesto. There is no evidence that he ever did this rather modern, abstract, and self-reflective thing. But Ephesians is a manifesto in effect because of the circumstances that elicited it.

83

Paul had heard about a group of converts to Christianity from paganism who were meeting in Laodicea. But he was the divinely designated apostle to the pagan nations set apart for this task from his mother's womb. Arguably only Barnabas was of equal stature (see Gal. 2:8–9). So these anonymous converts desperately needed to have their identities shaped by his views of what God was up to in Jesus in relation to the pagans; after all, his views were definitive. However, obviously Paul was unable to impart these in person, currently being a guest of the state and knowing that every incarceration carried the risk of execution. So he did the next best thing and wrote a letter, which was a time-honored way of speaking from a prison. Paul seems to have spent some months crafting and shaping this piece in the dark of his prison cell, reciting and polishing it repeatedly.

We can't undertake a blow-by-blow account of all the things Paul says about Christian identity in the letter. That would take at least a semester of close exegetical work (which I do recommend). But we can note some of its key emphases as it further reveals Paul's missionary system that we have already begun to put together from his early years of work and the two letters he wrote then.

Something old, something new

The agenda apparent in Ephesians largely confirms everything we have already learned, although the overarching story of God and humanity that Paul tells—and it unfolds in part through Paul—is now significantly deepened.

Paul is an emissary specially chosen by God to make known God's secret plan hidden from the foundation of the world but now revealed in Jesus. The triune God of Father, Son, and Holy Spirit has generously and lovingly chosen—"elected"—to gift humanity with salvation in Christ. Those who are responding to this generous gift are lifted from their old sinful existence that is destined for death into a new relational life. They are resurrected in Jesus, something they experience now as having a resurrected mind. Paul therefore expects the behavior of his converts to change, especially in terms of how they relate to one another. They are to be loving, kind, and appropriate in speech, as well as sexually disciplined. They will learn this behavior in a quite practical way by following their divinely appointed leaders who have been gifted by God in various helpful ways as apostles, prophets, evangelists, and teachers. Paul's converts should imitate these leaders who imitate Jesus, and thereby imitate Jesus himself. The Holy Spirit is intimately involved in this process as well.

A key result of this gift of resurrected life to the community is reconciliation between God's chosen people, the Jews, and those who have heretofore lain outside the boundaries of the holy people, the pagans. The new situation gifted in Jesus transcends this enmity; it is characterized by peace. However, the community is being attacked constantly by the evil forces who oppose God's cosmic plan, and it is called to stand firm in this fierce spiritual battle.

If this agenda apparent in Ephesians is basically the same as the system we have already reconstructed from Paul's activities in Damascus, Antioch, Galatia, and Macedonia, we might ask if anything is different—other, that is, than being laid out more fully. Two further things are worth mentioning.

Election

The Thessalonians knew that they were chosen by God. Paul highlights this at the very beginning of his first letter to them (1:4–5):

> We constantly give thanks to God for all of you . . .
> knowing, brothers, so beloved by God, his *choice* of you,
> because our joyful announcement did not take place among you in
>   words only,
> but in power, by means of the Holy Spirit, and with deep conviction.

It is clear here that God initiates his relationship with the Thessalonians. This tells us that love initiates. It reaches out, even to the unlovely. But Ephesians 1:4–5 shows us how this initiating love reaches right back to the heart of God before creation. It characterizes God's entire plan for the cosmos:

> He [God the Father] chose us in him [Jesus] before the foundation of
>   the cosmos
> to be holy and blameless before him;
> having chosen us in love to be adopted through Jesus Christ . . .

Paul is so excited about this overflowing benevolence and divine purpose that he can't quite finish the sentence he is writing about them. It runs on and on from Ephesians 1:3 through to verse 14 when his reader finally catches a breath. And this is all highly significant.

We often have to ask where exactly we should begin our story about God, Jesus, and humanity, and many interpreters think that this is best done from a human point of view. We begin as Paul's letter to the Romans seems to, with a struggling and sinful humanity (which is not wrong), which works out that it is under judgment and then seems ready to turn to the gospel as soon as it arrives. But this story is human-centered or, put slightly more technically, anthropocentric. It appeals to modern readers because it is a story that revolves around us, and it views us basically as individuals. It starts with our condition, and God arrives to sort things out. Modern reflection is remorselessly self-centered.

Ephesians stands strongly against this approach. It begins the story about God, humanity, and the gospel with God, specifically, with God's plan from "before" the foundation of the cosmos—"before" because there is no strict temporal before when time doesn't exist. God's plan was always to adopt us as children in his beloved Son Jesus. This has been a cosmic secret until its revelation now in the gospel, so the secret is finally out. But we don't understand this secret without the arrival of Jesus. He is the secret. So we can't work out the most important things about the meaning of the cosmos before the gospel arrives by beginning with our own situations. Proceeding in this way would miss the most important thing, which is responding to Jesus as we have been destined to. We must proceed in a Christ-centered way or Christocentrically, which is what Ephesians does. Christ is the key to the cosmos. This is where Paul's theological story begins.

Characterizing the community

The community that is called into being by God's work in Christ and Paul's work as an emissary is a relational network of people. It is also able to stretch across barriers of race and ethnicity. These are transcended by the wondrous new state of being resurrected in Christ, something that is experienced now by having a resurrected mind. But on the ground the new communities springing into being all have subtly different ways of doing things, and this all creates an interesting problem.

What is this new network, and how do we think about it? It isn't really "church" as we know it. On hearing this word most of us envisage a cute little stone building that people visit once a week—where, that is, we are not thinking of some walled compound or city. "Church" translates the Greek for "assembly" in Paul's letters, and it is not especially helpful to call the diverse network of communities we are trying to name an assembly either. Its communities assemble regularly, but this isn't the heart of the matter. They don't assemble together either; rather, they are spreading rapidly away from one another in geographical terms. We can't use ethnic or racial designations like Judaism anymore, or geographical ones. We are pushing through just these boundaries and barriers, including them within something bigger. This network is something new under the sun. In due course, we will draw a favorite image from church tradition and talk about a city (suitably defined!). Ephesians meanwhile gives us some of Paul's most compelling images for its description.

First, Paul describes it as a temple. This points metaphorically toward the purity and cleanliness of the community. Good and healthy relationships are pure; negative and destructive relationships are defiling. But the claim that the gathered community is a temple indwelled by the Holy Spirit has a radical edge. That God is fully present in a group gathering in a home suggests that God is not simply to be found in the Jerusalem temple, there to be approached by one person once a year, in the Holy of Holies, in a state of rigorous purity. An extraordinary geographical decentralization of God's presence has taken place. His followers no longer have to travel to Jerusalem to meet with him. They can travel out to those who do not yet know him, carrying his presence with them, rather as the children of Israel first carried God's presence with them through the wilderness of Sinai in the tabernacle. Moreover, if this is the case, communities no longer have to invest in capital-heavy projects to try to ensure that God will show up. Large buildings were redundant—a big change for Jews and pagans. God is traveling to where these small groups of people meet.

Second, in some distinctive passages—Ephesians 5:22–6:9 and Colossians 3:18–4:1—Paul lays out regulations for the key relationships within the community: between husbands and wives, owners and slaves, and parents and children. He is reflecting longstanding Greek practice here, so we can find a very similar arrangement laid out in Aristotle's *Politics*. Luther called these tabulations the Household Codes or House-Tables (*Haustafeln*) because they could be written up in a table of rules and hung on the wall of the kitchen to remind everyone of their roles in life. Originally, however, they were used to organize the ancient *polis* or city-state. They described its correct arrangement, and this is significant.[11] When Paul uses these rules to organize his communities, he is implying that the new network of Christians is a political entity. It writes its own rules and has its own rulers, ultimately being ruled by God. Christianity has its own politics, and Christians are citizens of another polity—another nation-state—from the one that they might think they occupy. Modern Christians accustomed to living in a society that separates church and state often forget this, but Ephesians and Colossians instruct us to remember it.

These passages contain challenges. They operate on a "command-and-control" model that offends many modern readers. Everything works smoothly within the city if people respect the roles they have been given and those roles are located within a great hierarchy of power. Some people have been placed in charge; they need to rule those they are in charge of wisely and compassionately whether they are wives, slaves, or children. Those who are being ruled need to respect their rulers; husbands, owners, and parents should ultimately be obeyed.

This plan for a harmonious community based on reciprocating compassion and respect has worked reasonably well for much of human history, and it is better than some alternatives. But relatively recently—at least in broad historical terms—the church has introduced some significant modifications. In particular, Christian groups campaigned steadily for 250 years beginning in the late 1700s to abolish slavery (sadly, often bitterly opposed by other Christians). And they were right to do so. Slavery is an abomination. We see in this abolition especially clearly that modern Pauline communities must differ in certain key respects from Paul's original communities. However, the tracing out of these differences is a difficult matter. To introduce this conversation now would take us a long way away from our main concern in this book, which is Paul himself. So, I must refer those who are interested in exploring this conversation further—a little reluctantly because I would dearly love to have this conversation now—to my next book, *Pauline Dogmatics in Outline*, which addresses just these questions. Suffice it to say here that for all the problems they raise for modern readers, the Household Codes tell us that Paul's communities were political. God is interested in the organization of every aspect of his people's lives.

Third, in some other passages, Ephesians develops one of Paul's most famous metaphors for his new network of communities: the body. Ancients thought about bodies differently from moderns. We tend to think of bodies as occupying a distinct space, with a volume and some external boundary or barrier—our skin. Ancient people viewed bodies as rather less discrete than this. They were more dynamic and fluid. Their boundary was less obvious. They were also more comfortable with tangible physical dimensions and more hidden spiritual dimensions interacting with one another to make them work.[12] This dynamic ancient notion of a body allows Paul to say several important things about his network of communities.

They are, precisely, a network, which is connected together. The communities are distinct, like the different parts of a body, but are irreducibly connected to one another as well—distinct but never separable then. This unity overrides local differences in status and cultural capital. However lowly or humble, everybody needs every part functioning well to function at all. Everybody needs everybody else. A basic equality is evident here. So the body speaks of a diverse and relational but utterly real unity.

In addition, the body metaphor speaks of the organic hierarchy in the community. Jesus is primary as the head is primary for the body. Everyone is connected to him and grows up into him; the connections here are quite concrete. But underneath him are other leaders who have matured more than their followers, and these leaders, gifted by the Holy Spirit, teach, encourage, and admonish the rest of the community. So the metaphor of the body nicely captures the elite, pedagogical arrangement of the community that we detected at Thessalonica, rooting it in Jesus himself.

Finally, the metaphor tells us something important about the foundation of the church. Later church tradition placed a great deal of emphasis on the apostles as the basis of the church, although it generally meant by this the writings of the apostles and some of their key followers, collected in the New Testament (and strenuous efforts were made at times in support of these authorships). It also emphasized the succession of church leaders—within a hundred years or so, bishops—that stretched back in an unbroken line of transmission to those original apostolic leaders authorized by Jesus himself. Irenaeus was highly instrumental in formulating and spreading this view as the church fought for its identity and direction in the late second century CE. But Ephesians encourages us to read this notion of an apostolic foundation slightly differently. It suggests that the basis of the church is a leadership group composed of missionaries, since apostles in Paul's day were basically missionaries. At the heart of the church is a group that is constantly in motion, reaching outside of itself to those who are not yet fully part of the Christian community. To lead the church effectively, at its highest level, is to be comfortable living alongside those who are not yet part of the church. What great criteria for the leaders of a community—outward looking and dynamic.

Several further important questions now open up before us, but for answers we need to move on to Paul's correspondence with Corinth. At Corinth more than anywhere else we see Paul navigating the challenges that can be posed by communities. As he does so we will detect some further factors that prove critical to the success of a Pauline community.

Questions

› Where was Paul imprisoned when he wrote "Ephesians," Colossians, and Philemon? Why was he locked up there? Where was he coming from and trying to get to?

› Who was "Ephesians" most likely sent to?

› Why did Paul write to Philemon? How did he know about this situation?

› What important elements within Paul's missionary approach does this little incident confirm?

› How much did a prison environment dominate Paul's letter writing?

› What three aspects of prison environments do we need to remind ourselves about?

› How did ancient Christians make the detentions of their leaders more bearable?

› Why did Paul lay out his views most systematically in the letter we know as Ephesians?

› What does Ephesians add to our previous understanding of God's election of us to salvation that we learned about in the Thessalonian letters?

› How does Ephesians help us to name and thereby to understand better the strange new thing that is Paul's spreading network of diverse relational communities? There are three important suggestions.

› The Household Codes tell us something positive and important about Paul's communities. What is it?

CHAPTER SEVEN

Culture Wars at Corinth

From Apamea to Ephesus

Paul was released from his imprisonment in Apamea, just up the road from Colossae. He walked for three days southwest to visit the Christian community there, and the Colossians now finally got to meet their founder in person. He then walked another day to the west to visit the mysterious pagan converts in Laodicea to whom he had written a letter. Acts says that he baptized a group at this time, so it looks as if they responded well to his manifesto (19:1–7). Then he visited Hierapolis, where a small group of Christians was meeting in Nympha's house. Hierapolis was a spa town up on a ridge overlooking a magnificent white thermal terrace. You can still see it easily today from the main road running through Laodicea. Then, as now, visitors bathed in its hot springs and mineral baths, so if I were Paul I would have hung around there for a bit and recuperated.

After reinforcing this little cluster of churches—which might have taken several months—Paul traveled farther west for a week or so, down the long Maeander valley, which exited to the coast at the city of Miletus. Miletus was a port just south of Ephesus, so Paul would have turned to the north at Magnesia and climbed out of this valley as it neared the coast. In this way he finally returned to Ephesus as he had promised. The stunning views of the Aegean Sea from what is present-day Turkey would have greeted him, and I have to say that a summer sunset facing west across the Aegean Sea is one of the great experiences in life. It had been a year and a half, but he was back.

Paul wanted to get down to some serious work in Ephesus, which was a highly strategic city of over 200,000 people crowded together. But he was supposed to be relaying instructions from the Jerusalem meeting he had just had.[1] Rather than visit all his communities on the other side of the Aegean Sea, in Greece and Macedonia, to give these in person, he did what any right-thinking ancient person would do and wrote them letters. The largest and most significant of these communities was in Corinth.

Paul wrote his first letter to the Corinthians, now lost, in the fall of 50 CE. The Corinthians pushed back quite hard. They wrote a reply to Paul with a number of questions. (We can see him answering these at various points in 1 Corinthians.) It was carried to him by an official delegation from the church led by Sosthenes. Some "people from Chloe's household" visited Paul during this time as well. They were slaves sent to give Paul the inside story on what was really going on.[2] As a result of all this, Paul had a pretty complete picture of the situation by the end of the winter. In the spring of 51 CE he wrote a long letter back, our 1 Corinthians. This is where we start to build up a more detailed picture of the community, and it is not a pretty sight.

Problems!

When we reach Corinth it is as if Paul's mission has hit the skids like a truck on a freeway hitting black ice. The church at Corinth was a mess, although it is a mess that will eventually tell us some important things about how to do church. I count fifteen distinguishable problems that Paul addresses in 1 Corinthians. (Technically, two of these aren't big problems yet, but they soon will be.) After listing them quickly we will try to press beneath the surface of the situation to identify the key underlying causes.

(1) Partisanship (1:10–4:21; 16:10–18). The Corinthians have factionalized behind different leaders. Some follow Paul, some Cephas/Peter, and some a rival called Apollos. Some might even have formed their own "Christ party." Disrespect for rival leaders extends to their followers, so, at the end of the letter, Paul has to ask the Corinthians to respect Timothy and the leadership of the humble household of Stephanas.

(2) Incest (5:1–13). A man is sleeping with his stepmother.

(3) Prostitution (6:12–20). Pagan society thought nothing of men visiting prostitutes, and some Corinthian men are continuing to do so.

(4) Celibacy within marriage (7:1–7). By way of contrast, some marriage

partners are withdrawing from sexual activity with their partners on "spiritual" grounds.

(5) Some Christians married to one another are asking about divorce (7:8–11, 39).

(6) Some Christians married to pagans are asking about divorce or they are being asked about divorce by their pagan spouses (7:12–16).

(7) Some engaged couples wish to marry (7:25–40). Their marriage arrangements have been on hold for reasons we will talk about in the next chapter when we address sex and gender. They want to move forward in their relationships to the next step. Some widows also want to remarry.

(8) Lawsuits (6:1–11). Some people in the church are litigating against one another. Second Corinthians suggests that the problem was a theft (2 Cor. 2:5–11; 7:11–13).

(9) Contact with idolatry (8:1–11:1). Some Corinthians are happily eating meat that has been purchased secondhand from the meat market. This meat has come from animals that have been sacrificed in pagan temples by priests to idols, so converts who are Jewish or who have Jewish sensibilities find this food offensive. It is polluted and contains blood. In addition, some Corinthians are feasting in restaurants located on temple premises, and even attending pagan worship events with their processions and celebrations and feasts. Those converts who are more respectful of Jewish traditions are again outraged by this.

(10) Some Corinthians are offended by the abandoned way in which women are praying and prophesying (11:2–16). Their clothing is slipping off, so perhaps think of someone worshiping up at the front of the church today like a pole dancer.

(11) The period of worship is chaotic (chapter 14). People are babbling in tongues and speaking on top of one another. Nothing is intelligible.

(12) The communal meal is a bring-your-own rather than a potluck meal, and significant differences are apparent (11:17–34). Some poorer participants are going hungry; others are feasting and getting drunk.

(13) Some people are denying the bodily resurrection both of Jesus and of Christians (15:1–58).

(14) Paul notes that a large sum of money is supposed to be collected that will be sent to Jerusalem to firm up his relationships with the other leaders of the early church who are based there (16:1–4). This is not a big problem yet, but it will shortly become one.

(15) Paul announces a change in his travel plans (16:5–9). He has canceled a direct visit to Corinth from Ephesus, substituting a route that will head

directly to his churches in Macedonia, and then down through Greece to Corinth at the end. He was always going to visit Macedonia, so this new plan means that the Corinthians are losing their first visit from him when he would have looped through them up to Macedonia and back. They will see Paul later and just the once now. Again, this is not a big problem yet, but it will shortly escalate into one.

Is it possible to simplify this shopping list of problems, bearing in mind that this is one of the most difficult challenges we face when reading Paul? I think so. When all is said and done there were four main difficulties underlying this mess:

(1) a basic failure in relating as Christians ought to relate to one another, with kindness or, as Paul puts it, in love;

(2) a dramatic failure of the local leaders of the church to act as Christian leaders ought to, considerately and self-effacingly; they were engaged in an intense competition with one another for status and influence;

(3) arrogant theological reasoning on the part of some that was both amateurish and overconfident, denying the importance of the body; we can call this "Christian intellectualism";

(4) tensions arising from the pressures Paul's teaching about sex placed on his converts after the passage of time, in addition to the pressures that pagan values and the basic realities of sexual activity place on people in any case.

Each of these problems would have been bad enough, but when they were all present together the combination was toxic.

We will look at the first three difficulties in more detail here in this chapter, and devote the following chapter entirely to sex and gender because navigating Paul's advice in this area is so complicated.

Problem 1: Christian relating

When we take a step back from all the ins and outs of the issues in the letter we can see that for much of the time Paul is urging something fairly simple on the Corinthians. In Paul's other communities a great deal that he says can be summed up in the phrase "appropriate relating," and 1 Corinthians is no exception. One of the letter's high points is chapters 12–13. Chapter 13 describes at length the principal Christian way of relating, which is with love. Its profundity is evidenced by the fact that it is still read out at weddings all over the world today.

> Love is patient, love is kind.
> It does not envy, it does not boast, it is not proud.
> It is not rude, it is not self-seeking, it is not easily angered.
> It keeps no record of wrongs.
> Love does not delight in evil but rejoices with the truth.
> It always protects, always trusts, always hopes, always perseveres.
> Love never fails. (13:4–8a, NIV)

Chapter 12 prefaces this appeal by laying out the way in which the community is all about relating together using the image of the body of Christ. No part of the Christian body is unimportant. Every part is linked to every other part, no matter how humble it might seem to be.

This advice is applied by Paul especially to the disorders in the Corinthians' communal meeting. This was a meal together at which the Lord's Supper was celebrated, followed by a period of worship with singing and the use of the spiritual gifts. People spoke in tongues, prophesied, and prayed for one another's healing (11:2–14:40). However, we have already noted how many problems are evident here. It is nevertheless amazing to observe how many of these problems—along with several others in the lengthy list we compiled earlier—would disappear if the Corinthians would just be nicer to one another.

People who love one another don't pray and prophesy in the communal meeting so that their clothing will become disarrayed and violate a viewer's sense of propriety; they don't shame their spouses publicly with their behavior; they don't bring lavish meals to a church picnic and gorge on them while other church members stand around hungry; and they don't babble in tongues on top of one another during the time of worship. Neither do they factionalize into bitter partisan disputes. They don't slander rival leaders but stay loyal to their original founder; they don't steal from one another; they don't mock people who are offended by a food item that they personally don't think matters; neither do they judge people who they think are ignoring something that should worry them.

It's not rocket science. So many problems in Corinth—and I suspect in many other places—are solved if Christians are kinder to one another, whether they are at home, out socializing, or at the weekly communal meeting. But something seems to be making considerate and appropriate relating especially hard at Corinth, and we don't have to look far to find out what that was.

The Corinthian church was unusually diverse, and the ethic of appropriate relating and kindness that Paul was teaching wasn't strong enough to overcome the tensions that these differences were bringing into the community. In this respect, Paul's greatest missionary success created his greatest challenges.

When the church was founded ten years before this exchange of correspondence, in the early 40s, Priscilla and Aquila worked with Paul to convert people in the handworker community, and probably just converted people off the streets outside the small factory-shops their handworkers labored in. These were out-and-out pagans. They were tough, poor, uncouth people. But Paul was more successful in the synagogue in Corinth than usual. Generally, he got expelled from the local synagogue after he had tried to convince everyone there to acknowledge Jesus as Lord, and sometimes he was quickly chased out of town.[3] But in Corinth he had some outstanding successes. He converted a wealthy God-worshiper, Gaius Titius Justus, and a Jewish synagogue patron, Crispus, and by the time he was writing his Corinthian letters, ten years later, another Jewish synagogue patron had been converted, Sosthenes. So there were Jewish converts and God-worshipers in the Corinthian church alongside the pagans. Equally importantly, some of these seem to have been wealthy, forming an additional contrast with the poor pagan handworkers and street converts.

Ancient society was marked by considerable differences in wealth. The top 1.5 percent in some cities monopolized at least 20 percent of all the resources. The rest of the top 10 percent owned the next 20 percent of income. The bottom echelon of society lived in constant hunger, literally "from hand to mouth," meaning that when they got any food they immediately ate it. By our standards, then, ancient society was extremely unequal. The elite were very wealthy and well connected compared to everyone else, and vastly superior to them in terms of power and status.[4]

To top it all off, Paul's converts were navigating relationships with people of different gender in all the complex and diverse ways that people usually do this—as singles, betrothed, and then in various married situations, whether happily married, unhappily married, married to another Christian, or married to a pagan. Every community is always involved with these powerful relational dynamics that do not always play out smoothly.

In short, the Corinthian church was crisscrossed by significant differences. It was composed of people who were from an utterly pagan background, who were half-Jewish pagans (that is, converted God-worshipers), and who were Jews. There were many poor converts but also a number of high-status and wealthy figures, along with their households. Further, and as always, there were complicated gender dynamics surrounding sexual activity. These diverse Corinthian converts brought all the hostility, suspicion, and misunderstanding, from these differences in race, class, and gender, straight into their Christian community, and Paul's exhortations to the Corinthians simply to be nicer to one another just weren't overcoming them. But there was a significant additional reason why this wasn't happening.

Problem 2: Leadership

Paul composed 1 Corinthians carefully in five blocks of argument, each one of which addressed a cluster of related problems.[5] But he began the letter with the problem that he identified as the heart of the matter. Paul's first major argument attacks the partisan divisions in the Corinthian community. The Corinthians are factionalized. They have split up behind different leaders—principally behind Paul and Apollos, but also behind Peter, whom Paul calls Cephas, and there is possibly even some independent "Christ party" in view (1:12).

On one level this partisanship is entirely understandable. Partisanship was a standard feature of ancient Greco-Roman city life and it hasn't exactly gone away. As I write these words the US has just voted in an extraordinary election in which both sides have vilified their opposition. But things were even nastier in the ancient world. There was no liberal veneer to cover things over. However, the bitter partisanship evident at Corinth is linked tightly with another feature of the community.

Life in the ancient city was a desperate struggle for survival, and an equally desperate climb up the proverbial greasy pole to the top. The tiny percentage of people who inhabited the top 1 percent were survivors. They were highly competitive, aggressive, tough people who sat on those beneath them and fended off their rivals ruthlessly. They also used the considerable resources of Greco-Roman rhetoric to mock and to denigrate their competitors. The unusual degree of factionalism in the Corinthian community is traceable in large measure to the handful of elite figures who are in it—the wealthy and highly educated converts that Paul and Apollos had made in and around the synagogue, including Gaius, Crispus, and Sosthenes. (The end of Paul's letter to the Romans, written in Corinth, mentions another local politician, Erastus.) These local civic leaders were acting as they usually did, striving with one another for attention and influence in an intensely competitive fashion, all the while preserving their privileges and status from the great unwashed who made up the rest of the congregation.

Moreover, another dimension in the poor behavior of the elite members of the Corinthian church comes through clearly in Paul's long responses. In addition to their competitiveness, the Corinthians have a cultural view of leadership, and this problematized their relationship with Paul.

Greco-Roman cities loved appearances. They loved what people looked like, how much money they had, their connections, and how they spoke. Fully trained rhetorical professionals could captivate audiences for hours. They were the rock stars of the ancient world, and they commanded huge fees for their performances. They looked beautiful and spoke beautifully.

In one of the most profound passages he ever wrote, Paul points out that the Christian God revealed in the crucified Jesus could not be more different from this (1:18–2:16). By journeying down into the human condition and ultimately accepting a shameful death, Jesus revealed that God was a reaching God, an inclusive and gentle God, who valued everyone, including the most despised and marginalized. Those whom society looked down on, God was especially concerned about and eager to reach. (The older theological term for this virtue was "condescension," but it has now been inverted into its opposite, being freighted with unhelpful connotations of superiority and haughtiness.) This is what a Christian leader should look like. It could hardly be more dramatically countercultural, and Paul lived this leadership style out in person.

He was not trained in the flashy tradition of Greco-Roman rhetoric. He had taken a somewhat unusual sectarian degree in advanced Jewish studies at an obscure regional university in Jerusalem. He was quite brilliant and a leader in his own tradition, being highly skilled in the things it valued. He could recall and manipulate scriptural texts at will. But he couldn't speak well, so he didn't sound like much to Greco-Roman snobs, and he looked like nothing. He was dirty, bedraggled, and unpaid. He labored away in small filthy workshops with his own hands. He might even have had an ongoing battle with some unsightly disease like acute conjunctivitus. This would have made his eyes red and weepy. In terms of appearances, then, he came across as a sickly handworker, and they were just one step above slaves.

All of this led at least some of the local Corinthian leaders to disrespect Paul, and some of them probably just despised him. They were embarrassed by his leadership and far preferred the more culturally impressive qualifications of a rhetor like Apollos (see Acts 18:24–28). They had no intention of following his example and acting like servant-leaders themselves—living alongside their humble converts and caring for those who were weak and shamed. They threw their weight behind alternative, far more attractive leaders at Corinth, vilifying their founder, and sharp divisions ensued.

In short, there was a dramatic failure of leadership at Corinth. The wealthy local converts who dominated the community were behaving as Greco-Roman leaders behaved. They were competing with one another for influence, status, and power—no love lost in this battle! Moreover, they were competing in the terms that their surrounding culture dictated, in terms of appearances and money, so they were undermining and criticizing Paul's leadership as they elevated the merits of their patrons. In addition, they were continuing to despise and humiliate their social inferiors.

Paul points out at the beginning of 1 Corinthians at length—returning to the theme at many later points in the rest of the letter—that this is a fundamental betrayal of Christian community. Christians are to love, support, and encourage one another, not compete with one another; and their leaders are to follow in the footsteps of the crucified Christ. The leader who reaches down to live alongside people, and who values and engages with the poor and the marginalized, is the true Christian leader. This is the "appearance" that matters.

We learn a lot from this Corinthian debacle. In small, relatively homogeneous communities like Philippi, Thessalonica, and Colossae, Paul's ethic didn't have to deal with the tensions created by deep social divisions. (This is one of the benefits of "homophily," as the sociologists put it.) At Thessalonica he had to deal with things like lazy community members. In a larger, more diverse church like Corinth, Paul's ethic of kindness faced much tougher challenges. It had to overcome deep divisions of race, class, and gender present within the fabric of the community. However, it is at this exact moment that we see both the importance of Christian leadership and its true nature. Christian leaders can manage and heal these divisions, provided they act appropriately. They are to humble themselves and to bridge existing social chasms of race, class, and gender, thereby drawing the community together behind them. But this type of leadership is deeply countercultural. It is hard even to recognize, while cultural accounts of leadership in terms of status, wealth, and influence directly undermine this authentic account. Such are the challenges of true Christian leadership, and the impossibility of true Christian community without it![6]

Sadly, there was another factor at work at Corinth that was closely related to the leadership failure that we have just been discussing, and it made things still worse. Some of the community leaders were intellectually arrogant.

Problem 3: Christian intellectualism

The elite status of some of Paul's converts presupposed an advanced education—the equivalent of a modern college degree—and some simply had the confidence that having a lot of money brings. They were local community leaders, players in the city's politics, and were used to thinking about things and proposing policies and judgments. But they weren't as clever as they thought they were.

In this I am reminded of the slightly overconfident students I have sometimes faced in seminars in various universities. They are often very smart, but they don't know quite as much as they need to. When they push back on the material we are discussing, written by some of the greatest minds of the twentieth century, they sometimes just haven't grasped the full depth and comprehensiveness of the material they are criticizing. They haven't read enough. Similarly, some of the Corinthians were inferring what they thought were theologically appropriate Christian actions and behaviors, but they didn't know enough either. They were jumping to conclusions and pushing them too hard, and the results of doing this were destructive.[7]

First, a group is correctly saying that food doesn't matter and that the kingdom of God isn't a matter of meat and drink, but they have turned this confidence into a weapon. As we know, some of the Corinthians were Jews or were strongly committed to Jewish ways of living. They shared the general Jewish revulsion to meat that has been improperly prepared. Such meat would have been quite literally a nauseating prospect for them, and I imagine that they looked down their noses at anyone eating it. But our amateur theologians are reversing this attitude and paying it back with interest. They are happily eating their idol meat and mocking those who have a problem with it. "Such scruples. What fools!" (1 Cor. 8:1–13).

Paul corrects this insensitivity with his basic relational argument. Although it is technically correct that food doesn't matter to this degree anymore, such arrogance hardly possesses relational integrity. The description of considerate activity in relation to God and Jesus that began the letter is not being followed here, as it should be.

In a second problematic act of intellectualism, this group is pushing another maxim to extremes. "Idols don't actually exist," as the Bible repeatedly says, so there are really no problems with attending idol feasts and worship events. It is not as if anything is actually there! In this way, the puffed up, as Paul calls them, could continue to attend the plethora of idolatrous events that structured the ancient pagan city—its processions, feasts, festivals, and sacrifices.

To deal with this problem Paul reintroduces the relationality and connectedness that these figures seem to keep overlooking. Idols aren't anything, but these pagan events are intertwined with the evil powers that roam the cosmos outside the church. Pagan culture might not be what it says it is, but it is still dangerous, and attending an idolatrous worship event is creating a foolish vulnerability to evil, as well as being deeply unfaithful to God. Can we really attend a black Sabbath and escape unscathed? Can we walk in a national parade, without thinking that a nation, a flag, or a history "is anything"? Paul instructs these particular Corinthians not to play with fire (1 Cor. 10:1–22).

Paul's final extended argument in the letter (15:1–58) addresses the denial of Jesus's bodily resurrection, and our intellectuals are probably in view here again.

Some strands of ancient Greek thinking disparaged matter and material things. They believed that only the unseen world of the spirit was important. Spirit was pure and eternal; matter was impure and transitory. Spiritual things had been trapped in material things rather as we might get our car stuck in a mudslide. So the right way forward was to get the car out of the mud and hose it off.

For people thinking in this fashion, Jesus's bodily resurrection made no sense. He was spirit. He had had his material things, including his body, hosed off by death, so technically there was no bodily resurrection. Who needs a bodily resurrection?! The whole idea is absurd.

Paul is rather horrified by this and argues at length that if Jesus has not been raised bodily then no one has been saved from their sins and their other problems, including from death. But he also argues that the body Jesus has been raised in is not like our bodies, which are mortal and die. It is a glorious, imperishable, spiritual body. Moreover, even as we occupy our present locations, we must pay constant attention to what our current imperfect bodies are doing. Paul has earlier spoken of being careful not to bring our bodies into contact with prostitutes and idolatrous worship festivals, so this is consistent (1 Cor. 6:12–20). Bodies matter. He has left some further awkward questions here unresolved, but we can tackle these when he starts to address them in more detail in his next letter, 2 Corinthians.[8]

The take-home from Corinth

The Corinthian situation teaches us a lot. Thus far we have learned three critically important things.

First, Paul's ethic of Christian love was deeply countercultural and highly demanding. Homogeneous and idealized communities mask how tough it is to practice this kindness and consideration across social divisions where it needs to bridge and heal and not merely to fit into a group that already gets along quite well. Corinth exposes this countercultural challenge.

Second, it is clear that local Christian leadership is critical to this process, and this leadership has to be formed on Christ's leadership, modeled by Paul and his students. Conventional assessments of value must be abandoned. Conventional competitive relations must be repented of. This recalibration of what an authentic leader looks like is so important to the health of the community and so difficult. Every community has elites, and invariably throughout history those elites have contested for status in terms of conventional markers. Paul is challenging the Corinthians and us to do things very differently. The deeply countercultural challenge of Christian behavior is exposed by Corinth here again, and it reveals as no other community does the need for good leaders if a diverse Christian community is to move forward.

Third, we learn that intellectualism—in the form of aggressive theological and ethical judgments that are separated from right relating and from the right depth in the Jewish tradition—is damaging. It creates further differences that become places of further tension, dispute, and conflict. Christian thinking must not be separated from (other) Christian acting in relation to other Christians. Neither must it be separated from a broader and richer account of the community rooted in Judaism. Above all, it must not suppose that our bodies do not matter! We act through our bodies, so everything they do is important.

In sum, the Christian way is fairly simple in theory. It asks all its followers to be kind and considerate toward one another. It asks its leaders to be sensitive to "the least of these," if necessary, living alongside them. But this is incredibly demanding in practice. These are deeply countercultural dynamics. If they are to take root, above all they require leaders, and the right sort of leadership. Christian leaders must help their communities to navigate their current locations ethically with due depth, sensitivity, and courage—something we will learn a lot more about momentarily.

But we have left one final complicating factor at Corinth out of consideration until now: sex. Questions generated by sex and gender roiled the Corinthians, and they roil us still today. This is such an important topic that we will devote the next chapter to it entirely.

Questions

- How many specific problems at Corinth does 1 Corinthians address? (Do you have a personal favorite?!) How many resonate with problems you have experienced at church, or at an institution that you work in?

- What was the first key underlying cause of all these particular disputes? What was Paul's main response?

- What was the second major problematic factor in play at Corinth?

- How did ancient pagan culture define leadership? How do *we* define leadership? How should Christians, attending closely to Christ, define leadership?

- What was the third major problem? Where did it seem to play out in strange specific claims and stances at Corinth? Can we think of analogous problems in our own day?

CHAPTER EIGHT

Navigating Sex and Gender

The Corinthian challenge

It is fascinating to see how Paul navigated the issue of appropriate sexual behavior with the Corinthians. The Corinthians were culturally a mixed bag. Many were pagans, arriving in church with all their local pagan sexual mores in place. Paul and some of the Corinthians were shaped by the rather different practices of Judaism. All of this was now intertwined with a new Christian angle on things. Pagan, Jewish, and Christian habits and instructions were all swirling around in a church characterized by insensitivity and rivalry: a recipe for disaster!

Sexual intellectualism

Some of the Corinthians were being too theologically aggressive. In chapters 5 and 6 of 1 Corinthians Paul addresses the way this aggression has led to sexually damaging behavior. Paul had taught the community that the Jewish food rules didn't matter anymore.

> The Kingdom of God is not a matter of eating and drinking
> but of deliverance and peace and joy through the Holy Spirit.
> (Rom. 14:17)

Another way of putting this would be to say "food for the stomach and the stomach for food" (1 Cor. 6:13). It goes in, it comes out, and has no religious significance. Who cares what we eat, where, or how? But what happens if we apply this adage to the penis? "The penis for sex and sex for the penis." Who cares with whom we have sex, where, or how?

The result of this bold theological inference is that converts from paganism at Corinth could keep doing what they had been doing all along, which was visiting prostitutes regularly. No big deal. (I assume we're talking mainly about men here.) But this theological boldness had an even more unhelpful application.

A man at Corinth is apparently sleeping with his stepmother. This may not be quite as shocking as it first seems. In the ancient world, women were married at or just before puberty, perhaps as young as twelve then, and often to much older men who had lost their first wives. If a woman's original husband had died, a stepson from a first marriage could have been older than his stepmother (although we don't know if the husband/father had died; the adage would apply whether he was alive or dead). And we can see now how the motto "the penis for sex and sex for the penis" underwrites this instance of incest, and the Corinthians who came up with this revolutionary practice are even quite proud of themselves for doing so!

Paul of course is not impressed and writes accordingly. He doesn't bother with any argument. The perpetrators just have to go. The community must expel them. He works harder on the problem of prostitution (6:12–20).

That he doesn't appeal to heterosexual monogamy suggests that the problem might be currently single men. He pushes back here on the notion that our bodies are irrelevant, and this issue comes up again at the end of the letter. The connections we make through our bodies affect us, and a sexual connection affects us at a particularly deep level. Uniting with a prostitute sexually disrupts and contaminates the unity we have with Christ and the Spirit. What a self-destructive thing to do!

If this first cluster of sexual indiscretions at Corinth came from an overly aggressive theological application, coupled with a lack of depth—that is, from intellectualism—the second cluster, which Paul addresses in chapter 7, comes from a different direction.

Staying where you are

Previously we had too much sex going on. Now, in chapter 7, we have too little. Some women are refusing to have sex with their husbands on spiritual grounds. "It's good for a woman not to be contacted sexually by a man," they are saying (7:1). A woman might have been justifying this because she has become an ascetic and wants to discipline her body to attain to spiritual experiences. We know that some of the women at Corinth were active in worship services and interpreted this as being in touch with angels. It would have been entirely normal to have adopted an ascetic lifestyle to try to deepen these experiences. There is a lot of evidence for this sort of behavior from later on in the church.[1]

Paul would not have a problem with this if the person involved was single, but if she—and perhaps he—is married, then Paul expects the spouse's sex drive to be satisfied by a willing partner. This is just a part of a normal marriage, and this leads us to an important discovery. We begin to uncover here the way in which all Paul's advice, whether earlier on in relation to incest and prostitution, or here countering too much asceticism, is structured by typical Jewish categories, with one or two key variations.

Insofar as people occupy their current fleshly bodies—and they do have bodies and always will, so bodies are important—marriage is between a man and a woman, as the Bible says right at the start, in Genesis 1–3. There are some important additional biblical rules, however. The relationship must not be incestuous. The book of Leviticus defines this. All cultures have a strong incest taboo—it is part of basic human programming—but all cultures define incest at its boundaries slightly differently. Leviticus clears this up for Paul as it does for other Jews. Moreover, marriage is to be enduring and faithful. Paul quotes a rule from Jesus here (see Mark 10:2–12). The results of this modified Jewish pattern? No sleeping around, no prostitution, and no incest. But within this arrangement partners should have sex and try to procreate, so no ongoing asceticism for the married either, and no divorce. A fundamentally Jewish view of sex and gender holds all these different instructions together. Finally, marriages are constructed in an orderly, hierarchical fashion. Men rule their wives, and parents rule their children. Wives obey their husbands just as children obey their parents. This arrangement is evident underlying the situation at Corinth, and, as we saw earlier, it was spelled out clearly by Paul in his programmatic instructions in Ephesians and Colossians.

As we read on in the letter, however, we find that Paul supplemented this basic configuration with an important additional rule when he converted people. Albert Schweitzer dubbed this "Paul's law of the *status quo*."[2] Grasping this explains the remaining sexual pressures that are upsetting the community at Corinth. If sex is hot water for a community, then Paul's law of the *status quo* puts it in a kettle, slams on the lid, and leaves it boiling on the stove.

Paul's law of the status quo

When Paul first founded the community, 1 Corinthians reveals that he said,

> let each of you lead the life that the Lord has assigned,
> to which God called you.
> This is my rule in all the churches. (7:17)

> Let each of you remain in the condition in which you were called.
> (7:20)

Paul clearly thought that this law had a key advantage. It encouraged singleness. Paul was single, although we don't know whether he was single all along or widowed. He believed that this was the best way for Christians to live if they could handle it, and he was right. Edgy missionary work is dangerous. It's much harder to deal with all the rigors of travel, imprisonment, and public scorn if spouses and children are in tow. They make missionaries vulnerable. His "stay where you are" rule encouraged Christian converts who were single to stay that way, and it even put engagements on hold. Technically, betrothed Christians never needed to get married, and they stayed single too. In this way, everyone was ready "to go to the front," unencumbered by family distractions.

But while Paul's view here is understandable, it was too much for most single people at Corinth to cope with as time passed. Because of the sex drive, along with the broader process by which people mature from childhood into adulthood and then parenthood, most people just don't stay in a state of singleness. As they are programmed—except for the 1 percent who are genuinely celibate—they grow up, fall in love, get together, and have kids (not necessarily in that order admittedly). Human sexual relationships are dynamic. So the passage of time posed a difficult challenge to the various groups of singles at Corinth. Who knows how long some couples at Corinth might have been engaged to marry but put that happy event on hold because of Paul's stay-where-you-are law? A young couple in love might have converted when Paul first arrived in Corinth in 41 CE, and be grimly hanging on, betrothed but in an unconsummated relationship, ten years later, in 51! Clearly the tensions were beginning to build.

So Paul does the practical thing in 1 Corinthians and says that they can get married if they really want to. It's better not to, so he doesn't concede his main position. But it's okay to marry now since this move, which is not technically staying-where-you-are, is still staying within the basic Jewish framework for marriage that he has been advocating all along. I can imagine that this advice came as quite a relief to some, although if it were me who had been betrothed and waiting for ten years I would have wanted to punch Paul in the nose.

However, there was another point of tension at Corinth. A standard feature of marriages, universally observable cross-culturally, is that many of the men and women who pair up, and usually have children, get unhappy over time and part. Around a third of marriages dissolve (speaking very generally). A common rule of thumb is at the four-year mark, which is when infants first reach a level of viability, and culturally this results in the phenomenon of divorce.[3] Time has passed at Corinth, and so some couples are moving in this direction too, including Christian marriages, in which both partners were Christian, and mixed marriages, in which only one person was a Christian. Paul responds to these two categories in ways that might seem to be initially surprising.

He quotes a rule by Jesus that Christian couples must not divorce. This would accord with his underlying Jewish framework. Divorce was deeply frowned upon, and often opposed unilaterally, rather as John the Baptist called out Herod Antipas for dumping his first wife and marrying his sister-in-law, Herodias (Mark 6:14–29). But when it comes to mixed couples comprising a marriage between a Christian and a pagan, Paul counsels flexibility. Apparently, strict marriage rules apply strictly only to those within the community. The stay-where-you-are rule doesn't apply so firmly either. Spouses in mixed marriages are "called to peace" and are allowed to figure out what will work best on quite pragmatic grounds, taking due account of any children. They should navigate forward through the specifics of the situation in a way that will result in maximum harmony relationally, changing their situation and their roles if they have to, that is, *not* staying where they are if this is the best thing to do.

By the end of chapter 7 Paul has addressed most of the sexual problems at Corinth—and there was quite a list. He prohibits incest, prostitution, abstinence within a marriage, and Christian couples divorcing. But he allows Christians in mixed marriages to work out the best thing to do even if that means divorcing, and he reluctantly allows engaged couples to marry. Sex comes up again in passing from time to time in the rest of the letter, but Paul is generally just worried that his pagan converts will lapse back into bad pagan habits, indulging in sex at pagan parties and festivals and visiting the brothel down the road because they lack the self-discipline to do otherwise. Underlying all Paul's advice is a traditional Jewish framework: marriage is between a man and a woman, for life, provided they are not too closely related to one another. Anything outside this arrangement is aberrant and to be prohibited. Divorce, incest, homosexuality, polygamy, polyandry (!), and infidelity in the form of using prostitutes are all consequently outlawed.[4]

The big Christian twist in all this is singleness. By freezing all existing arrangements at conversion, Paul holds any single people in place, whether they are single or betrothed, on the assumption that this will make them more mobile and less vulnerable. Clearly he was not expecting the church to last more than a generation then, or, alternatively—and equally unrealistically—he was expecting it to grow by conversion alone.

With these realizations in place it is time to devote some attention to how Paul navigates questions of gender at Corinth.

Navigating gender

I have used "sex" up until now to denote the sex drive and sexual activity associated with that, although stepping over at times into the analysis of what scholars call "gender" or "gender construction." The expression of the sex drive always has an institutional form, and a broader picture or construction of gender, and this is very important. People get offended when their forms are flouted because they are bound up with powerful emotions and hormonal surges, although cross-cultural study has revealed that forms vary enormously from culture to culture.[5]

Women were part of the disorderly and insensitive worship service at Corinth that Paul wanted to pull back into a more mutually respectful and decorous event. They were speaking in tongues in such an abandoned way that their scarves were slipping off and their hair becoming unbound. This was a very bad thing.

In Paul's day chaste women wore a headscarf called a *pulla* rather as women in Pakistan today wear the *dupatta*. It covered the head, shoulders, and neck, not the face, as the more comprehensive Iranian *burqa* does. Women also wore their hair neatly coiffed. It was plaited and arranged, held in place with pins, and wealthy women had particularly elaborate configurations. Only lengthy attention from dedicated slaves could produce these, so they signaled the status of their wearers instantly as much as large diamonds and Gucci bags do today. The latest hairstyles were circulated and copied from the picture of the Roman Empress stamped on coins—the ancient equivalent of *Vogue*.

Conversely, women who were losing their clothing and had bedraggled hair were acting like *maenads*. In ancient Greek culture *maenads* were the female followers of the god Dionysus, known literally as "raving ones." (Dionysos was an exuberant partying god.) They were drunk and on the loose!

Any husbands in the room at Corinth were being horribly humiliated by the abandoned behavior of their wives. Paul tries to rein this in in 11:2–16 by appealing to the story of Adam and Eve. Adam got made first, so he is in charge. It's not a great argument, but we'll worry about that some other time. The key point for now is the realization that here Paul is allowing the women to continue to speak in tongues. However, they must do so in a way that does not shame their husbands. Perhaps think then of a modern pastor asking women who are speaking in tongues in church so vigorously that their blouses are slipping off to do so in a more restrained way. It's reasonable.

But someone might ask if this is really the case when Paul famously forbids women to speak at all in 14:33–36. Paul's short aside here has been widely represented as a command that women should be silent in the congregation period. But this isn't what he is saying. As we have just seen in 1 Corinthians 11:2–16, and as we read at length in 1 Corinthians 14, women are fully entitled to speak through the Spirit in tongues or in prophecy. It's just that they are not to question and to interrupt other people speaking in church. They are not to interrogate the preacher. Consequently, Paul never silences women in church altogether. Far from it. He silences those sitting in the pews. So in fact most churches today have followed this advice to the letter—although most of the men must now remain silent as well!

The Christian city

We can see by this point that the Christian community was doing things very differently from the pagan community that surrounded it at Corinth—or that it was meant to do so! It seems to be a city within a city, a city living by very different rules.[6] Its basic shape and dynamic are simple. Its citizens are to be relational and considerate, not aggressively competitive. They are to reject cultural markers of status and to adopt an incarnational leadership style, walking alongside those whom society despises. In the same way they are supposed to try to bridge painful differences in class, status, and race. They are to think about appropriate Christian behavior in a mature, grounded, and constructive way. They are to navigate forward, locating sexual activity firmly within the marriage covenant and rejecting promiscuity. But the details of that covenant can be softened as the Spirit leads, whether in relation to getting married or getting divorced, and some of the basic cultural expectations of gender itself can be modified under pressure from the Holy Spirit, such as women speaking publicly.

As we move on to the next major phase in Paul's interactions with Corinth we will learn about two further areas in which the community was supposed to be countercultural as well—two really big issues that any city has to deal with all the time: its handling of money, and its handling of conflict.

1　　　　　　　　2

Questions

‣ What had Christian intellectualism led to at Corinth in relation to sexual practices?

‣ What is Paul's basic road map for instructions about appropriate sexual activity and about gender? What is consequently allowed? What is prohibited? Where does this come from? What are his distinctive Christian additions?

‣ Why did Paul think that the "law of the *status quo*"was a good idea? What areas of sexual pressure emerged? How did Paul eventually advise people to navigate these?

‣ How did Paul allow Christian women at Corinth to step outside the traditional view of what a woman was allowed to do in terms of gender expectations? What behavior did he shut down? What do his principal concerns here seem to have been?

CHAPTER NINE

The Christian City

Leaving Ephesus

Before Paul wrote 2 Corinthians tumultuous events broke out in Ephesus. (Second Corinthians was the third in the sequence of letters written to Corinth over these months, but it is the second letter we have preserved for us in our Bibles.) The book of Acts tells us about three dramatic episodes that led to some stunning successes but ended up with Paul having to run for his life (Acts 19:8–41).

The drama began when an exorcism at Ephesus went wrong (Acts 19:13–16). Some Jewish exorcists were involved with a particularly difficult case. A demon was refusing to leave a man, so in a fit of desperation the magicians abjured the demon to leave "in the name of Jesus whom Paul proclaims." This proved to be a mistake. The demon responded, "I know Jesus and I know Paul but I don't know who you are!" He leaped up and beat them, chasing them naked and bleeding down the main street. Naturally, everyone heard about this. It was the talk of the town, and it made Paul famous. But why? To grasp the reason for this we have to enter into the mentality of ancient people.

Most people in Paul's day lived in a world that they believed was densely populated with invisible spiritual beings, and many of these were capricious and malevolent. But they could be manipulated. We have hundreds of magical spells written on papyrus that were designed to make a girl fall in love, to attack a rival across the street, or to protect one's family and business from harm. People wore protective amulets and purchased the services of spell-casters. They cursed one another and tried to ward off the returning curses. This was all frowned on—or ridiculed—by the intelligentsia, but most people were deeply invested in these activities.

The manipulation of beings in the spiritual realm had rules. It was all about power. The gods were the most powerful beings, but there were legions of other spirits and influences, and this explains why Paul became famous indirectly when this exorcism went wrong. The demon the Jewish magicians were trying to cast out was so strong that he overcame seven grown men. When he said "I know Jesus and I know Paul," he was saying in spirit-talk that he respected Jesus and Paul. The word in Greek suggests that he "acknowledges" Jesus. He was admitting that if Paul had been present, commanding him in the name of Jesus to leave, he would have had to go. But the group of seven magicians lacked the power to get him to do anything. That an enormously powerful demon capable of beating seven men, speaking from the spirit world, had acknowledged the authority of Jesus and of his servant, Paul, did not just impress a great mass of Ephesians; it struck fear into them. Huge numbers converted. Then another interesting thing happened.

The Ephesians brought their magic scrolls and spells and burned them in a great bonfire in the street (Acts 19:17–19). Acts suggests that the pile of material might have cost, in today's terms, as much as six million dollars. (It was fifty thousand times the daily wage of a skilled laborer.) Even if the author is exaggerating a little, this is a huge sum of money being incinerated. Paul had made an impact! Try to imagine something similar happening in your town one day. The main street would be closed as six million dollars' worth of porn videos, computer games, and insurance policies went up in smoke. That would make CNN. The bonfire also tells us something interesting about the things Paul was preaching.

The Ephesians were burning their magical scrolls because they no longer needed them. They were now being protected from demons and curses by the God revealed in Jesus for free. He was clearly an extremely powerful God who could shield them from any spiritual aggressors.

These sorts of shifts within a city's population have significant economic and political consequences, as the third episode in the Ephesian drama shows (Acts 19:23–41). The burgeoning popularity of the Christian movement now stirred up an even larger social reaction.

Paul's Christian communities worshiped a God present in their midst who was not imaged. They were like the Jews in this respect. Their meeting places contained no statues of gods that were prayed to and venerated. Moreover, they condemned worship events involving idols. These were dangerous. When you sup with Satan you use a long spoon. But ancient cities were centered around temples that housed images, and Ephesus housed one of the wonders of the world, the

temple of the goddess Artemis, who had "fallen from the sky." It was internation-
ally renowned for its ranks of beautifully carved green marble columns. People
traveled from all over the world to seek the favor of its great goddess, probably for
help especially with fertility, and they bought small images of her made by local
tradesmen to take back home to continue to pray to and worship. However, these
tradesmen saw a problem looming, and quite rightly. If Christianity succeeded
in taking over the city, as suddenly seemed likely, their industry would be wiped
out. Idols would be abandoned, their temples neglected, and their livelihoods, as
well as the heart of their culture, would wither and die.

Faced by this crisis, the craftsmen did what large groups of angry people
generally do to gain attention. They rioted in the streets. They rushed around,
made a lot of noise, and tried to find someone to beat to death. Half the city
packed the enormous theater—which is still standing—and screamed their
goddess's cult chant for two hours. "Great is Artemis of the Ephesians! Great
is Artemis of the Ephesians!" Emotions were running high. Fortunately, they
couldn't find Paul, who was restrained from rushing into the fray by wise
friends. City officials managed to calm the people down by offering the mob
due process, and Paul eventually slipped out of the city.

The seriousness of this event should not be underestimated. This riot was
what the Romans called a *seditio* or "sedition." This was a grave enough disturbance in civic order to draw their military attention. Troops would march,
order would be restored, and a lesson would be given to the local inhabitants in
the form of mass crucifixions. Moreover, Paul was somehow involved in this.
He looked like an instigator. If anyone ever succeeded in pinning this event
on him before a Roman tribunal, he was a dead man.

Consequently, Paul headed off to Macedonia a little earlier than he had
anticipated. As he had said in 1 Corinthians in the spring, "a great door of opportunity had opened up" in Ephesus—perhaps the largest and most rapid
door-opening he ever experienced (1 Cor. 16:8–9). But in 2 Corinthians we read,
looking back on subsequent events, that a massive resistance had opened up
as well—"a great pressure beyond our ability to endure so we despaired of life"
(2 Cor. 1:8). Paul had almost been broken. But he had escaped and was heading
to Corinth, although there were plenty of unresolved troubles there as well.

Wooing Corinth

We now see a carefully constructed strategy unfolding designed to regain the
Corinthians' trust. We see Paul here at his cleverest and most tactical. He

knows that some Corinthians are disloyal and hostile, being followers of a rival teacher, and he knows that he has sent a stinging letter in the form of 1 Corinthians, so his own followers at Corinth are possibly quite offended. Paul has further hurt them by changing his travel plans and canceling a direct visit (1 Cor. 16:7). This must have felt like an insult. Moreover, his rival will shortly go back to Corinth for a return visit. Paul now hatches a plan to repair all this relational damage with Corinth in stages.

The first thing he does is to change his representative at Corinth. Previously the timid Timothy represented him. Now he sends Titus. We don't know much about Titus. Second Timothy 4:10 says that he left Paul for "Dalmatia" during Paul's last imprisonment, so perhaps he was a convert from Paul's mission up the east coast of the Adriatic. Paul mentions a mission here in Romans 15:19 when he speaks of reaching "Illyricum," which was the ancient name for Croatia. Perhaps think of Titus then as a tall and somewhat intimidating Croatian arriving in Corinth as Paul's new representative. Paul sends Titus directly westward to Corinth at the same time that he escapes from Ephesus and heads north to Macedonia. The idea is to rendezvous together there.

At the planned rendezvous Titus brings excellent news. At least some of the Corinthians have responded well to 1 Corinthians and its aftermath. They have addressed some of the issues it named, and they received him well. But there are clearly some problems still present. After this welcome news, Paul doubles-down on this strategy that seems to be working. The Corinthians seem to be responding better to his letters than they do to him in person! So he writes another letter and sends it back with Titus. In a stroke of genius, he sends a delegation from the Macedonian churches along with him.

Paul is occupied at this time with raising a large sum of money for the poor members of the church in Jerusalem. Corinth contains his key donors, but he has alienated them by insulting and upbraiding them in his scathing letter. Unsurprisingly, the gathering of money in Corinth, which is supposed to be taking place weekly, has stalled. He prods them into action by manipulating their competitiveness. Paul sends some Macedonians to Corinth from the poor churches in that region, who have already raised a decent sum, knowing that the Corinthians will die rather than be outdone in their fundraising. "Outraised by a group of poor handworker Macedonians?! No way!" But not only is this Macedonian delegation certain to spur the wealthy Corinthians into action. It will provide him with a loyal base of support when he arrives shortly in person. The Macedonians will have his back. It is a brilliant plan—and we see later on that it worked.

In the events leading up to and just following 2 Corinthians we see Paul's courage and his cleverness in play. It is worth drawing attention to these, because he writes a lot about the nature of Christian leadership in the letter and these two qualities are prominent there. Where relationships have been strained, Christian leaders need to pursue reconciliation; differences caused by conflict need to be bridged. But as they do so, they also need to be brave and smart. "Be as innocent as doves and as cunning as snakes" is how another writer in the New Testament puts this on one occasion (Matt. 10:16).

It is time now to ask what 2 Corinthians adds to our developing picture of the Pauline city.

Leadership

We have already seen that a key factor underlying the problems at Corinth was a failure of leadership. We can infer directly from this that a key factor in the establishment of a successful and authentic Pauline community will be appropriate leadership. As soon as a community confronts social differences, whether of race, class, or gender—and they often arrive together—leaders will be critical to any forward movement. Christian leaders must consequently be courageous bridge-builders, able to leave their own comforts and familiarities and to reach out to others who are different, holding people together.

Paul articulated the heart of this type of leadership in 1 Corinthians 1 and 2 when he spoke of Jesus being crucified especially for the poor and the marginalized within humanity. In the same way, authentic Christian leaders reach alongside those whom society is uninterested in. They abandon their own cultural capital, if they have any, and live alongside those whom God has called into their community. This is how Christian communities are supposed to be established. It becomes increasingly apparent in 2 Corinthians that the way Christian leaders act externally, when communities are being founded, is also the way they need to act internally once those communities—along with all their awkward differences—are up and running. When missionaries reach out to others in friendship, bridging into awkward spaces, they get alongside people. Paul is now applying that approach internally, to the Corinthians. This approach can lead a community forward, despite its differences, and hold it together as it navigates the unsettling impact of the Spirit on its cultural forms. The leadership modeled in the cross applies everywhere. But this sort of leadership makes genuine Christian leaders vulnerable, which is probably why so many people avoid it.[1]

They will be exposed as they travel, leaving behind all that holds them safe—all the things that they might have accumulated to protect them and to ensure future success. They will be exposed to misunderstanding, to cultural hostility, and to physical challenges. Furthermore, their leadership will be vulnerable if those they convert do not reevaluate their own cultural markers of success and realize that God is calling them to abandon those. Converts tend to bring their prejudices straight into the church, leaving them behind only slowly after a long period of teaching and adjustment. If they do not abandon these cultural values—perhaps because the wrong leaders are modeling the wrong things for them—they will horribly misunderstand who should be leading them. In local cultural terms, Christian leaders look like nothing, and if they are authentic Christian leaders that is just what they should look like. They abandon pagan markers of leadership, which are invariably tied to some ascent to fame, status, and fortune. Fake Christian leaders, however, will probably look and sound great and will appeal to any converts who have not had their values reshaped. In so doing they will nevertheless betray the true nature of Christian leadership. This was the main battle that Paul was fighting at Corinth.

It is possible to evaluate Christian leaders in the suffering and the costliness they endure. A Christian leader must evidence faithfulness. She must walk obediently in the footsteps of the one who endured homelessness, rejection, and a shameful death. Christian leaders evidence grace under pressure. These are the markers of authenticity, and the church went on to map them in stories of martyrs.

It is vital to appreciate that this vulnerability does not mean that Christian leaders have abandoned power, except in the conventional social way that this might be exercised as bullying or force. They still possess leadership, which means that they influence and guide others as their superiors. But the power they use is the power of God, by appointment, and exercised principally by example and persuasion, not by resources or force. Paul is engaged in a power struggle at Corinth; have no doubts about that. And he is not surrendering his leadership of that community but is fighting hard for it. But the way his power is exercised is folded into his account of how authentic Christian leaders lead.

Fortunately, the triune God has not left Christian leaders alone in their vulnerability. Another important marker of authenticity is the activity of the Spirit. The Spirit is the Spirit of Jesus, so where Jesus went, reaching out to the unlovely, the Spirit of Jesus goes as well. Consequently, as apostles, which is to say, missionaries, travel into difficult and challenging spaces, the Spirit is there attesting to their authenticity by touching those who are listening to them. "These people don't look like much and, even worse, they talk about a

God who was crucified, but something dramatic and divine happens as they teach us. They say that resurrection is on the other side of all this and I see my Aunty Janelle has been healed from her gout, and my Uncle Sam is speaking some strange heavenly language and falling on the floor, which really isn't like him. Perhaps they are right."

The countercultural nature of true Christian leadership is the main lesson of 2 Corinthians. But some other gems are buried in its extended discussions. Two in particular are extremely important. A Pauline community is a Christian city being built within a larger pagan country, and it does things very differently from its surroundings. Second Corinthians tells us that it does things very differently with money and with conflict. If things were countercultural before, they are about to get even more so.

Money and gift

In the middle of his letter, in chapters 8–9, sandwiched between his two discussions of Christian leadership, Paul stirs up the Corinthians' commitment to his great collection, and in doing so says some fascinating things about money. We glimpse here how a Christian economy should work.[2] Its basic principle is giving. Unsurprisingly, the heart of the matter is again found in Jesus. Paul describes the key dynamic in 8:9.

> For you know the gift of our Lord Jesus Christ:
> that though he was rich, yet for your sakes he became poor,
> so that by his poverty you might become rich.

Paul points out here in a statement of deceptively simple profundity that God has abandoned the equivalent of unimaginable wealth and entered our condition in person, thereby entering unimaginable poverty by comparison. He did this because he loved us and wanted to benefit us, ultimately gifting us with his presence and then with the wealth to which he returned. We need to ponder this statement carefully.

Love for people entails getting alongside them and abandoning cultural capital so they are not coerced or overwhelmed. But once in that place, in the friendships that result, we can and obviously should, if we are able, continue to gift our friends with what they need out of our resources. Love is generous and not merely kind, as Paul has already said in 1 Corinthians (13:4). But love is not compelled. So such generosity is free in the sense of being voluntary and uncoerced, Paul points out (2 Cor. 8:3, 17; 9:7). It keeps no measure of raw totals. Generosity in a gift is always proportionate to the resources of the giver. Neither should it create entitlement. We are not to impoverish ourselves so that others might be greatly enriched. But it should create equality, and this makes perfect sense.

A community of mutual commitment and kindness should be a community that gives to its members generously and shares its resources happily. One person enjoys largesse at a given moment. He ought to help others who at that same moment are in need. Hence the wealthy Corinthians should give to their poor community members and to the poor in the community at Jerusalem. This is not a law or even a fixed pattern. It's an interpersonal dynamic that adjusts as circumstances adjust, bearing in mind that the resources to give are ultimately supplied by God. God is fundamentally a giving God who gives of himself and continues to give. Jesus is a gift, freely given and immeasurably enriching. The economy of the Christian community and its handling of money is all about giving, and about this sort of giving.[3]

As usual, it's so very simple and so very hard.

I imagine that Christian communities through the ages have done what the Corinthians did, generating a hundred and one different reasons to avoid this economy of free, generous giving to all, with the ultimate end of equality. But there is no escape. A Christian economy, for the soundest theological reasons, is redistributive. It is this because it values its members, and their bodies, and so gives, and does so as God has given to us—freely, extravagantly, and without conditions.[4]

A series of quick caveats are in order, though, before we move on.

Paul generally talks about needs, and these should be distinguished from wants. God is presumably interested in needs rather than wants, but Christian communities—and especially those living in the modern western world—often get very confused between the two nevertheless. The cultural reevaluations we have noted already can help us here.

The sort of cultural capital Paul rejects at Corinth is often very costly. Things like status, education, and appearance take effort, connections, and a great deal of money. As Christian leaders learn to reverse these valuations and engage with those on the margins, an education into authentic needs should unfold. Jesus lived a very simple life, as did Paul. We can learn from this that we may need less than we think we do. Moreover, grasping all this might help us to break out of a mentality of deprivation and scarcity into a mentality of sufficiency and abundance. A great deal of modern society is premised on a false sense of scarcity. The wealthiest society in human history—the USA—is obsessed with how much it still needs! This mentality leads us to accuse God of failing to show up when our expressed needs are not met. How many of our prayers are requests to God to give us something that is ultimately about money? Our expressed needs, which may be little more than thinly disguised cultural expectations, may need to be reeducated by a community that is generous but also trusting and simple. Grounded in the lives of those living on the outside, Paul has a firm grip on the frivolities of life and on what he really needs. As he says famously in Philippians 4:11b–13:

> I am not saying this because I am in need,
> for I have learned to be content whatever the circumstances.
> I know what it is to be in need,
> and I know what it is to have plenty.
> I have learned the secret of being content in any and every situation,
> whether well fed or hungry,
> whether living in plenty or in want.
> I can do all this through him who gives me strength.

I suspect that our modern culture desperately needs leaders that are similarly grounded.

Paul's teaching in 2 Corinthians 8 and 9 reveals that a Christian community's attitudes to money and economy are shaped by the generous Lord it worships, and those attitudes may end up being strongly countercultural. His teaching in chapters 2 and 7 discloses that his approach to solving conflict will likely be the same.

Restorative justice

All communities and societies have procedures for resolving conflict, although we also need to speak from this point onward of "disputes." "Conflicts" denote fundamental axes of difference characterized by ongoing hostility, anxiety, and the threat of violence. In a conflict there may be no actual incidents or specific fights taking place at a given moment, just ongoing hatred. "Disputes" are specific disagreements. These might be as minor as arguing with a waiter about the accuracy of a restaurant bill, or as major as shooting someone you have caught sleeping with your spouse. Conflicts and disputes can be related. A dispute within a broader conflict will most likely be escalated, and an ongoing conflict will lead to a higher number of disputes. So it is especially important to try to resolve conflicts because of the way they inflame and multiply actual disputes. But there doesn't have to be a conflict for a dispute to break out. People can have a fight over anything, and frequently do, while some conflicts roll destructively on, the sides festering with hatred, with few or no disputes.

Disputes are costly. So are conflicts.

They cause emotional and relational pain and rupture, and they can result in material and bodily damage. A divorce is a "solution" to a marriage that has descended into irresolvable conflict, but this spiral is punctuated with disputes, and can originate with one. Children, money, perhaps houses, families, and entire rhythms of life, are caught up and twisted around by this spiral.

To avoid the great costs that disputes and conflicts entail, communities always have some way of trying to deal with them. But these are not always especially effective. They might be discriminatory, impractical, expensive, and even counterproductive. Christian communities tend to shy away from facing this challenge presumably because it is unpleasant to acknowledge that Christians often fight with one another. But the price for this is poor dispute and conflict resolution. In fact, dispute resolution and conflict resolution pose the most acute if often unnoticed challenges to Christianity.

The Christian community is premised on the fact God has resolved a dispute with humanity in person. This is not God's only reason for being involved with us. This resolution restores a relationship and a plan that have been in place from before the foundation of the world. But resolution is clearly a key part of it. The plan has to be brought back on track if it is to move forward. Christians proclaim, at the heart of their message, that God has dealt with the sins of the world through Jesus's life, death, and resurrection. But this is just technical Christian language for the claim that the relationship between God and humanity has been restored and the estrangement between them resolved. *The* conflict at the heart of the universe has been resolved. Hence when we fail to resolve the smallest disputes within our communities effectively, not to mention their ongoing conflicts, this is an ongoing disconfirmation of the truth of what we are saying. Moreover, clearly this shortfall cripples the ability of Christians to offer anything useful to the rest of the world in the way of peacemaking. It is vital to see, then, that in 2 Corinthians Paul offers us a model of dispute resolution as it was widely practiced in ancient societies. This can be highly effective, but it has been overlaid by modern bureaucratic and institutional methods in our day that are arguably much less constructive. What a revolution it would be if Christians took back dispute resolution from the state and learned how to do it properly. The Christian city must, in short, face the fact that disputes happen, along with conflicts, and that resolving them involves certain techniques, skills, and a lot of hard work, which it is incumbent upon Christians to learn.

First Corinthians raised a lot of issues and asked the congregation to organize itself to address them. In one instance, instead of taking a grievance to court, the Corinthians were to appoint even those of low status—"men of little account" (6:4 NIV)—to adjudicate it. Many of the Corinthian converts were made off the street. It is likely that someone had stolen something. Thieving was (and still is) endemic in hierarchical societies. It is one of the ways that the humiliated and disempowered get back at their superiors. Perhaps surprisingly, however, the Corinthians seem to have met this challenge. We learn from 2 Corinthians 7:11 that the "case" has been dealt with. "You have proved yourselves to be innocent in every way with respect to the matter of the court case." Paul is possibly a little over the top praising the Corinthians for this act, but he is trying to be affirming. They haven't got much right. But we learn from this that Paul clearly expects the Christian city to resolve its own disputes in a Christian way. To allow external pagan courts to resolve matters is shameful! But what does this resolution look like in practical terms?

In 2 Corinthians 2 Paul writes about someone who has caused grief both to him and to the rest of the congregation through some offense. This could be the thieving offender we just noted, the incestuous stepson of 1 Corinthians 5:1–11, a dedicated visitor to the local brothels addressed by 6:12–20, or all three. In a certain sense it doesn't matter. What matters is that this behavior has hurt Paul and has damaged the congregation. So the Corinthians have visited disapproval and shame upon the perpetrators, and shame is the most unpleasant emotion that people can experience. Paul now says that this is sufficient. The one who has grieved others and is now shamed must be restored, and the community's love must be affirmed. The Corinthians must forgive and encourage so that the people in question are not overwhelmed, and if the congregation fails to do this, it is being outwitted by Satan's schemes!

This is all very intriguing. These Corinthian actions gesture toward something we now know as "restorative justice."[5]

Indigenous people in various places have long practiced communal dispute resolution. Offenders and the offended are brought face-to-face to process a damaging incident. Deep shame results for offenders. But it is this very experience that leads to learning by offenders and keeps them from further offending. Moreover, when someone who has been hurt, and who has been supported by the community, confronts an offender, he or she is empowered, dignified, and healed from much of the trauma that the offending has caused. It is a profoundly restorative practice, and I think we see it peeping through the cracks of the Corinthian community's actions here. And all this is just what we would expect from a Christian community.

God has taken the initiative to reach out to a hostile and offending humanity, reconciling us to himself in an immensely costly act. We have not just been forgiven. We have had our relationship restored. The damage has been undone. We have been reconciled. In just the same way, Christian communities should organize themselves and practice reconciling their own members together when they have disputes. When they do this, they are participating in the triune God's relationality that restores relationships and heals them when they are damaged. When they do not do this, they undercut their witness to the reality of this God at the most fundamental level. We don't often hear this said—the community at Corinth is normally the poster child for what not to do—but here we need to follow in the footsteps of the Corinthians.

Arrival in Corinth

Paul deepens his important account of what a Christian leader should look like in 2 Corinthians. Christian leaders don't look like much to the outsider, and they shouldn't. They are meant to get alongside people, no matter how humble, so they need to abandon most cultural markers of leadership that are based on status and capital. We must learn to radically reevaluate authentic Christian leadership in terms of Jesus. But we learn two further highly significant things from 2 Corinthians about the Christian city: about how it handles money, within an economy of generosity and giving; and how it handles disputes, with a process of restorative justice. Moreover, we see a healing process unfolding around this letter as Paul woos Corinth and restores his relationship with them after his stinging previous letter. With patience, diplomacy, perseverance, and not a little cunning, Paul stitches his relationship with the Corinthians back together.

Paul finally arrived personally in Corinth midsummer in 51 CE. Much had happened through the spring. He had sent a deeply challenging letter to the Corinthians from Ephesus, risking losing the participation of his wealthy but squabbling clients there in his great collection for the poor in Jerusalem. Around the same time he had experienced an enormous success in Ephesus—an evangelism explosion—followed by a traumatic reprisal that forced him to flee the city for Macedonia. But in a series of steps he had succeeded in drawing most of the alienated Corinthians back to the point where he could stay with them again. Looking down over the azure Corinthian gulf from Gaius's villa, the summer sun baking the hills and surrounding Achaian plain to a dry brown, he must have taken a great sigh of relief. Things were back on track.

How wrong he was.

The most serious challenge of his ministry was about to strike him in Corinth like a tidal wave, having already wrought destruction through his other congregations all the way from Jerusalem around to the Aegean. Paul had to spring immediately again into crisis mode.

Questions

> What three events led to a stunning expansion of Christianity in Ephesus, followed by Paul's speedy and secret departure from the city? How do we need to think like ancient people to understand these events?

> How are Christian leaders supposed to copy Jesus's leadership when they encounter people and plant communities?

> How does this quality also help communities to navigate their internal differences and conflicts?

> Why do Christian leaders often not look like much? How can authentic Christian leaders be recognized? What sort of power do Christian leaders exercise? What sort of power should they avoid?

> What sort of giving should characterize authentic Christian communities, and why?

> How does authentic Christian community educate us into the difference between needs and wants?

> Why is it so important for Christian communities to embrace the need to become skilled at conflict and dispute resolution?

> What is the difference between a dispute and a conflict? What difference does it make if a dispute takes place within a broader conflict?

> Where do we see a Christian community at Corinth addressing an incident and an offender? What offenses might specifically have been confronted? How was this done (insofar as we can tell)?

> What does Paul strongly urge the Corinthian community to do to and with an offender after the incident in question has been addressed?

PART 2

CHAPTER TEN

Enemies

Conflict

The new conflict threatened to split the entire early church apart. But to understand it fully we need to flash back two years to Paul's first arrival in Ephesus, on the other side of the Aegean Sea from Corinth, in 49 CE. When we talked about this in chapter six we noted in passing that something forced him to break that mission off. He only finally made it back to Ephesus one and a half years later, at the end of 50. What was the intervening event in 49, something so significant that Paul left an important mission and was diverted for over a year? Something serious.

The diversion began when a report reached Paul's ears in Ephesus of a major problem in the church in Syrian Antioch. Syrian Antioch was a strategically critical church. It had been the cradle for Paul's revolutionary missionary breakthrough over a decade ago, so it was the mother church for the pagan mission in the way that Jerusalem was for the church as a whole. Then it had been his base when he looped out for the next two years to evangelize Cyprus, Galatia, and Pamphylia during what most of us now know as Paul's "first missionary journey" (see Acts 13–14). The disturbing report concerned Peter, Barnabas, and some emissaries from Jerusalem. They were all in Antioch and had all turned their backs on Paul's approach to mission. They were now insisting that any pagans converting to Christianity had to go the whole hog, converting fully to Judaism. This new protocol basically eliminated Christianity and undermined Paul's original missionary breakthrough along with the legitimacy of his whole approach—a crisis if ever there was one! Paul dropped

PAUL: AN APOSTLE'S JOURNEY

everything and headed for Antioch to address the situation. He was accompanied by some supporters, including his taciturn Croatian coworker, Titus, who
happened to be uncircumcised. Would Peter, Barnabas, and James's emissaries
insist that Titus had to be circumcised if he was to be saved?

When Paul arrived in Antioch he didn't hold back. He confronted the
other leaders. He accused Peter of vacillating and play-acting, and he rebuked
his old friend Barnabas as well (although they had already had their disagreements).[1] But things were not resolved because it turned out that the person
behind the situation was James, Jesus's brother, who was allied with a group of
newly converted Pharisees back in Jerusalem. This group lay behind the delegation to Antioch that had stirred up this trouble. All the leaders in Antioch
realized that they had to travel to Jerusalem to hash the whole thing out with
James and his new friends face-to-face.

We tend to be on Paul's side here because we read about these events
mainly from his point of view. To grasp what was going on fully we need to
appreciate what James, the leader of the messianic Jews, and his new conservative Jewish converts, were feeling at this moment.

An astonishingly successful mission has suddenly exploded in Utah.
Young ministers, graduates from a well-regarded divinity school and thus
highly trained in the importance of noncolonial sensibilities, have been sent
there by their bishop to do mission work, and people have begun to flood into
the Methodist churches in and around Salt Lake City. The mission's success
verges on being a revival. The bishop is initially very pleased. But then disturbing reports begin to reach him.

Apparently, these flocks of new converts all happily confess that Jesus
is Lord and endorse the triune God of grace. But no one is being baptized or
taking the Lord's Supper. These rites have been abandoned. Moreover, churchgoing with special linen undergarments is viewed as acceptable if not as standard. Sayings from the book of Mormon are being quoted liberally in the
church alongside quotations from the Bible. Most disturbing of all, there are
rumors that polygamy has been ruled acceptable, and many male converts with
multiple wives are coming tearfully out of the closet and living and worshiping
openly with their impressively large families.

The bishop contemplates simply excommunicating the young missionaries and their new congregations immediately. But he generously sends a
letter along with a small delegation of trusted co-workers, ordering all those
involved to return to traditional Christian practices without further ado.

To his surprise, the missionaries involved confront his representatives
very directly about these instructions and a heated public argument ensues.

128

The orders are rejected by the Utah missionaries in no uncertain terms, with copious quotations from Scripture and tradition in support of their radical departures. Fortunately, all the parties concerned agree to journey back to their home state to meet together with the bishop to try to decide what should be done. They will seek the will of God together concerning this entire controversy.

In just this sense but more so, Paul's Christian communities were a shockingly radical departure from standard Jewish practices. Many of the things that Jews hold most dear were not being taught. It is no surprise then that the conversion of Jewish leaders to the new Jesus movement back in Jerusalem resulted in a clampdown at Antioch. But Paul was no pushover. He was ready to defend his turf, and we pick up his story again in Jerusalem, where he, Barnabas, and Peter had traveled from Antioch to discuss these questions with James and his influential new converts. One of the most important meetings in the entire history of the church ensued.

At the end of what were presumably some long and occasionally heated discussions, the Jerusalem leaders, Peter, John, and James, shook hands as partners with Paul and Barnabas. The Jerusalem apostles, led by Peter, would evangelize Jews while living as Jews, and Paul would continue to head up a movement evangelizing pagans, living if necessary like a pagan during this work although observing key rules. Any pagan converts would avoid things like blatant idolatry and sexual immorality. To cement the deal, Paul would travel back through all his churches to gather a large amount of money for the poor that the community in Jerusalem was caring for. This is the collection that in the previous chapter we saw Paul bringing to a successful conclusion at Corinth. James, following in Jesus's footsteps, had a heart for the poor.

Underneath all this we can detect a classic "live-and-let-live" deal, but this was a courageous decision by all involved. It was brave of Paul to evangelize pagans in this way, and it was brave of the early church leaders, who were Jews running a Jewish mission in Judea, to let him do so. Two things now need to be noted carefully.

First, as a result of this deal, the early church was fundamentally diverse. The church as a whole was a partnership between messianic Jews, who lived fully committed Jewish lives, and converted pagans, known at this time as Christians, who in certain respects did things very differently. And it still is (or at least it should be). This profound diversity framed by an even more fundamental unity is built into the very foundations of what the church is all about, although it is hard to appreciate it when the importance of fully practicing messianic Jews within the body of Christ, and of Jews in general, is not recognized. In fact, these groups are not just important. As Paul puts it in Romans 11, they are the tree-trunk into which Christians are grafted as a motley spread of unnatural branches. Any branches that have cut themselves off from their new Jewish root and wandered off in a striking bid for pagan independence have, to modify the idiom, sawn off the very thing they need to sit on. There is absolutely no erasure of Torah-observant Judaism in Paul, although he makes the same curious claims as every other Jew in the early church: that Jesus, the crucified carpenter from Nazareth, was Israel's long-awaited Messiah and its Lord.

Second, not everyone accepted the Jerusalem deal. As is common in deep conflicts, a small militant faction did not accept the decision of the majority at the meeting and set out to undermine it. I am reminded here of the "Good Friday Agreement" that brought a lasting peace to the conflict in Northern Ireland shortly after my family and I arrived to live in Great Britain in 1996. The Irish Republican Army—the terrorist wing of Irish resistance to British rule known as the IRA—signed off on the deal. But an IRA faction was unhappy and split off to continue terrorist activities, styling themselves "the Real IRA." The unhappy figures in Jerusalem were the Real IRA of the early church, and they were very like Paul when he was Saul—learned, sincere, zealous, deeply dedicated to God, and completely wrong. We will call them "the Enemies," since this is what Paul calls them once in an uncharitable moment.[2]

About a year and a half after the Jerusalem conference, the Enemies set out from Jerusalem to reverse the damage they thought Paul had inflicted on the Jesus movement. They traveled through Paul's communities in 51 CE, exhorting everyone to convert fully to Judaism as the only path to salvation. In other words, they ignored the Jerusalem deal and its terms and set about undermining it. If round one between Paul and the Enemies had been in Antioch, and round two in Jerusalem—at which point Paul was clearly ahead on points—round three would take place in Paul's own churches, and it would be a fight to the death.

Paul's last three letters

We noted earlier that Paul arrived in Corinth in mid-51 CE after a very difficult year. He had been expelled from Ephesus and had worked through a crisis in his relationship with the Corinthian church. Just as things seemed to be calming down, however, he learned that this group of militants was going to each of his congregations behind his back to undo the work of the council. Just when he thought everything had been settled! The resistant splinter group that we are calling the Enemies started their campaign through Paul's churches in 51 CE, just over a year after the important Jerusalem consultation. Sadly, this delay, along with one or two other snippets of evidence, suggests that they had spent the intervening time persuading the Jerusalem leaders to turn on Paul and to renege on the critical Jerusalem deal.[3]

Paul couldn't be everywhere at once, putting out these fires as they were lit on all sides, so he did what he always did and wrote letters, dispatching them like blasts from a blunderbuss. Congregations en route to these letters' final destinations were supposed to read, copy, and study these letters as well, so in this way he covered everybody. We have one of the letters from this volley preserved in our Bibles, and part of another one.

Paul wrote a storming letter to his churches up in Galatia, fearing that they were already lost—the letter that Martin Luther loved so much.[4] He wrote an equally strong letter to the Philippians.[5] This letter has been lost, but he quotes a piece of it again in a second letter he wrote to the Philippians shortly after this, which we do have preserved in our Bibles. The quotation from the first letter can be found in the scathing section 3:2–4:3 that has always puzzled scholars. There is a sudden shift to a rather vitriolic argument that is out of keeping with the surrounding discussion, but a quotation from an earlier letter when Paul was feeling deeply vitriolic explains this shift nicely.[6] Finally, Paul confronted the Enemies personally in Corinth, where things were about to take an especially nasty turn.

The Enemies, like the young Saul, were zealots, which means that they were prepared to kill on God's behalf, and they certainly wanted to kill Paul. He was a traitor to his people, to his people's customs, and ultimately to God. But they couldn't just murder him, stoning him in a public street. That would elicit Roman reprisals. So they did the next best thing. They would bring a court case against him before the Romans on serious charges and hope that the Romans would execute him for them. If money had to change hands to convince a Roman official that Paul was a no-good, it was a small price to pay for his head on a platter.

The Enemies duly accused Paul of seditious behavior in Corinth, and he was jailed pending trial. We know this because he wrote the letter to the Philippians that we have preserved in our Bibles at this time, thanking the Philippians for their support during this imprisonment and urging them to stand strong against the Enemies' views. It is in this letter that he calls the militants "enemies of the cross" (Phil. 3:18), having just called them "dogs, evildoers, and mutilators" (3:2)![7] No love lost there then. As Paul anticipates in this letter, however—and he was very experienced in these matters—he was exonerated. I imagine that the wealthy Corinthians could have matched any bribes that the Enemies could offer. Equally importantly, Paul's judge, a Roman aristocrat named Gallio, refused to be drawn into this fight. He ruled that the dispute between the Enemies and Paul was a matter internal to Judaism and should be handled by that community. Roman officials, operating at a higher civic level, need take no part in it.[8]

After his release Paul realized that he had to travel back to Jerusalem again. He couldn't tell if the leaders there had backed out of their deal and betrayed him, factionalized themselves, or disapproved of the militant Enemies but lacked the power to stop them. So he determined to travel again to the mother church located in Judaism's holy city with a group of supporters, easing his reception by taking the promised haul of money that he had collected by now. (His friends must have had stacks of gold coins wrapped around their waists in belts under their dingy tunics, and if they were wise they carried stout staves to ward off bandits.) Surely someone who cared so much about the poor could be trusted? But this was an awkward change of direction for his missionary project.

Paul had been wanting to go to Rome after his most recent visit to Corinth. He wanted to dispatch the money to Jerusalem, to the east, with some letters and some trusty money-bearers, and to head in the opposite direction himself, to the west, to Rome in Italy, and then ultimately beyond Rome to Spain. Rome was a missionary paradise and the epicenter of the empire. From there the gospel could spread to the other three corners of the empire that Paul hadn't evangelized yet—Egypt, Africa, and Spain. It was also a huge opportunity in its own right, dwarfing all other cities in size with its million or so inhabitants. But now Paul is in a dilemma. He simply has to go back to Jerusalem to find out what is going on, and this is in the exact opposite direction from Rome. It will take weeks if not months. And it is risky. There is a good chance he will be caught and killed in Judea. This is the Enemies' home turf. Even if all goes well, the long journey to Jerusalem and back will allow his Enemies the opportunity to get ahead of him. They can travel to Rome and poison that entire critical missionary field against him before he arrives—an awful prospect. What is he to do? What he always does, of course. He will write a letter. But this was no ordinary letter.

Paul's letter to the Romans had to explain everything in full to any converts there rather as "Ephesians" did for the new Laodicean church that Paul had not yet met. Few of Paul's Roman readers had met him or heard any of his teaching before. So what he could just summarize in his other letters to his own converts he had to spell out completely in Romans. Moreover, he had to describe and, if possible, destroy the teaching of the Enemies. *And* he had to defend his own gospel against their criticisms of him. A full dress rehearsal of his own gospel and of the deficiencies of the gospel of the Enemies, and a defense of his gospel against their not-unintelligent charges, make Romans the most extensive and theologically dense letter Paul ever wrote, and it is a masterpiece. Like all masterpieces, however, it goes far beyond the circumstances that elicited it, and it can be difficult to grasp in all its complexity.

The Christian city continued

As we turn to look at the content of Romans in more detail, it is comforting to note how it says many of the same things about the Christian city that we have already learned from 1 and 2 Thessalonians, "Ephesians," Colossians, Philemon, and 1 and 2 Corinthians. The same goes for Galatians and Philippians, Romans' sibling letters. These last three letters all deal in one way or another with the Enemies. But they still build the Christian city as Paul understands it, further emphasizing some of its key features.

Galatians gives a punchy outline of Paul's radical approach to Christian ethics in its final major section (5:1–6:10), and we have already appealed to its pithy summaries like 3:26–28 and 6:14–15. We also sense Paul's Corinthian difficulties peeping through the cracks, which is not surprising. He wrote Galatians in Corinth, so in parts of Galatians he is talking to the Corinthians who were sitting around listening to him compose and recite the letter, and who would have made copies of it and continued to study it. "If someone is caught in a sin, you who are spiritual should restore him gently" probably references the thief of 1 Corinthians 5, who was admonished in 2 Corinthians 7 but was supposed to be reintegrated into the community according to 2 Corinthians 2 (Gal. 6:1). We see here again the city's important practice of restorative justice. Meanwhile, "Do not use your freedom to indulge the sinful nature . . . [in activities like] sexual immorality, impurity, and debauchery" refers to just about everyone at Corinth. This reemphasizes the Christian city's strict sexual ethic (5:13, 19). However, the rest of Galatians addresses the position and the counter-charges of the Enemies, so we will postpone a look at those until we get to Romans, which lays out the same things at more length.

Philippians wraps a charming letter around an anti-Enemy portion from a previous letter, present in 3:2–4:3. Above all it emphasizes the humility of Christian leaders as those relational qualities are rooted in Christ himself. Christ lowered himself—as Paul puts it "emptied himself"—taking on the human form and then accepting a humiliating execution (2:5–11, esp. v. 8). These are astonishing acts of solidarity, of getting alongside the unworthy, and ultimately of love, and Paul weaves together through the letter the way he and his genuine co-workers like Timothy, and even the suffering Epaphroditus, model these virtues too (2:19–30). The Philippians seem to have been experiencing a painful internal dispute between female leaders (which is very interesting; see 4:2–3). Paul calls them to respect one another, to serve one another, and to rebuild a community that ought to evidence the overflowing joy and peace of God (4:4–7).

Romans is much longer and fuller than Galatians and Philippians. It is helpfully constructed in four main sections: chapters 1–4, 5–8, 9–11, and 12–16 although, as usual, a more practical letter frame wraps around these arguments that make up the body of the letter.[9] Chapters 5–8 have already been discussed in our earlier account of the breakthrough that occurred at Antioch (see chapter two). They are the fullest account that we ever find in Paul of the resurrected ethic that undergirds Christian behavior. They could be titled "How to be ethical without being Jewish—although in such a way that Jews can still be Jewish."

The baptized have had their corrupt bodies of Flesh executed and buried in Jesus. They have been resurrected and re-created through Jesus's resurrection and ascension thanks to the plan of the Father and the work of the Spirit. This resurrected reality introduces the all-important interpersonal dimension to Christian life that sits lightly to the form of various practices—things like food and calendrical observances—but is very concerned with how people relate to one another. The ethics of the Christian city are further developed in the letter's fourth subsection, chapters 12–16, which we have also dipped into already from time to time. Paul speaks there of the congregation in familiar terms as a body led by leaders who have been gifted with diverse roles from the Spirit; of the importance of love and its implications; and of the critical importance of kindness in the face of different practices.[10] As at Corinth, at Rome some Christians stand closer to Jewish customs than others, observing the Sabbath and avoiding impure food. Paul urges due sensitivity to this.[11]

So a good half of the letter is detailed but familiar. But what of the other half, chapters 1–4 and 9–11, and of the material we haven't discussed in Galatians, chapters 1–4, so around two-thirds of that letter? And what of the storming section quoted in Philippians from a previous anti-Enemy letter to Philippi (3:2–4:3)? Do these sections add anything to our description of the Christian city?

It depends.

New material

An argument about Paul's authorization is apparent in Galatians 1:11–2:14, but I don't think we need to spend too much time on it here.

Paul clearly felt that he had to defend himself in Galatians against the charge of being some sort of renegade. His Enemies seem to have said that he was authorized as an apostle by the leaders of the early church in Jerusalem, Peter, James, John, so those leaders outranked him. Further, Paul has now gone well and truly off the reservation and so they—the Enemies—have been authorized by the Jerusalem leaders to follow around behind Paul cleaning up his mess. They will instruct his converts more thoroughly in the ways of Judaism and the Torah. Paul outflanks this account of his authority brilliantly in the opening argument of Galatians by attributing his apostolic office directly to God. *Jesus* commissioned him, not the Jerusalem leaders, on the road to Damascus, and not back in the Holy City, which he didn't even visit until two years after his divine commission. Paul has obviously visited Jerusalem since then from time to time but only to discuss things as equals and to coordinate working within a partnership of mutual recognition. When he has to, Paul will even rebuke a leader like Peter to his face for being wrong, as he did at Antioch.

Is there anything else that is new?

There are two types of new material present in the distinctive sections in these letters. They overlap with one another a lot at first glance because they both engage with Jewish material.

There is a peculiar argument in which Paul opposes "justification" achieved by doing "good works" as instructed by the Jewish law to a justification bound up with "faith" and with Jesus.[12] The need for male converts to be circumcised comes up a lot as well. Paul clearly doesn't like the justification that is supposed to come through instruction by the law and advocates faith and Jesus over against it. This is discussed mainly in Galatians 2–4, Romans 1–4, and Romans 10.[13] There are some very vestigial appearances in Philippians 3:6 and 9 and Ephesians 2:8–10, so in five more verses, and that's about it.[14] Paul's use of what we can call "the justification opposition" is consequently quite peculiar to Galatians and to Romans, while something behind Ephesians and Philippians leads him to mention it in passing.

Abutting these passages are other discussions about Israel that have a different shape ("Israel" being the Hebrew for "God's people"). Paul tells stories in them about Israel, especially its inception with Sarah and Abraham, although the other ancient mothers and fathers of Israel are often in view as well. Paul sometimes extends the story through the next great turning point in

Israel's history, the time of Moses, which included the exodus from the tyranny of Pharaoh in Egypt, the sojourn in the wilderness, and the giving of the law on Mount Sinai. Sometimes he briefly alludes to the exile and to God's saving of a Jewish remnant from Babylon, events that occurred much later in Israel's history. His stories extend to Jewish reactions to Jesus in the present day although he doesn't stop here. He pushes on to talk at times about Israel's future. A long panorama of Israel is consequently discernible, although it appears in a patchy way in Paul's highly circumstantial letters. He seems to draw on bits of this story as and when he needs to. These contrasting, story-like discussions can be found mainly in Galatians 3–4 and in Romans 4 and 9–11,[15] although we shouldn't forget some contributions from the Corinthian letters.[16]

We're going to spend a bit of time unpacking these two neighboring clumps of material—Paul's famous opposition between justification through works of law and justification through faith, and the stories he tells about Israel's past, present, and future—and there are two important reasons for doing so. We might be forgiven for thinking that there should be just one. Wouldn't we read these texts to find out some more about what Paul thinks about the law of Moses and about Israel? He hasn't talked about these important subjects much at all in his other letters. We might learn some key things here about handling the Old Testament in our Bibles, and about the people that those books talk about but who seem to be strangely absent from our churches, the Jews. And certainly this is one of our reasons for paying careful attention to these passages. The Christian city needs its account of preceding Jewish history. It is built, after all, on Jewish foundations, and a lot of the city in Paul's day was Jewish. But there is another critical reason for this attention.

Much interpretation of Paul has gone disastrously astray at this moment and I mean disastrously. To use one of Paul's own metaphors, the description of his gospel has wandered drastically off course to be shipwrecked and destroyed (Rom. 9:6).[17] One of the most important challenges we face when we read Paul is avoiding the danger that lies in wait for us here, maintaining the course that we have been on up to this point in our discussion as set by his other seven letters. To switch metaphors back to one we have already been using: we already know how Paul builds the Christian city. It is a friendly city with open borders. Its leaders, the apostles, are seldom even at home but are visiting other cities as missionaries and diplomats where little colonies of resident aliens are being set up. (They tend to slip into these cities' more unsavory quarters, to be sure.) It is like a modern city, then, with highways and transport routes flooding in and out, thick with traffic. At its center it is, as the book of Revelation also sees so profoundly, ruled by a lamb who has been slain (Rev.

5:6). It is ruled, that is, by a victim, not by a perpetrator of violence. However, if we deviate from our course and then run aground on the hazard that awaits us in these passages in Galatians, Philippians, and Romans, we will wall our city in and install a new ruler. Moreover, this new ruler is not characterized by compassion, inclusion, and healing, but by retribution, exclusion, and, if necessary, by punishment. Our city will be ruled by a lion, not by a lamb. It will be demarcated and punitive. It will be another city entirely.

The danger lies in the first group of passages we just described that oppose justification achieved by works to justification obtained in relation to faith. We can get Paul's arguments here very wrong, so we need to spend a bit of time learning to read them in the right way. In order to do so, however, we will need to grasp a very basic and important theological distinction. It was the Enemies' failure to grasp this distinction that led to their confrontation with Paul.

Questions

› What was the challenge facing Paul at Antioch, and then in Jerusalem?

› What were Paul's opponents probably worried about?

› What was in the Jerusalem deal?

› What did the early church basically look like?

› When did Paul's troubles with the Enemies begin?

› When and how did Paul learn that people had rejected the Jerusalem deal, and were undermining his churches?

› What particular challenge did Paul soon face in Corinth from the Enemies?

› The last three letters written by Paul that we are dealing with here—Galatians, Philippians, and Romans—all come from different phases within this period. When and why exactly were they written?

› Why does Galatians begin with a long biographical section? Why do some of its ethical exhortations sound Corinthian?

› Why does Philippians contain a distinctive and strong, central subsection (3:2–4:3)?

› Why did Paul write Romans? Why is Romans so comprehensive?

- There are two types of material present in these three letters that we have not encountered before in the other seven letters (or at least not very much). What characterizes the first type of material? Where is it found? Why is it important to handle this material carefully?

- What is the second type of material? Where is it found?

CHAPTER ELEVEN

Covenant versus Contract

The unconditional gospel

Paul's gospel proclaimed a God who is for us. He was for us before we were for him. He reached out to us while we were still estranged, hostile, and sinful, going to extraordinary lengths to draw us back. The Father and the Spirit offered up their only beloved Son to die for us. The Son accepted the will of the Father and the Spirit and obeyed this fate, becoming one with us and dying for us. This tells us that God loves us, and loves us before he does or is anything else. God is love all the way across and all the way down. This is the extraordinary and highly counterintuitive message of texts like Romans 5:5–6 and 8, although we have seen how it permeates almost everything else that Paul says elsewhere in his letters.

It follows from this that God's relationship with us is unbreakable. Because God loves us this much, God will never let us go. If we think of a healthy family that is loving and committed—and I realize that many people, sadly, do not come from families like this—we can see that the parents are irrevocably committed to their children. Their relationships with their children are covenantal. They are unbreakable. Damageable, yes. Frequently bruised and hurt, yes. But breakable, no. These parents can never rescind being parents. They are parents forever. Their children will always be their children, and vice versa. I am the parent of two children and will never not be their parent. Never. Are they perfect? No. Are our relationships free from difficulty, hurt, and disappointment? No. Am I committed to them permanently and irrevocably? Of course I am. This will never change. These sorts of covenantal relationships—

of utter loving commitment—lie at the heart of all healthy relating. They do not have to spring only from families. Paul had no spouse or children but he had friends who would die for him and he for them. Covenantal families and friendships foster all true human flourishing.[1]

In the light of this it is tragic to see how often people alter these arrangements and claim that personal flourishing must take an altogether different form. When this happens we are no longer teaching the gospel at all. The gospel has been altered into something we can call religion. But how exactly do we transform the gospel into religion? It's very easy. *We insert conditions.* This move transforms unconditional familial relationships of love into conditional and legal relationships of limited obligation. The covenantal forms of the gospel are replaced by the contractual forms of religion. It's a small step for a religious person but a giant leap backwards for humankind.

Religion

All human societies function conditionally and legally in certain respects, and states have a particular fondness for doing things this way. Few have been as organized as ours. The reach of modern bureaucracies can be a little terrifying. But all states have rules that are enforceable if they are broken. Moreover, commerce generally depends on contracts, and our modern society is again rife with this mode of relating although it is by no means unique. In a commercial contract we undertake to fulfill certain conditions to receive things in exchange. If we don't fulfill the conditions then we don't receive what we contracted to get and vice versa. This all feels very natural to us, although it is entirely cultural. But what happens if we structure God's relationship with us in this way, contractually, because we think deep down that God relates to us like a ruler upholding some program of law and order?

If God relates to us conditionally, through a contract, in a religious way, then God no longer loves us. We must be talking about another sort of God. Certainly we are not talking about the God who is definitively revealed by Jesus.

Love is not conditional. We have just seen this when we talked about healthy families and deep friendships. Love is irrevocable. It is unconditional. It never gives up, never lets go. If we introduce conditions into our relationships with people then we only love them if they fulfill those conditions. If they break those conditions we stop loving them. If God only loves us when we fulfill certain conditions then God has to be conditioned into loving us, and this is quite a limited situation. God's fundamental attitude toward us—to which he will immediately return if the right conditions are not fulfilled—is something different from love, and is presumably just. This is, moreover, how God relates to most people since most people in history have not been members of the church. Now justice is okay, but it can be very harsh, and it certainly isn't love; and love based on the fulfillment of certain conditions isn't love either. I am not a husband or a parent who loves his family *because* my spouse and my children fulfill certain conditions. Our relationships are not based on contracts or justice. My family can do nothing to break this relationship. It is a covenant, not a contract, and God is just the same. Love is higher than justice as the heavens are higher than the earth.

Is the God revealed in Jesus fundamentally loving or not? Of course he is loving! He is love all the way down. We know this to be true. The Father offered up his only beloved Son for us while we were still hostile to him. The Son died for us while we were still resistant and alienated. This God is love to a degree we struggle to grasp. So the suggestion that God has to be conditioned into love, and otherwise, underneath it all, is merely just, is deeply destructive. It undermines the gospel at its heart and hideously misrepresents what God is like. We must resist this move at all costs, which is what Paul had to do when his Enemies came into view. But before we see exactly what he said about all this we need to consider an important objection quickly.

Many people become anxious at the thought that God might be unconditionally and permanently committed to us in love—strange but true. They worry that people will take God for a ride and misbehave. If we are permanently in God's good books, then why would we want to do the right thing and respond to him and to others as we should, sometimes in costly actions of kindness? The concern here, in other words, is ethical. Does this understanding of God undercut ethics? Will we stop behaving well because we are under the gaze of a covenantal God? This was probably the concern that Paul's Enemies had.

I understand these concerns, but they are the absolute opposite of the truth. A covenantal relationship exerts the strongest possible ethical pressure on its partners. Abandoning a covenant, conversely, and structuring relationships with a contract, relaxes those pressures and allows unethical behavior in all sorts of ways. It is, paradoxically, religion that is unethical! Let's trace its thinking through for a minute and see where it gets us.

Religious ethics

Religious people try to avoid supposed ethical abuses by introducing conditions into their relationship with God. If and only if you fulfill certain conditions, religious people say, will God then stay in relationship with you, be nice to you, and reward you. If you don't fulfill them, then the hammer will drop. Ethical behavior is encouraged here by building it into the conditions that save. Ethics is loaded into God's saving contract with us. The hope is that connecting these things together will motivate the ethically abusive to behave well, if only out of self-interest. "If you don't do X, Y, and Z, then you won't be saved!" In Paul's day people probably said that converts should avoid bad behavior because if they don't then they might be sentenced to death on the Day of Judgment. "Do the smart thing and avoid hell and get to heaven. Act rightly! Do everything that the law says!"

But let's think carefully about what we are saying when we urge people to be good so that they can get to heaven because of a contract that God has made with them. Why exactly are they going to be good? If it is because they hope to get some future reward then it is a selfish decision that now has nothing to do either with the goodness of the behavior in question or the God who is asking them to behave well. It is purely self-interested.[2] Similarly, if they behave well only to avoid a negative outcome, they are not behaving well because that activity is good and the avoided activity is evil, or even because they care about it particularly. They are just trying to save their own skin.[3]

Imagine I am heading off to a conference in Amsterdam, famous for its fleshpots (which in fact, as I write this, I am; a New Testament conference is about to be held there). I am a happily married man, and a faithful one. But why should I remain faithful in Amsterdam while my wife waits patiently and innocently for me back in North Carolina? For contractual or for covenantal reasons?

Thinking contractually, I could reason this way. "I must not indulge myself in the fabled fleshpots because I could lose the reward of heaven and might get sent to hell. Moreover, I might suffer some practical, this-worldly losses as well. My wife might find out and would probably divorce me. I would have to pay her a great deal of alimony. And I would be lonely once I got back to North Carolina." I might reason that there is not much likelihood of her finding out, and I could take the risk—many do presumably. I would just have to lie about it all when I got back to the USA. However, I might then think the risk is too great. How would I disguise the costs on my credit card or my large withdrawals of cash? So I refrain from visiting a brothel and come home ethically triumphant.

My wife meets me at the plane and says, "Did you indulge yourself, dear?" I reply, "No, I thought the risk of you finding out if I did so was too great, and the financial inconvenience would be too high." I could have added, "Those risks apart, of course I would have," at which point, any right-thinking wife would divorce me in any case. So clearly I haven't done the right thing here even though technically I behaved in the right manner. My contractual motivations undercut my action's goodness. I did the right thing superficially, but even then it wasn't actually right. A contractual approach has weakened my good behavior in every possible way.

How would I approach this situation covenantally?

As I sit on the plane and contemplate the fleshpots of Amsterdam I think to myself, "If I indulge myself with one of these women, I betray my wife whom I love dearly. I inflict awful hurt on her, and damage my covenant with her deeply and possibly fatally—and much of this irrespective of whether she ever finds out. I love her and want to be faithful to her and so will skirt these fleshpots like the plague, since that is what they are." This of course is the right way to act and involves the right reasons. Moreover, the pressures on me to act in the right way are far stronger than any pressures I feel if I am just thinking contractually—and it is the same with God.

We do not behave in the right way because we covet or fear the final consequences of this in terms of going to heaven or being cast into hell. To behave in this way is a betrayal of our relationship with God. Reasoning in this fashion, we don't care about God, and we don't care about the good either. We are behaving selfishly, and if we behave correctly for this reason we still sin. We should behave in the right way because we love God and want to do what pleases him. He has shown us what the good thing to do is and we want to do the good thing to please him. Christian ethics is covenantal because it flows from personal relationships—our personal relationship with a loving God—and we must hang on to this, earnest religious ethicists notwithstanding.

In sum: to be covenantal is to be ethical in the deepest possible way. To be contractual, supposedly on ethical grounds, is to weaken ethics drastically. So I am going to stay covenantal and read Paul in that way too, not least because I think he was so ethical.

The "gospel" of the Enemies

Grasping the distinction between a covenant and a contract is critical when we read the texts that contain Paul's justification opposition. These do have a religious element but now we know why. The Enemies were religious! They linked salvation and ethics together in a contract, so when Paul describes their program in his letters he writes about a religion. Paul's enemies probably didn't understand the distinction between contractual religion and the covenantal gospel as clearly as he did. But by their actions they ended up advocating religion and undermining the gospel.

The Enemies traveled around insisting that Paul's converts from paganism adopt Judaism fully. The men had to be circumcised and to join the local synagogue.[4] Everyone had to start reading Torah assiduously (which is not a bad thing if it is done for the right reasons, but here it isn't). They had to eat the right food, to avoid contaminated wine and idols, to avoid sexual immorality (which they were already supposed to be doing although, again, it needs to be for the right reasons). And they had to follow the Jewish calendar, lighting the Sabbath lights, resting on Saturdays, and observing the Jewish feasts. Reading between the lines, Paul's Enemies thought that only circumcision and complete commitment to the Torah would generate right behavior. If people did all this and lived righteous lives, they would show up before God's throne on the Day of Judgment and be pronounced righteous, and this was pretty important. Only the righteous entered the kingdom of heaven. By teaching this, however, we can see that the Enemies understood messianic Judaism conditionally. Its participants had to do things to be saved. If converts did not act in a certain way, then God would not save them. This made salvation insecure and pushed it into the future. We know for sure only on the Day of Judgment if we make it in, and this current insecurity is a hallmark of conditionality.

In short, by insisting on Christians converting fully to Judaism, which they understood conditionally, the Enemies had replaced Paul's gospel with religion. The covenant was displaced by a contract. "If you don't do all this, then you will be condemned to hell," they said. "If you do, then you will get to heaven—and not otherwise." They were a variation then on good old-fashioned turn-or-burn theology, although here Jewish turn-or-burn preaching with a pinch of Christianity thrown in.

It follows from this that religion is present in Paul's texts when he talks about the gospel of his Enemies, although, as he remarks caustically in Galatians 1:7, it doesn't deserve the title of gospel at all. It is hardly good news. The phrase "You will be justified by doing the works taught by the law" is a summary of the religion of the Enemies. What this means is: "If you do works as taught by the divinely revealed lawbook, then you will be saved on the Day of Judgment. You will be pronounced righteous by God because you are! You will receive a verdict of 'righteous' in that court because a court is what decides these sorts of things." This is the claim that comes up in Romans 1–4, 10, Galatians 2–3, and vestigially in Ephesians 2 and Philippians 3. We can see it quite clearly in a text like Galatians 2:15–16.

Galatians 2:15–16

I would translate this text as follows:

> We who were born Judeans and not pagan sinners,
> knowing that a person is not delivered by doing works as instructed by
>   the Torah [only]
> but also by the fidelity of Jesus Christ,
> even we believed concerning Christ Jesus
> that we are delivered through the fidelity of Christ
> **and not** through works as instructed by the Torah,
> [and understood further] that [as Scripture says]
> "all flesh will not be pronounced righteous through works as
>   instructed by the Torah."[5]

The position of the Enemies here is fairly obvious, although Paul is clearly denying it. No one gets saved on the basis of some contract with God, by doing lots of good works and then showing up on the Day of Judgment, and then hoping that God pronounces him or her righteous. Paul says this three times in one sentence just so we don't miss the point. But if we read this passage carefully we can see that Paul is denying this claim because of a more important underlying position. We get saved in another way, through Jesus, and any alternative system like the teaching of the Enemies must therefore by definition be wrong. "Even we Jews know this . . . ," says Paul. "God has chosen to give us resurrection and new life by means of his Son, Jesus, whom he has resurrected already. This was God's plan, so anything you might come up with simply has to be wrong whether it looks Jewish or not. Get with the program." "If deliverance comes by means of the Torah [and its works] then Christ died gratuitously," Paul says shortly after this (Gal. 2:21), which basically means, "Christ died to save us, therefore salvation does not come through the Torah." This is Paul's basic position, although we should note a couple of its details more carefully before we move on. These will help us to read his justification opposition correctly whenever we run into it in the various passages in Romans and Galatians where it occurs.

The faithfulness of Christ

Texts like Galatians 2:15–16 are often translated so that they speak repeatedly of our faith in Christ. But although Christian faith was very important for Paul, introducing that notion unilaterally can be a mistake and end up obscuring Paul's broader argument. To appreciate exactly what he is suggesting we have to realize that one of his key phrases is best translated "the fidelity of Christ Jesus."[6]

Paul obviously intends to out-Scripture his opponents in passages like Galatians 2:15–16, and this phrase, which he uses a lot, alludes to Habakkuk 2:4, a text Paul read as a prophecy about the coming of the Messiah. He quotes it in full in 3:11. The text from the prophet says, "The Righteous One *through fidelity* will live." For Paul this Scripture is a prediction of the saving story of Jesus. "The Righteous One" was a title that the early church often used for Jesus. Its use was influenced by Isaiah 53. This was a very important text for the early church because it talks about a righteous person being led like a lamb to the slaughter while bearing the sins of others. This seemed to point very clearly to Jesus. The fact that the same title came up again in Habakkuk 2:4 would have led early Christians who knew their Scriptures like Paul to link these passages together and to find Jesus in this text as well. "Fidelity" in Habakkuk 2:4 speaks of the way Jesus obeyed his Father and endured the cross like a martyr. "Live" speaks of how Jesus was resurrected on the third day, because of his obedience, and enthroned in heaven as Lord. Habakkuk 2:4 is consequently the short version, drawn directly from the Jewish Scriptures, of the story Paul tells slightly more fully in places like Philippians 2:5–11. It follows from this that whenever Paul speaks in Galatians 2:15–16—or anywhere else—of "the fidelity of Christ," he is alluding to this scriptural verse and by implication flagging the entire story of Jesus—his obedience, death, and resurrection.[7] In fact, he flags it three times in this important sentence.

It follows from this realization in turn that "faith" in these texts does not tell us what we have to do to become a Christian. It does not speak of a condition for salvation.[8] Faith speaks first of the faith of Jesus himself, allusively implying his death, burial, and resurrection as well, and Paul's sentence is running the argument we just noted. Paul knows that salvation does not take place by means of obedience to the Torah. Salvation means "resurrection," and God has effected resurrection for us through Jesus. So we are saved by being connected to him. His resurrection opens up the way for our resurrection. We will live because he lives. Now if this is God's plan, it's a really bad idea to go off and come up with our own, no matter how pious it looks. But this is just what the Enemies had done. "Good luck," Paul might have said, "but I'm staying to take my chances with Jesus. He is, after all, God, so his plan is probably going to work best. In fact, it has worked!"

Christian faith

Paul doesn't just talk about Jesus's faith in his letters. He talks a lot about Christian faith too (see especially Gal. 2:16 and 3:22). So how do these faiths connect together?

It's pretty straightforward. In the same way that we get our love from Jesus's love and our obedience from Jesus's obedience we get our faith from Jesus's faith. He is the source of all our goodness. The Spirit gifts us these virtues as well. As a result of this, any faith we have is a reflection of the character of Jesus in our lives. Our fidelity echoes his fidelity. It bears his imprint. And this allows Paul to fashion a further useful argument against the teaching of the Enemies.

The Enemies were arriving and telling Paul's converts that they needed to do a lot of additional things to be saved. The men had to be circumcised, and everyone had to start studying the teachings of Moses and obeying them. Paul has just said that this is a bad idea because it sets aside what God has done to save us, through Jesus. But it is also unnecessary. The faith of Paul's converts shows that they are saved already.

"Our faith is evidence that God is already connected to us and at work within us," he might have said. "It is proof that we are saved, and assures us that full resurrection and life lie just ahead. Jesus was faithful and then God the Father resurrected him and glorified him. He has been saved. And we are now joined to Jesus. We are sharing in the first part of his story, in his faithfulness. Death and resurrection may lie ahead of us then, but our faith shows that we are bolted onto Jesus, and in view of this we know with certainty that our resurrection and glorification will follow shortly as we have seen that it already has for Jesus."

This argument must have greatly reassured his converts. It is as if Jesus has already ridden the elevator to the party on the top floor of a big hotel. We have just stepped into the elevator down on the first level—the most boring part of the journey. We are going to be locked into a small box for a bit. But we know where the elevator is going because we have seen Jesus at the party already and we know that he took this elevator to it. That we are standing in the elevator feeling its hum and rise is proof that the party is waiting ahead of us as the door finally opens. This is how faith works for Paul in these passages. It is the elevator. It proves that we're already on our way. Salvation is assured.

This is still a useful argument to recall at times today because religion is alive and well in the modern church. I sometimes call religious versions of Christianity "Jesus-but" theology. Any time someone says the name Jesus, thereby referencing what he does for us, and goes on to add the little word "but," we are most likely in the presence of Christian religion, not the gospel, and this is, as religion always is, unsettling and destructive.

A good old-fashioned Southern Baptist preacher comes to a church of devout Episcopalians. He preaches for forty-five minutes—church members blanching in their pews as he roars well past the usual twelve-minute cut-off—speaking passionately about how God has done everything for us in his Son by way of his Spirit. "Jesus is all that you need . . . but you have to be baptized properly to gain his benefits, as the good book says. You must be fully immersed after making a free decision for Christ. Only then are you truly saved." The poor Episcopalians are shaken by the Baptist's learning and fiery conviction. They have, after all, only been sprinkled as unthinking infants and never properly immersed in water as confessing adults. However, before submitting to another baptism down at the local river, they write to their bishop for clarification.

She is, it turns out, deeply versed in the distinction between a covenant and a contract, having read Karl Barth's *Church Dogmatics* before going to sleep at night for many years. She writes to her troubled flock and simply asks them the following: "Do you believe in your hearts that Jesus is Lord, and that God raised him up to sit at his right hand as Lord? Do you confess this truth every week and maintain it faithfully?"

They write back and reply even more simply, "Yes."

The bishop suppresses a chuckle and writes back the following. "Then you need not fear. You already bear the marks of Jesus's person in your character and your behavior. This believing—this faith—is evidence that Christ's character is already imprinted upon you by the Holy Spirit. Like him, you will one day be resurrected and enter into glory. God is already among you! God has already saved you! Have no fear! Nothing can break this relationship that God has established with you. You don't need to be afraid of some future Day of Judgment when God might exclude you. He loves you. He has already sent his Son to die for you, and this when you did not even know him but despised and reviled him. Get baptized if you want to avoid causing offense, or if you feel the Lord has called you to. But don't do so from fear. You have been called to freedom, not to bondage. You are participants in a gospel, not in a religion."

This is how Paul's arguments in these texts are supposed to work. His emphasis on Jesus's faith points to him as God's appointed way to life and resurrection as predicted by the Scriptures. His emphasis on Christian faith is then supposed to generate assurance. The Galatians do not need to adopt all the practices of the Jewish Torah to guarantee their future resurrection. They are on course for resurrection already. Their faith attests to this, proving that they are walking in the footsteps of the faithful Jesus who has already been resurrected. What has happened to him lies just down the road ahead of them. Resurrection is locked in.

Now that we know how to read Galatians 2:15–16 constructively, along with all of Paul's other similar oppositional texts by implication, we are ready to turn to consider the new vistas that open up for us as Paul considers Israel, past, present, and future.

Questions

> What does healthy parenting teach us about the nature of covenantal relationships?

> What is a contractual relationship? How is this relationship fundamentally different from a covenantal relationship?

> What attitude or disposition lies at the heart of each type of relationship?

> Why do we sometimes resist affirming a covenantal relationship with God? What do we fear?

> Why is it problematic to act in the right way simply to fulfill the conditions of a contract that will save me? What does my good behavior really consist of given this motivation?

> What motivations and pressures do a covenantal relationship place on my behavior?

> Is the common ethical anxiety about covenantal relationships valid?

> Why do we find religious and contractual elements in Paul's texts when we read the passages that contain his justification opposition?

> What were Paul's Enemies—possibly to a certain extent unwittingly—teaching? Why was their program ultimately contractual?

▸ How do these realizations help us to read texts like Galatians 2:15–16 constructively?

▸ How does Paul prove that believing Christians can be assured of their salvation already, in the here and now, and don't have to wait nervously for some future judgment to find out if they are saved?

▸ When might this argument by Paul still help Christians today?

CHAPTER TWELVE

Israel Past and Present

Paul's view of present Judaism

One of the unique contributions from the cluster of letters we are now considering—Galatians, Philippians, and Romans—is the window they open onto Paul's view of Judaism. The Enemies were learned messianic Jews advocating a conditional understanding of salvation. Paul thought this was just dead wrong and he was right to fight them so determinedly. They were peddling religion, and he was offering something very different in the gospel. But the Enemies gave a religious account *of Judaism*. They spoke of its Scriptures, its present customs, and the future of its people. However wrong they were, squeezing these into a contract, this mistake forced Paul to provide his account of these important matters in debate with them. In Galatians, Philippians, and Romans we discover what Paul thought Judaism was, what it is, and where he thinks it is going.

The first big advantage flowing from a clear identification of the Enemies within the arguments of these letters is that we no longer need to include their material in a description of Paul's view of Jews. The Enemies are not legitimate interpreters of the inner truth of Judaism, just as they fail to understand the gospel. All the textual data that describe their teaching—attempted justification through works of law—can be sidelined. This material looks Jewish, and in a certain sense it is, but it is not Paul's account of Judaism.[1] It is an account he spent much of his life opposing. What was Paul's view of Israel?

Where Paul starts his account is, as always, very important. He begins with his present situation, baptized in Jesus, with a renewed mind gifted to him by the Spirit. From here he looks back to his ancestral traditions, interpreting them from this new vantage point.[2] Naturally not all modern Jews or even modern interpreters will share this starting point. However, for Paul the personal presence of the God of Israel in Jesus was a given. It was bedrock. It was non-negotiable. And God gets to say what Judaism is all about. It follows from this that Paul's view of Judaism, past, present, and future, will be deeply informed by Jesus.

From this starting point, present Judaism divides for Paul between those who have confessed Jesus's Lordship and those who haven't. The former are in the minority, so he uses the biblical motif of a remnant to describe them in Romans 9 and 11. Remnants were small groups of things left behind after a devastating experience from which new life could later flourish. The prophet Isaiah speaks of a tree stump that has been cut off.[3] Fresh growth and another tree will eventually spring from it, evoking the way a small group of Jews returned to Jerusalem after their seventy-year exile in Babylon and flourished again. Messianic Jews like Paul exist, even if there aren't very many of them, and their presence suggests that a great future flourishing of messianic Judaism within Israel could take place. However, before we think about this future possibility some more in our next chapter, it is important to emphasize that messianic Jews within the church are Jews.

They are not Christians. Paul expects them to live like Jews. We can detect moments when messianic Jews are called to Paul's mission among the pagans. They then live—to a degree—like pagans.[4] But otherwise we see that messianic Jews in the early church, and even Paul when he moves through Jewish situations, live in full obedience to the Torah's instructions. According to the book of Acts, Paul takes a Nazirite vow twice during two trips to Jerusalem. He shaves his head, avoids corpse impurity, avoids alcohol, then shaves his head of its unkempt hair and makes an offering of it when he arrives in the temple in Jerusalem. This is pretty Jewish. He circumcises Timothy who was technically a Jew, being born of a Jewish mother, but who had not been circumcised. He observes the Passover in Philippi. He debates from the Jewish Scriptures in synagogues on the Sabbath. Such is his commitment to his own people that he endures the frightful community discipline of thirty-nine lashes from them five times.[5]

In the same sense, we get no hint at any time from Paul that he expects missionaries to the Jews in the early church, led by Peter, to abandon the Torah or to teach the same to their Jewish converts. They are not to extend that lifestyle into his Christian mission when pagans have converted and make it mandatory everywhere. Pagans can stay where they are, with some adjustments. But Jews are to stay where they are when they were called, which means living as good Torah-observant Jews. There is a conundrum here, however, that we should face before we go any further.

Given that Paul does have harsh things to say about the Jewish Scriptures, which played such a key role in guiding the lives of pious Jews (and still do), we need to find out if his position is unstable, collapsing on itself unworkably. Was he actually quite confused here? Or does his position have some rationale that allows Jews to still be Jews following both Jesus and the Torah, despite the difficulties Paul sees within this arrangement?

Using Scripture

On the one hand, Paul is quite clear that Scripture can kill. If the Roman Christians try to obey the tenth commandment, avoiding coveting, they will inevitably sin and thereby lapse into the desperate condition of the Flesh (7:7–25). They will die. If Paul's Galatian converts undertake circumcision as prescribed by the Torah, Christ will be of no use to them (5:2–4). The Mosaic Torah was a ministry that brought death, he says in 2 Corinthians 3. In Galatians 4 it is an enslaved existence that aligns more with Hagar and Ishmael than with Sarah and Isaac (vv. 21–31; Genesis 21). In 1 Corinthians 15 it is the power behind Sin, which has a sting that kills (vv. 54–56).

On the other hand, Paul clearly loves Scripture, frequently appealing to biblical sayings and stories in relation to his converts. Paul speaks of various exodus events to the Corinthians in 1 Corinthians 10 and 2 Corinthians 3; of patriarchal stories in relation to the Galatians—the promise to Abraham, the conception of Ishmael, and the miraculous birth of Isaac; and of the births of the other patriarchs when writing to the Romans, extending his analysis to speak of the exile and the remnant. Jesus is witnessed to by the Torah and the Prophets (Rom. 3:21). The Roman Christians should attend to everything that has been written because it provides instruction and encouragement, thereby facilitating perseverance and hope (15:4). This presumably is why Scripture is cited over fifty times in this letter. This usage can be stern. Paul threatens the Corinthians with plague and death if they do not desist from idolatry as exemplified by the Israelites who worshiped the golden calf during the exodus (1 Cor. 10:1–11). But even this stern usage is instructive and ultimately supposed to be positive, like a sour-tasting pill that is meant to cure an illness.

What is going on here? Paul seems to be all over the place.

Rather than ascribing a horrific confusion to him at a very basic level, it seems that Paul distinguishes between *the Spirit's* use of Scripture to mediate the commands and teachings of the risen Jesus and his Father, and *other* uses of Scripture, which are then pretty much our own idea. These last uses can be taken hostage by the flesh and the evil Powers that live in it.

Instructions governed by the Spirit are recognizable because they give life. They build up the body of Christ and guide it on the pathways of obedience. When Paul uses scriptural texts to teach, they all basically speak about a God revealed in Jesus and working through that person. "Whatever promises God has promised to us they are 'Yes' *in him*" (2 Cor. 1:20). As a result, the "Torah that is Christ" is our primary teacher (1 Cor. 9:21; Gal. 6:2).[6] Christ speaks *through* Scripture, and this is not just acceptable; it is critical. Christians and Jews need written texts to shape their language. But the one who speaks ultimately is God. "You received the word heard from us *about* God not as the word of a person, but as it truly is, the word *of* God, which is also working within you who believe [in it]" (1 Thess. 2:13).

The second, human use of Scripture, however, is vulnerable to exploitation by evil Powers. It leads ultimately to death, and the teaching of the Enemies would be a good example of this. This is why the death-dealing aspect of Scripture comes up so clearly in the letters Paul wrote to deal with the Enemies, and why we are addressing it here. If we doubt the importance of this type of scriptural activity we need only to recall quickly the way the Scriptures were extensively used to sustain the cause of the Confederacy during the American Civil War, principally by endorsing the ongoing existence of slavery. This exegetical work was by no means irresponsible. It was careful and nuanced. Consequently, generations of scholars, teachers, and preachers in the southern states taught that the word of God had no problem with slavery, and even more than this; the Bible encouraged it. Yet the church today would universally recognize this use of Scripture in defense of slavery as demonic. Scripture can kill.[7] But how does this manipulation of Scripture by evil forces actually work?

Paul's template here is the command that was manipulated by the evil Powers present in the Garden of Eden. He sees these Powers working through the snake, which he later dramatizes as "Sin" with a capital "S." Sin deceived Adam and Eve by means of their divine instructions and thereby unleashed sin, suffering, and death, on the whole cosmos (Rom. 5:12–14; 7:7–13). The presence of the commands from God—in particular, the instruction not to eat from the tree of good and evil—was what created the opening for the evil Powers to deceive and ultimately to kill humanity. Paul sees this dynamic at work in all subsequent uses of Scripture that are not taken up by God—he uses the tenth commandment's prohibition of covetousness—and it is a sobering thought. Fleshly interpretation is open to seduction, manipulation, and colonization by the evil Powers that roam our cosmos, and they like nothing better than to oppress, to enslave, and to kill.

When pondering this dynamic I cannot help remembering the PREA training I first experienced several years ago. PREA, which is short for the Prison Rape Elimination Act, is a well-intentioned piece of legislation introduced in 2003. Sexual abuse in prisons is common and the Bush administration was rightly outraged by this and tried to do something about it. However, it did so in a fashion that ignored the lessons of Romans 7. In typical contractual fashion it made all sexual activity with a person in detention an automatic felony. People doing time were defined legally as unable to give consent to such an act, and there is a truth here. Correctional and detention officers (COs) have such power over people in detention that consent can easily be coerced, or simply retrospectively asserted after a rape. So the Act defined this consent out of existence. Abusive COs could no longer appeal to consent if they were caught having sexual contact with people doing time. (The legislation did not address sexual abuse between detainees.)

It followed that all visitors to prison on a regular basis who assist with programming and the like had to learn about this new Act and sign off on it. "People in detention cannot by law give consent to sexual activity, so if you have sexual activity with such a person you automatically commit a felony. If you have sex with someone you will end up in here alongside the people you are volunteering to visit and not just visiting any more. . . ." But this Act opened up an area for potential manipulation. If a person doing time could elicit sexual contact with a CO or volunteer, then they created a hold over the person they had had sex with and could manipulate them, perhaps to smuggle in contraband or perform other illegal activities. Disclosing any sexual activity would automatically convict the CO or volunteer of a felony. So the PREA training, which volunteers must endure annually, included a number of short movies—not, to be sure, Oscar-worthy in quality—that ran through different scenarios whereby people in detention could manipulate a correctional officer or volunteer into illicit sexual contact. These were fascinating.

Half a dozen different situations were acted out in the short clips, and by the end of the education into what not to do all the volunteers were stunned by the various opportunities to engage in sexual contact that they had previously had no idea at all existed. The level of ingenuity in these situations was remarkable. Even if I had put my mind to it I would never have come up with some of them. And yet here I was being handed all this information on a platter. Of course, I was being told that I shouldn't do any of it. But I had had no idea previously about any of it and so wouldn't have done it anyway. Now I knew exactly what to do. The instructions about what not to do, in all their stunning details, told me *exactly* what to do. All that information was now imprinted indelibly on my mind. It is this sort of situation that Paul seems to be thinking of when he writes in Romans 7 about how the tenth commandment can be manipulated by evil powers to lead people into sin despite what the text is saying directly.

It seems, then, that the words spoken in the past by God and now treasured up in a written form as Scripture, are not the words of God if they are not spoken again by God. Without the animation of the Spirit and the summons of Christ, they are just words that have been written down by human hands with pen and ink and parchment—treasured and valuable to be sure. They were the words of God, after all. However, words about God's former wishes drawn from the handwritten texts that record them are sadly open to demonic exploitation unless God reiterates them overtly for us again. In particular, when Scripture says not to do something it makes a direct suggestion in that very moment about how to sin. The command not to covet as it is written in the Scriptures immediately suggests all sorts of sins—desire for a neighbor's house, spouse, servants, donkey, ox, property, and much else besides.

I wonder if the underlying experience that led Paul to this insight into the potential destructiveness of Scripture was not his persecution of the Christian community prior to his call. Paul undoubtedly learned a lot from this.

Prior to the revelation of Christ on the road to Damascus, as chapter one already noted, Paul was a deeply devout servant of God but understood this to mean being prepared to kill on God's behalf, and doubtless he buttressed his persecutions of Christians with scriptural citation. He was a Bible-believing Pharisee after all. Perhaps he quoted the story of Phinehas, who impaled an immoral Israelite as he was sullying himself with a pagan woman in his tent (see Num. 25:1–9; Ps. 106:28–31). But this action in Paul's earlier life, along with this use of the Bible, was not godly. It was satanic. And I think that Paul learned a permanent lesson from this.[8]

The Scriptures themselves should not be used independently of God. When used by the flesh, they serve the flesh; hence their usage must be guided by the Spirit of Jesus. When it is, they are a good and helpful thing. It follows that Jews can still be Jews, studying their precious Scriptures and obeying their instructions, provided those instructions are mediating the commands of Jesus, and for much of the time I am sure they are. But a chasm yawns just to the left of this footpath where scriptural interpretation veers away from the voice of the living God and is taken hostage by the flesh and its occupying evils.

There religion awaits with all its hypocrisies and cruelties. Paul's Enemies had slipped into this abyss.

With this sobering lesson in mind concerning the dark side of scriptural usage, we can turn to consider a life-giving example of scriptural teaching in Paul's account of Judaism's past.

Israel's past

We might ask first why Paul even talks about the past. Isn't it just past? Paul has a lot to be getting on with in the present, and he would encourage us to focus on the same. But Paul has some important reasons for talking about the past on occasion.

If God is a faithful God we would expect his plan that takes effect through Jesus to be in continuity with what he has been doing up to Jesus's arrival. After Jesus has come we shouldn't expect a new plan or, still worse, an entirely new chosen people. This would call God's character into question. Alternatively, anyone proposing a radical shift in God's plan can be called into question, and Paul runs this risk because of his highly innovative conversion of pagans. His converts are not joining God's people in history as they have traditionally been organized, as Jews. This does look pretty strange. Surely he is an apostate or some sort of renegade? Paul faces a real challenge here. How does he handle it?

He retells the story of Israel. Israel's history as he narrates it is smoothly continuous—now that the figure to which everything has slowly been building has been revealed. In the light of Jesus's climactic resurrection Paul sees faithfulness and resurrection inscribed into Israel from its very beginnings. Israel began when it was called into being in the household of Abraham. Abraham, known as Abram at the time, was promised seed and land by God. "I will make you into a great nation and I will bless you; I will make your name great, and you will be a blessing. I will bless those who bless you, and whoever curses you I will curse; and all peoples of the earth will be blessed through you" (Gen. 12:2–3). God reiterated these promises in a subsequent chapter. "Look up at the heavens and count the stars—if indeed you can count them. . . . So shall your offspring be" (15:5).

These promises had translated by Paul's day into entry by Abraham and his seed into the life of the Age to Come through resurrection, and the inheritance of that perfect world forever. But there was a technical problem. He had no direct heir with Sarah, his wife. Nevertheless, at an extraordinarily advanced

age, having soldiered on in faith for sixteen years or so after the last promises, God miraculously gifted the couple with Isaac, an heir through whom
Abraham's seed would descend and the promises be fulfilled. Paul describes
Abraham's old loins and Sarah's barren womb as "dead," so the conception
and birth of Isaac were literally an event of life from the dead or resurrection.

Note carefully now what account of past Judaism Paul has created. The
basic story has God placed centrally as the key actor, as is appropriate. God
calls Judaism into being through its original ancestors, then promises future
life to them. In this fashion they are "elected" or chosen. God initiates this
relationship and gifts Israel with existence and purpose. Abraham responds
faithfully to this relationship after his call, trusting God. God then fulfills
his original promise in an act of resurrection in Isaac that opens up new life,
although this only foreshadows the main event that will come much later, at
the end of the Age. In just the same way, God calls Isaac, and then Jacob, the
younger son of Isaac, over Esau, gifting them also with seed and inheritance.

In view of these origins in the patriarchs and matriarchs, it now seems
like the most natural thing in the world that Jesus has come—God in person—
and opened the doorway into the promised new life through his resurrection.
Another faithful figure has arrived who has endured suffering and then been
gifted with resurrection, although this time life has been given in the Age to
Come and not merely anticipated. The promises have been fulfilled!

Paul is even able to slip his mission to the pagans into this developing
story. God did not just promise Abraham seed, which is to say, descendants,
and land, meaning in its later, expanded sense, the Age to Come. He promised
to bless Abraham as the father of many nations—the pagan nations! Abraham
was told repeatedly, "All the nations of the earth will be blessed through you"
(Gen. 12:3; 18:18; 22:18). Consequently, Paul's mission to the pagan nations
is just the outworking of this original blessing. The pagans too have gained
entry into the life of the Age to Come through Abraham's most important
descendant, Jesus, although the way they live now, without fully adopting
Jewish customs, is unexpected. But this inclusion of the pagans by God into
the people who will be gifted life in the Age to Come is in continuity with these
foreshadowings in Abraham. God calls his people into existence. Presumably,
Paul adds in Romans 9, he is free to include whomsoever he wants to as long
as he doesn't turn his back on his original people—and he doesn't.

This is a controversial retelling of Jewish origins and subsequent history.
Although Paul knows the Mosaic stories well, and appeals to them from time
to time as he needs to, he has defined Israel in terms of its origins, using the
stories of the patriarchs and matriarchs. This marginalizes the story of the exo-

dus and the giving of the Torah on Mount Sinai more than many other Jews in his day would have been happy with. Moreover, the gift of the Torah is, as we have seen, a double-edged sword. It is not just a treasured repository of God's instructions about right living, although it is these things. It is an opportunity at the same moment for the evil Powers working within human nature to seduce and deceive people into sinning—a reading informed by other aspects of Jewish tradition and principally by the tragic story of Adam and Eve. New information in the Torah about right living is also new information about wrong living. So Paul's history of Israel reduces the gift of the Torah—which remains a good gift—to an interlude between the patriarchal origins of Israel, with all their anticipations of resurrection, and their later fulfillment in Jesus's arrival, death, and resurrection. Moreover, it draws that negative interlude into the negative story defining humanity as a whole based on its descent from the original transgressor, Adam.

At bottom, then, past Israel is depicted by Paul as having a *telos* or goal, the overarching goal that is the resurrected Christ. With the arrival of that goal Paul sees the previous history of Israel as building toward it. It is only a plausible narration for those who believe in the goal, but he, along with all the other followers of Jesus, did. Clearly Paul tells the story of Israel backward. He looks back from Israel's fulfillment and sketches in its antecedents. Hence if that fulfillment is true, it follows that his sketch of antecedent Israel is correct. If it is not, then his sketch is not.[9]

Unbelieving Jews

The result of these realizations is a particular view of what unbelieving Jews in the present are. The Jews are very much God's people still, called into being through Abraham and Sarah. They are first and foremost the people to whom God came in person—the people God took up and assumed. What a privilege! Further, that divine person, a resurrected Jew, is now the template for all of humanity who will populate the Age to Come. Even now they remain the heart of the church or, as Paul puts it, its tree trunk. Converts from paganism are included as an unnatural addition to the Jewish tradition, which was established in Abraham and Sarah. They are guests invited from abroad and welcomed into this Jewish history, there to take up, among other things, the Jewish Scriptures, learning from that faithfully preserved treasury. Consequently, the pagan debt to Judaism is incalculable.

It is extraordinary to think, then, that instead of acknowledging this

Christians would negate Jews, erasing their practices and identity, judging them inferior, immoral, and irrational, and eventually herding them onto cattle cars to be transported to camps for enslavement and eradication. (This testifies to the shocking capabilities of the fallen Powers that roam the flesh.) Although Paul has been read in a way that endorses this evil behavior, this is a reading of Paul that he himself would be horrified by.

In short, Paul viewed all Israel as privileged and irreducibly special. This was a Christ-centered view. It was rooted in the most powerful revelation of the God of Israel that Paul knew, when the God of Israel had come to Israel in person, so it was an explicitly theological construction. But it was, for just these reasons, non-negotiable, not to mention, unshakeable. And it was fundamentally and relentlessly positive.

Nevertheless, a major objection can be made against our developing reading. Someone could say that there are plenty of harsh judgment texts in Paul suggesting that Paul's God is, in the end of the day, conditional. You have to do certain things to make it into the people of God and be guaranteed resurrection, whether as a messianic Jew or as a Christian. At the least, you have to believe in Jesus. If you don't, then it sure looks as if you will ultimately be judged and excluded as Paul's judgment texts suggest. Not everyone makes it into the saved box, and if that is the case this just looks like a big contract on some level. Moreover, it looks as though unbelieving Jews do eventually get thrown under the bus, along with all the other unbelieving pagans that Paul can say some pretty harsh things about on occasion.

Now is the ideal time, then, to discuss Paul's view of Israel's future. This will help us to see that, although this objection has elements of truth, it is not the whole picture.

Questions

> Why do we get so much information about Jews, Judaism, and Israel from Galatians and Romans and not as much detail, if any, from Paul's other letters?

> What information in Paul's texts can we remove from any account of his view of Jews and Judaism?

> How is present Judaism currently divided, according to Paul?

> Are messianic Jews really Jews or are they Christians?

‣ What two types of scriptural use are detectable in Paul? What explains this? When have you experienced life-giving and death-dealing uses of Scripture?

‣ Have you ever experienced a situation in which a well-intended or fundamentally good instruction led to the opposite effect?

‣ What situation(s) might have led Paul to realize that sometimes Scripture can be used destructively?

‣ How does Paul tell the story of Israel in the past? What is the key to his account? Do you think this is valid?

‣ How should Christians view and treat unbelieving Jews, and why?

CHAPTER THIRTEEN

God Wins

Judgment

There can be little doubt that Paul saw the future playing out very differently in relation to two contrasting groups of people. The chosen will be saved. They are marked now by the Holy Spirit and are supposed to live spotless lives. On the last day they will be resurrected and glorified, along with the suffering cosmos, or simply transformed in the blink of an eye if they are still alive, and be presented blameless before God. Shockingly, Paul made this offer indiscriminately to pagans, and, in a double shock, his definition of righteous living did not include many standard Jewish activities. But Paul clearly held that the rest of humanity, lost in idolatry and general wickedness, will be destroyed by a fiery cataclysm. Sin, death, evil, the powers, Satan, corruption, and the entire world of the flesh will be annihilated. Paul expected this extinction to include a vast number of idolatrous pagans—especially those who had been nasty to his small Christian communities. (See for example 1 Thess. 5:1–3; 2 Thess. 1:6–10.)

So the stakes were fairly high for becoming a Christian or a messianic Jew loyal to Jesus. Only this could guarantee eternal life. This seems to suggest that there might be something like a contract lurking in Paul's theology. Certainly Paul attributes the responsibility for ending up unsaved largely to a refusal to accept the offer of the gospel. Satan plays his part (see 2 Cor. 4:4). But Paul's longest discussion of rejection and its causes is in Romans 10, where he discusses the rejection of Jesus by a large number of Jews. He places the blame for this squarely at the feet of those who have rejected Jesus. God has come right down to his people, reaching out to touch their hearts and minds, both in person and through chosen messengers, and they have pushed all these overtures stubbornly away. It is their fault.

Does this mean that deep down Paul thinks about salvation conditionally, that salvation is structured like a contract, and that people have to do certain things in order to be saved, failing which they are struck down on the Last Day? If you get damned for not doing something, then doesn't it follow that you will get saved by doing something, at which moment we have a contract? Not necessarily, although there are some real challenges here that we need to face.

It is entirely possible for people to push an arrangement away, however destructive and irrational that rejection might be. This refusal does not mean that the overarching arrangement is a contract, as any parent of a troubled teenager knows. They could be pushing a covenantal arrangement away and refusing to live out of that basic reality. If people reject these arrangements and turn away, then they lose the benefits of living in these arrangements. This does not mean that a contract is in place though. It's just the universal reality of consequences.

Jessie was born to a stable and happy family. Her parents were kind, faithful, and consistent. But for whatever reason she was angry and decided as a teenager to explore drugs. She pushed her parents away and spiraled into serious substance abuse, eventually becoming deeply depressed and ultimately vagrant. At any moment she could have entered a rehab clinic and engaged in recovery with a fully supportive family. But she refused. One day an acquaintance asked her, "Where are your parents?" She replied, "They are dead. I have no parents. I am all alone. Nobody loves me."

This was a lie. She has parents who are still her parents and love and support her unconditionally. They have not withdrawn from her and are ready to stand by her during any attempted recovery at a moment's notice (and the addiction specialists tell me that they will need to be ready to do this for the seven times that most addicts take to make it through recovery fully). Jessie is located in a covenantal relationship. But she is rejecting that relationship and refusing to live out of its reality. Her rejection of this reality and its gracious structuring of her life does not mean that she can do anything to reestablish the relationship itself and thereby turn this covenant into a contract. The covenant is still in place. It is there. It is always there. She is just rejecting and abusing it. She should *respond* to this covenant as is appropriate, and in doing so she would stop damaging herself as well as the other people who love her and are engaged with her. It is this dimension in the situation that she is messing with, and she is experiencing the consequences of doing this.

The fact that large numbers of Jewish people contemporary to Paul were rejecting Jesus and courting the consequences does not mean that they are in a contract. They were in a covenant. That's what made the rejection so acutely painful and incomprehensible. Covenants can be violated and damaged. They are restored when they are recognized and people turn from their foolish ways—when, in other words, they repent. But have we answered our challenge here as we need to?

Not fully. We still need to ask if God can really be covenantal and loving all the way down if he lets people perish in a final fiery cataclysm, even if that's what they apparently want. If this is the case, won't God's love have limits? Won't the unbreakable covenant break? Or can God's covenantal commitments and relentless love overcome the human rejection of that commitment and love? I think Paul provides an indirect but clear answer to this important question.

Who wins?

We saw earlier that Paul gives an account of the problem facing everyone in terms of Adam, in counterpoint to an account of the solution in Christ. In doing so, he claims that Christ's solution is humanity-wide. It corresponds to Adam, the original image of all humanity. Paul goes out of his way to affirm this in 1 Corinthians (1 Cor. 15:22; see also vv. 45–49):

In Adam all of us die.
In the same way, in Christ all of us will be made alive again.

In Romans 5 he goes even further. He writes that Adam is only a "type" of the one who comes later. He is an inferior negative copy of an original in the sense that a carefully carved and molded stamp can be used to press imprints into small discs of metal to make coins (Rom. 5:14). Ancient coins were never as clear and sharp as the original—and they face in the opposite direction. Christ is primary then; he is the stamp. Adam is secondary; he is the inferior negative imprint.

Paul goes on to argue in this paragraph that Christ's solution to Adam's problem is so superior it is almost incomparable to it. It is vastly greater both qualitatively and quantitatively. Only when this incommensurability has been grasped from verses 15–17 can we proceed to a parallel comparison between Christ and Adam in verses 18–21, although this is surely what we would expect from a personal intervention by God into a problematic situation.

But the gift is *not* like the trespass.
For if the many died by the trespass of the one man,
how much more did God's grace
and the gift that came by the grace of the one man, Jesus Christ,
overflow to the many!
Nor can the gift of God be compared with the result of one man's sin:
The judgment followed one sin and brought condemnation,
but the gift followed many trespasses and brought justification.
For if, by the trespass of the one man, death reigned through that one
man,
how much more will those who receive God's abundant provision of
grace
and of the gift of righteousness
reign in life through the one man, Jesus Christ! (Rom. 5:15–17, NIV)

It stands to reason that God acting in Jesus must be vastly superior to
the created but corrupt situation that he is engaging with. After all, he runs
creation. When it comes to God getting involved with creation as a person as
against a person dictating the future of humanity, God's person is going to be
bigger, better, and more important. The formula is: Christ > Adam, although
it is more like

Christ > Adam

This all suggests that God's plan being effected in Jesus is going to work
better than anything that might happen to us in Adam, and God's plan for us
in Jesus is saving! Moreover, to leave any loose ends unresolved would imply
that God's solution was, to this degree, ineffective. We would be faced with the
awkward conclusion that God's plan centered in Jesus, having been disrupted
by evil, is never completely executed, and this despite God's personal involvement. This will happen, however, if any people who were created good are
eternally lost, ultimately to the nothingness of death. Evil would be victorious
to this degree. The extinction of the personal would have succeeded. God's
plan for fellowship, reestablished in the face of evil by a personal intervention
and salvation, would have failed in relation to these particular people. The
rescue mission didn't work here. Imagine a hostage rescue attempt in which
the commandos saved two out of two hundred captives. Would we view this
as a success?

If we placed this problem to Paul in this exact form, one wonders how
he would have reacted. "Paul, did God's plan to rescue the world through his

own Son come up short? Did it fail to some degree? Was it perhaps as much as 40 percent ineffective? Or more? Was it—if we are deeply committed Calvinists—perhaps 95 percent ineffective? Are God's created acts ultimately more extensive and effective and important than his redeeming acts?"

I imagine his answer would have been "Hell no!" If God is going to win, and his plan be brought back on track, we must expect everyone to be drawn back into fellowship with him through the work of Jesus. Jesus's mission was perfect. It was complete. No one gets left behind.

However, we have another quite strong card to play in this particular hand. There is some fairly clear evidence that Paul viewed God as being capable of overcoming human resistance when he wants to.

Unbelieving Israel

In Romans chapter 11 Paul spends some time arguing that unbelieving Israel will eventually be saved. The conundrum that many Jews rejected Jesus as both Messiah and Lord was a painful problem for Paul, and he basically throws the kitchen sink at it. Over the course of this long chapter he makes numerous arguments, large and small. But most of them are designed to take his listeners to the conclusion that "all Israel will be saved" (11:26a), and this despite the fact that presently they are largely hostile to God acting in person in Jesus.[1]

First, Paul points out, using the motif of the remnant, that God never lets go of Israel (11:1–7; see also 9:27–29). As we have already seen in chapter twelve, the existence of a remnant indicates God's commitment to the wider group from which the remnant comes. It is preserved precisely in order to preserve the future of the broader group, which will sprout from this stump despite its experience of being cut off in judgment. Hence the existence of a remnant indicates that God has not let go, and will not let go of Israel, but will bring a future flourishing to his presently truncated people. Second, Paul argues cryptically that if the firstfruits of an offering are holy then the entire mass is, and that if the root of a certain tree is holy, the branches are as well (11:16). (Paul's claims here are best explained by some technical Rabbinic arguments.)[2] He then adds, third, that God is able to graft broken branches from a cultivated olive tree back into their own tree since there is something natural about this reinsertion (11:24b). It is, after all, their own tree, so this is easier than grafting unnatural pagan branches into the trunk.

As we read on, however, we discover that these three organic images in Romans 11 are grounded by a fourth argument that reaches all the way back to Romans 9: Israel will be saved in its entirety because the later descendants of the patriarchs are beloved on account of the patriarchs. God's gift of life to the ancestors of Israel—to Abraham and Sarah, Isaac and Rebekah, and to Jacob and Leah and Rachel—is irrevocable and unchangeable (11:28b–29; 9:5–13). This then is the holy offering of firstfruits that sanctifies a polluted offering, the root of a tree planted on holy ground that sanctifies the branches that spread into unclean space, and the cultivated and fruitful olive tree into which broken branches can be regrafted. The irrevocable election of Israel's founding families also undergirds the preservation of a remnant, which continues the existence of Israel after it has strayed into disobedience and fallen under judgment, thereby guaranteeing its later flowering into full fruitfulness. And this all makes perfect sense.

Paul's God is a covenantal God. This God calls people into existence, loves them, enjoys them, gives to them (see 9:3–4), and never lets them go. He gifted life to the patriarchs and matriarchs and called Israel into existence. He preserved them through their rebellions and hostilities. And he will draw them back to him in their fullness because he is this sort of God. His love never gives up, never lets go.

We don't know exactly how this will happen, or when. Scripture tells Paul that "the rescuer," who is probably Jesus, will turn ungodliness and transgressions away from the descendants of Jacob. (So this really has to be Jesus.)

> As it is written: "The deliverer will come from Zion;
> he will turn godlessness away from Jacob.
> And this is my covenant with them—
> when I take away their sins." (Rom. 11:26b–27)

But we don't know any more than this. This could refer to a future personal visit by Jesus; or it could refer to an obedient response to his original presence and work; or perhaps to something else again. However, we do know that it will happen. Paul is quite clear about this:

> All Israel will be saved. (Rom. 11:26a)

We are now in a position to draw the key inference for our present discussion. Paul is facing the fact of widespread Jewish rejection of Jesus (9:1–3; 10:1–3; 11:28a). Few Jews have, like him, become messianic Jews or missionaries to the pagans, and perhaps very few. The vast majority of Jews seem to be unbelievers. But Paul is confident that all Israel will eventually be saved.

Why? Essentially, because of the nature of the God who summoned Israel into existence in the first place. God called Israel into being and loved Israel by way of its famous ancestors. He gifted Israel with existence and life at that time and will now never let go. He is this sort of God, a God who lovingly elects and then maintains this commitment in spite of any hostility and foolishness in the objects of his love. His love will eventually triumph over Jewish unbelief. In short, in the contest between divine benevolence and human recalcitrance fought out in the space that is Israel, God will win. All Israel will be saved.

But there seem to be no good reasons for withholding exactly this narrative from humanity in general. (Paul himself did withhold it, but we are extending him here consistently.)

God created humanity, lovingly electing them into existence and fellowship, preserving them through their self-destructive hostility and foolishness, and refusing to let any of them go, as seen especially in the great outreach of the mission to the pagan nations. God loves humanity as much as he loves Israel, Israel standing as a remnant and hence as a saving sign in relation to the rest of humanity just as the believing Jewish remnant stands as a sign to the rest of Israel. God's Son came to save the human race, undoing the destruction of Adam, not just the destruction of Jews. Hence it seems that exactly the same rationale should apply. God will not let humanity go. In the contest between divine benevolence and human recalcitrance fought out in the space that is the human race, God will win. All humanity will be saved. And we can be confident, in view of this, that God really is a covenantal God, committed to us all permanently and irrevocably.

We still need to know how to handle the Scriptures that push against this view, and many do. But we should recall at this moment that Christians should read the Scriptures in the light of Christ and at his command. They cannot be used to go against him or to correct him. If he wants to save everyone, or seems poised to, we must learn to read the Scriptures accordingly—and there are lots of ways of handling Paul's judgment texts, along with the other judgment texts in the Bible, constructively.[3] It might be helpful to recall at this moment too that a healthy approach to Christian ethics is covenantal and not contractual,[4] and that people who resist joining God's people are only hurting themselves and damaging those they love. They are struggling through the challenges of life with no assurance, no guidance, *and no hope*. No one in their right mind would choose to live like this—which just goes to show that when we sin we are not in our right minds.

But this still leaves us with what Paul actually said. He himself was not an explicit universalist. However, we are I think entitled to suggest that he is one implicitly. If we do not infer this, we unleash the horrible internal contradictions that we have just tabulated. Christ is qualitatively and quantitatively superior to all of humanity as represented by the story of Adam, not inferior. His story, which is God's story, must dominate the story of Adam, and not the other way around. Moreover, Paul is explicitly universalist in relation to unbelieving Israel. In view of this tension in his writing it does seem necessary to push through his deepest insights, which are grounded in the God revealed by Jesus, so here Paul reinterprets Paul. God really is love all the way across and all the way down. The covenant is unbreakable, and ultimately enwraps us all in the gracious purpose of God that was established with us through his Son before the foundation of the world.

I am not going to insist on this. This view has to be suggested and left largely at that. My insights are always distorted and limited; the events in question have not happened yet; and I am not in charge of them when they do—and they are massive, namely, a full unraveling of all of history through time and space! What I can say with confidence is that there is every ground for hope, and that we can trust the one who is in charge of this process to do a good job on that day. More than this does not need to be insisted on. Having said this, however, I do worry that I am being just a little bit cowardly.

As soon as the dreaded word "universalist" is used, a lot of people just get off the train. But I hope it is obvious by now that this is unnecessary. Even more than this: it might be necessary to stay on the train to preserve God's integrity, along with the integrity of Paul's gospel. Universalism (in the sense I am using it here) is a defense of God's integrity. We shouldn't want God's plan to fail. God is God. God gets what he wants, eventually. And God's work is compassionate and perfect. It follows that we should resist reducing Christ in size, making him smaller and less significant than Adam and his work. This is to get things the wrong way around. The plan in Christ is far bigger, better, and more glorious, than anything that happens foolishly because of Adam and Eve. So perhaps we need to put things slightly more strongly.

Let me say that I know as yet of no good theological arguments that lead me to expect another outcome regarding the scope of the future resurrection besides universalism. No other scenario seems to be grounded in Jesus so strongly. I expect everyone to be raised in glory, although some rather more shamefacedly than others.[5] The caveats just noted still apply: limited theological insight on my part; the events have not taken place, and they are enormously complex; and I am not the one who makes them take place. I am not in a position either to know everything about this or to insist on this scenario. But I am quietly confident.

God is love.
Love never lets go.
Therefore God never lets go.

Questions

› How does Paul see the future playing out in relation to how he divides humanity into two main groups—believers and unbelievers?

› Does the possibility that some unbelievers might be annihilated on the Last Day mean that Paul does think in conditional or contractual terms about salvation?

› Does the possibility that some unbelievers might be annihilated on the Last Day mean that there are limits on God's love?

› How does Paul portray the relationship between Christ and Adam?

› Do we expect God's plan for us in Jesus to succeed or not? What happens if there are any loose ends here, so to speak? How would Paul probably react to the suggestion that God's plan partly failed?

› Where does Paul make an extended argument for God's ability to overcome and save people who are resisting him and hostile to his purposes in Jesus?

› What is Paul's main argument for the claim that God will not abandon unbelieving Israel, but all Israel will be saved?

› Are there any good reasons for refusing to extend this argument to humanity in general?

› If we can't extend Paul's argument, how does this change our understanding of God?

CHAPTER FOURTEEN

The Last Journey

The author of Acts

By this point in our story we have processed all the letters Paul wrote.[1] We now lose sight of him insofar as he himself gives us information about what he was doing. But we are fortunate to have a long account of the next phase in his life from the book of Acts in chapters 20 through 28. Acts picks up very neatly from where our letters leave off. There is a ton of detail here—so much so that I won't spend much time recounting it. The best thing to do is to pick up the book of Acts and read it. But I will say something first about the author of Acts. We need to work out how reliable his information is.

Almost all of the narrative in the final long section of the book of Acts is written in the first-person plural: "*we* did this, then *we* did that, then this happened to *us*, and *we* did this . . ."[2] What does this signal mean? Many scholars stand within a tradition of highly skeptical scholarship and think that this is a literary device meant to convey vividness. They are confident that Acts was written much later than the life of Paul and so it can't have been written by someone who was with Paul at the time of these events. If it was written some time after 100 CE, and Paul's journeys being described here took place in 52 and 54 CE, then an eyewitness would have waited a strangely long time and been very old by the time he actually got around to writing things up. The "we" is more likely to be a literary device. However, I find the reasons supporting this late date for Acts weak and the general accuracy of the book to be very high. It is not in a strict historical sequence, but the episodes are remarkably accurate when we compare them with Paul's accounts of the same events. My judgment is that this "we" material was written by someone who was part of Paul's circle and who accompanied him during this last difficult period in his life. The author was there and that is why he says "we."

The author slips some subtle clues about his identity into his story. Although the first-person narrative is dominant for the final phase of the book, we encounter a small patch earlier on in chapter 16, and nowhere else. In chapter 16, Paul and his missionary companions, Silas and Timothy, have set out from Galatia and ended up rather unexpectedly looking out across the Aegean Sea from the massive Roman port of Troas. (Troas is, incidentally, a huge, overgrown, and largely unexplored ruin to this day, and the harbor is still clearly visible. I ran around the inner harbor just for fun when I went there in 2015. Enormous broken columns still lie around its former docks.) Paul had a dream in Troas in which a "man of Macedonia" begged him to cross over to Europe to preach the gospel there. The text continues, "*we* got ready at once to leave for Macedonia, concluding that God had called *us* to preach the gospel to them" (Acts 16:10). This "we" continues until Paul leaves Philippi. The narrator is suggesting then that he was part of Paul's missionary party at this time, when it evangelized Philippi.

I have already talked about the delightful episode that unfolded at Philippi when Paul converted Lydia because it is a nice example of the network evangelism he used. But a further fascinating detail can now be added to that story. Paul, his anonymous companion, and the rest of his missionary team met Lydia outside the city at a Jewish place of prayer. Moreover, after her conversion, Paul and his companions continued to go to this Jewish location, Acts tells us (16:16). This all looks very Jewish to me. This hunch is confirmed when the "we-sections," as they are often called, resume in 20:5. The "we" begins again in Philippi. Paul is now on his final journey to Jerusalem. Acts notes his many companions—no less than seven other men. The book does not give the reason for this but we know it from Paul's letters. This group is carrying a load of gold coins to Jerusalem—Paul's great collection for the poor in that church! On arriving at Philippi, however, Paul sends his missionary party on ahead, while he and his anonymous companion celebrate the Passover together in Philippi, suggesting fairly directly that this anonymous figure was, like Paul, a messianic Jew.[3]

It seems likely then that this messianic Jew joined Paul's work in Troas and accompanied him to Philippi. We don't know if he converted in Troas or not, or if he simply met Paul there. But it seems that he stayed in Philippi until he rejoined Paul's roving missionary work during the apostle's last fateful journey to Jerusalem, which was a good twelve or thirteen years later. Paul evangelized Philippi in 39 CE and passed through again, for his last visit, on his final journey in 52 CE. So this figure may have stayed in the interim to help that small Christian community to thrive as one of its shepherds or servant-leaders (see Phil. 1:1).

If so, it is possible that he is named in Paul's letter to the Philippians, which was written just before Paul's final swing past the city. Is he Clement or Syzygus (literally "yoke-fellow"),[4] I wonder? We cannot be certain but it is an intriguing thought. More important than his name, however, is his Jewish identity. We know now why the book of Acts, and its companion Gospel, are so steeped in Jewish concerns, themes, and cadences. They were written by a Jew, although by no means by a typical Jew. This was a Jew who had met and worked alongside Paul, and who then accompanied him during his darkest hour.

Paul's last journey

I cannot improve upon the storyteller who wrote Acts. His last chapters on Paul's journey to Jerusalem and its aftermath are among the most gripping and vivid narratives preserved from all of antiquity. But some comments are in order. First, the story in brief.

Paul was heading back from his Aegean communities to Jerusalem in the spring of 52 CE with a large collection of money, as he had promised at the important conference that took place over the winter of 49–50 CE. Further imprisonments, evangelism, and court cases had delayed its collection. Originally, Paul did not want to accompany it himself since he planned to head to virgin territories for more missionary work, most notably to Spain, the farthest reaches of the empire. But the irruption of the Enemies into his churches told him that something had gone badly wrong back home. So he knew he had to delay his further work until he had traveled again to Jerusalem, delivered the collection, and argued once more, if necessary, for the legitimacy of his revolutionary approach to mission.

After leaving from Corinth for Jerusalem Paul looped up through Macedonia and then down the eastern coast of the Aegean, stopping in the towns of Troas, Assos, Mitylene, and Miletus, and then on the islands of Cos and Rhodes. This route makes as much sense as someone living in Miami wanting to visit New York and deciding to drive there by way of Dallas, until we realize that this diversion allowed him to steady most of his churches against the seductions of his Enemies as he headed back to the holy city. That he didn't visit

Galatia or mention the Galatians' participation in the collection in his letter to the Romans suggests that they may have been lost. Moreover, Acts subtly indicates that Ephesus was still far too dangerous for Paul to enter. He stopped south of Ephesus in the port of Miletus and sent for the Ephesian elders to travel down so that he could speak to them there rather than set foot in a city where he would be torn limb from limb on sight—almost a 300-mile journey there and back, taking at least three days of good sailing.[5] (Presumably the Christians in Ephesus were keeping a low profile too.)

Acts hints that after reaching Jerusalem, Paul's collection might have been rejected by the other leaders of the early church. Acts doesn't talk about the collection but it does speak of Paul bringing alms for the poor. These were deposited in the temple, which was not Paul's original intention, although this could be the author of Acts making a complicated church deal rather easier for his later readers to understand (21:24; 24:17). Whatever the details, Paul went to the temple, as any good Jew should, and was arrested after a riot. We now see him caught up in a series of arrests, imprisonments, and trials, which provide further insights into this repeated feature of his missionary work. Paul cleverly disrupted his trial before the Judean ruling council, the Sanhedrin, by appealing to the resurrection. The council was split in fierce partisanship on both sides of this question. He also avoided an assassination attempt and was sent by armed guard from Jerusalem to Caesarea, a coastal city that was the seat of the Roman governor.

At this time the governor was Felix, who is notorious for his stupidity and corruption in all the ancient histories that mention him.[6] Acts says that Felix held a hearing about Paul and then left him languishing in jail, hoping for a bribe, which seems completely in character. And Paul had arrived in Jerusalem with a great deal of money. Unfortunately, he had given it all to the poor, and the early church was either unwilling or unable to bail him out. So Paul languished in jail until Felix's replacement, who arrived in 54 or 55 CE, roughly two years later.

Felix was recalled to Rome at this time to face corruption charges, but his older brother, Pallas, was one of the most powerful men in the empire and so Felix escaped with a warning. At Paul's end of things, in Judea, a much more competent governor called Festus arrived. Festus tried Paul again, and during the course of the trial Paul appealed to the judgment of the Roman emperor. Paul was a Roman citizen and technically a citizen of the city of Rome, so he was allowed to make this appeal. Governors did not necessarily have to honor them, but Festus seems to have been an upstanding fellow, so Paul was duly sent to Rome.

Paul's voyage was an arduous one. It was late in the year, and seafaring in ancient vessels on the Mediterranean was much riskier during the fall and the winter. South of Cyprus his ship was caught in a sudden and terrible storm. It tried to stabilize itself with a sea anchor because ultimately the sailors feared being destroyed on the coast of what is present-day Tunisia. Its massive cliffs and rocks were a graveyard for scores of ships, old and new. Fortunately for Paul's vessel it ran aground on Malta—a near-miraculous occurrence, because a couple of miles on either side it was open sea and then the Tunisian cliffs. The ship was destroyed and the voyage interrupted, so Paul and his companions, both Christian and military, wintered on the island and then set off for Rome the following spring.

Acts finishes its account by documenting the calmness of Paul's arrival in Rome. There was no opposition apparent there—something the book goes out of its way to emphasize, suggesting that the author knew all about Paul's Judean enemies—and both Jews and pagans were open to hearing Paul proclaim the gospel as people visited him in his captivity. This went on for two years and then the book closes. But we are left with little doubt that after this period of time Paul's appeal failed and he was executed. This was particularly clear when he made a speech to the elders of the Ephesian church whom he had met at Miletus at the start of his dramatic final journey to Jerusalem. They were grief-stricken, we read, when he said, "I know that you will never see my face again" (Acts 20:25). At that point in the story this statement is innocent enough. It suggests that Paul will head so far away on mission work that a return to the area will be impossible. But in retrospect we see that the author has presaged Paul's death. As the prophet Agabus also warned him later in his journey (21:10–11), he had, like Jesus, been bound hand and foot by the inhabitants of Jerusalem and handed over to the pagans to be executed.

We lose sight of Paul in 57 CE as he preached "without hindrance" from his house arrest in Rome. And I can't help wondering if the astonishing growth in the Roman church that took place up to the persecution of "myriads" of Christians in 65, as recorded by Tacitus in *Annals* 15.54, was partly due to this introduction of the revolutionary and highly flexible Pauline missionary system into the area. We can assume, however, that in 57 or 58 CE Paul was executed. He was probably beheaded, which was the quick, clean death appropriate for a Roman citizen. If this process was not honored, however, then he may have died in the arena, like so many Christians in Rome did after him.

Two things are worth emphasizing as we bid Paul's life farewell.

The last virtues

When Paul first set off for Jerusalem in the spring of 52 CE with his posse of companions wearing belts of gold, he never dreamed that from the middle of that year through to 57 he would be incarcerated. At the height of his missionary powers, as he was about to open up a major new front in Spain for the growth of God's kingdom, he was to be locked up and locked down for five years, after which his career would be completely halted by execution. It is hard to comprehend the frustration and anger he might have felt toward his captors, his fellow Christians, and perhaps even toward God. What was God thinking?! But God did have other ideas.

Paul saw himself as a church-planter. God saw him as a practical theologian. The letters Paul had written to his struggling communities were to become one of the most important and influential literary legacies in human history. His influence would be vast—and yet Paul had no idea at the time that this was what would happen when he was writing the letters, grieving and praying over his churches, or thinking later during long years in prison about what the point of his life was. "How unsearchable his ways," he might have exclaimed had he known this.

This long incarceration and final execution also wrote martyrdom into the church's definition of leadership. Paul's faithfulness and courage must have impressed if not chastened the other leaders of the early church. He had endured a great deal and then died for his Lord—more than most of them had yet done, although several would eventually join him. Paul's martyrdom would have sealed the sincerity and power of his mission in his own blood. Moreover, it wrote the importance of being prepared to die into the church's leadership manual. And embracing this narrative would prove crucial to the survival of the church during the centuries that followed (and it still does). Paul, like Jesus, modeled a willingness to die on behalf of God, which meant a willingness to face down charges and trials, to endure imprisonments, and to refuse to be frightened by death, all the while eschewing the weapons of the world. Paul no longer killed for God; but he had learned that he needed to be willing to be killed for God. It is this type of leadership and this narrative that allows minority Jewish and Christian groups to continue to survive in the face of acute pressures from the powers that rule pagan-majority cultures. Church leaders must be prepared to stand firm whatever the cost inflicted on them— the story of the martyr. This is Political Survival 101. The church remembered Paul as someone who would endure prison, which meant enduring arrest, intimidation, interrogation, trial, and the threat of punishment. In so doing it was equipped to survive everything the Roman empire, and every other empire, could fling at it.

Furthermore, we never see the importance of the Christian virtue of faithfulness more than we do in Paul's long final imprisonment, and we never see more than here the way it is grounded in the faithfulness of Jesus himself. Paul never expected that he had to summon up this fidelity—this courage and trust and superhuman endurance—from his own meager fleshly resources. This had to be the gift of God, and all gifts of God ultimately come through Jesus, the great gift from God, and from their Spirit. We can be faithful ultimately only because he has been faithful, and yet because he has been faithful we can be faithful to an extraordinary degree. This is the final theological lesson we see figuring forth from Paul's final biographical chapter. And with these last realizations—somewhat bitter because we have learned them at great cost to Paul—our journey through his extraordinary life is over.

Questions

‣ Why is the long final section of Acts (chapters 20–28), which describes Paul's last journeys, written in the first person, with frequent uses of "we"?

‣ Can we detect further clues in the story concerning the identity of this figure?

‣ What happened to Paul during his journey to Jerusalem, and just after his arrival? Where did he end up, and when?

‣ What clues in the story suggest that Paul was executed shortly after it finishes?

‣ What was Paul probably feeling and thinking during his long incarceration?

‣ What was his most important activity and impact on the church?

‣ What does this teach us about how much we know about the significance of our lives, and about how God works?

‣ What does this final challenging part of Paul's life teach us about church leadership?

‣ Where did Paul get his astonishing faithfulness from?

Conclusions

This book has traced Paul's journey, which covered an astonishing distance in a day when people traveled mainly by walking or by hitching rides in small flimsy wooden ships. Paul was dedicated! But while we have followed his journey through space and time we have also tracked the journey he undertook in his thinking as he learned how to establish and to maintain Christian communities. I have traced out these intertwined journeys here because of my deep conviction that we still have a lot to learn from this outstanding missionary and practical theologian.

We have learned from Paul about God. We've learned first about how we learn about God. The truth about God is in the hands of God! It is revealed definitively, moreover, both in and by Jesus. The doctrine of the Trinity ultimately explains this approach to truth since the Spirit discloses the truth about Jesus to us wherever we are. But the Trinity opens up into a series of fascinating insights into people. We have learned that we, made in the image of the triune God, are relational, loving, and covenantal. This is God's will for us and for our behavior—a certain way of relating—while God's ultimate plan for the universe is to gather us all up into a joyful play of communion together.

It is this divine reality and accompanying ethic that lies behind the diversity we see in the early church. Jews committed to Jesus and pagans converted to him coexisted within a common loving relational pattern that was nevertheless open to their cultural differences. The church lives out of its resurrected location, beyond many of the structures shaping our current life in the flesh. This allows God's will to be expressed and obeyed diversely among different people. However, this is no flight from bodies. Our present bodies of flesh experience the empowerment of a resurrected mind and the pressure of a God who draws us ceaselessly into loving relationality.

We discovered quickly, however, that Paul's development of these lofty theological insights was supremely practical. A relational God reaches out to include those who have not yet heard about God's gift of life and fellowship in Jesus, and here the means is the end. People are included relationally. We have seen Paul networking deftly between communities and opportunities, playing missionary "snakes and ladders" around the northeastern quadrant of the Mediterranean Sea. And this was no colonial mission. It was a sensitive and incarnational outreach. We have seen in Thessalonica how Paul worked alongside his poor converts, as one of them, and in Philippi, with Lydia, how he initiated friendships across difficult social barriers. After he had converted his new friends, Paul called them to live in communities of loving mutuality. They were to imitate his ways and the behavior of his leaders, and to pursue virtuous lives. We have seen this sequence of community establishment and community nurture in the first letters he wrote, 1 and 2 Thessalonians, which come from a remarkably early period in the church's history, around 40 CE.

Paul passed into shadow after his missions in Athens and Corinth, the cities he evangelized after Thessalonica and Berea—a time we infer was a long, hard, and largely fruitless struggle. He returned to view seven years later in the Roman province of Asia where he is in prison. Paul's message was generally inflammatory enough to cause local disturbances. Jews objected to his inclusion of pagans in the Age to Come and to their rather un-Jewish way of life. Pagans objected to his denunciation of temples and idols. Paul wrote three letters from this particular imprisonment, in Apamea, just to the east of the Lycus valley: the letter we know as "Ephesians" was most likely sent originally to the Laodiceans; Colossians addressed a small Pauline community founded by proxy in the city of Colossae; and Philemon exhorted a member of the Colossian church to receive his troubled slave, Onesimus or "Handy," back with kindness. These fascinating texts shed light on what it was like to endure an ancient imprisonment. They open up a window on the challenge of navigating slavery. And amidst these practical local challenges, the nature of Christian community comes more sharply into view. Christian communities are novel—something new under the sun—so it is hard to know sometimes exactly how to describe them. Ephesians articulates how this spreading network of diverse but overlapping communities is helpfully understood as a body. Like a body, as ancient people understood them, it has various diverse members but a deeply unified nature and spirit. We also see in these letters how the emerging early church can be thought of as a city—a Christian city—that rises up within a pagan land. It has its own distinct way of life.

The blueprint for building the Christian city continued to unfold at Corinth, although the Corinthian community's diversity tested the quality of Paul's construction. We learned from 1 Corinthians that the partisanship and rivalry endemic to pagan culture were present within the church. Its members were harsh with one another, some of its relatively wealthy members were intellectually pretentious, and everyone was having trouble navigating Paul's instructions concerning appropriate and inappropriate sexual activity. In the light of these struggles we learned how important leadership was to a successful Pauline community—Christian leadership. We learned, moreover, that Christian leadership has a distinctive mode. Such leaders abandon any perceived advantages in status they might have to get alongside different community members in just the way they get alongside people to befriend and to convert them in the first place. Christian leaders build bridges and span divides although they court vulnerability by doing so. This is not leadership as the pagan world viewed it, hence the difficulties some of the Corinthians had in recognizing their real leaders and copying them. But without this type of leader it is clear that the Christian city as Paul built it will struggle. We also saw at Corinth, from 2 Corinthians, how the Christian city is in charge of its own business. It has its own economy, an economy of giving, and it has its own legal process. It resolves its own disputes, and in a restorative fashion. By the end of this sequence of letters we gained a clear picture of what the Christian city looks like. We could see clearly both its structure and some of its key challenges.

A significant shift in Paul's journey then took place. Previously Paul had been on a literal physical journey planting and then nurturing communities. His main problems had been moderating their internal problems. But now we encounter a danger of a different sort and from farther afield. Paul was attacked by formidable messianic Jewish militants who rejected his flexible approach to the conversion of pagans—the Enemies! They posed a deadly challenge.

Paul responded as best he could. He defended himself in court, wrote letters, collected money, exhorted his communities to stand firm, and resolved to travel to Jerusalem to have another meeting with the other leaders of the early church—a torrid one if necessary. Galatians, Philippians, and Romans all attest to different moments in this struggle. These letters thereby reveal something we have not seen much of thus far: Paul's ongoing care for Jews and for Judaism. The Enemies challenged Paul to articulate his view of his own people more clearly.

It is easy for Paul's later readers to lose their way in this material. A trap lurks here for the unwary in the passages that develop a justification opposition. But once the distinction between a covenant and a contract has been grasped—between an unconditional gospel and conditional religion—we can see that these passages oppose Paul's gospel to the religion of his Enemies. They say nothing more, and nothing less, than this. Nestling alongside these polemical texts, we read as nowhere else of Israel's past, present, and future as Paul understood them in the light of Jesus. The Jews, his people, are the tree trunk into which his later pagan communities are grafted as unnatural branches are cut into the trunks of ancient olive trees. Hence Israel has a privileged, precious, and irrevocable history and destiny, and this despite the current hostility of some Jews to Jesus. The love of God will triumph over their folly, as it will implicitly triumph over all human stupidity.

This final challenge effectively closed Paul's ministry. He was arrested during his journey to Jerusalem and incarcerated, as a companion on the journey helpfully recounts for us in the book of Acts. Long imprisonments in Judea and in Rome followed, punctuated only by dangerous travel and corrupt trials. Paul's life ended shortly after the book of Acts closes, with his execution. But in this final tragic period in Paul's life, when he was either held stationary or forced to travel against his will, we see the importance of steadfast faithfulness and of the virtues of the martyr. It is clearer than ever from this period in his life that Christian faithfulness in this sense—a faithfulness willing to endure long incarceration and death—originates from the preeminently faithful one, Jesus himself.

We also learn more from this period about the inscrutable ways of God. Paul, the preeminent missionary, must have been deeply frustrated by his final incarceration. Unbeknownst to him, however, his legacy would live on in his letters, which would find their way into the heart of the New Testament and become one of the most influential literary collections in human history.

The Pauline gospel that we see emerging from these haphazard communiqués to various struggling Christians in the first century CE is a marvelous thing. It journeys into unnoticed corners of the world to meet and to make friends. It plants and builds the Christian city, and it defends this city against its religious assailants, whether those come from without or within. May we be brave enough now to follow Paul's example and to set out on this journey ourselves.

Notes

Notes to the Introduction

1. Romans, 1 Corinthians, 2 Corinthians, Galatians, Ephesians, Philippians, Colossians, 1 Thessalonians, 2 Thessalonians, 1 Timothy, 2 Timothy, Titus, and Philemon.

2. Few people grasp the deep interconnectedness of thought, activity, and story better than Stanley Hauerwas. See especially his memoir, *Hannah's Child: A Theologian's Memoir* (Grand Rapids: Eerdmans, 2012).

3. I have tried to supply a definitive biographical framework for Paul's life based solely on the evidence of his letters in my *Framing Paul: An Epistolary Biography* (Grand Rapids: Eerdmans, 2014), and I am still reasonably confident that it holds good. Further key chronological analyses and detailed arguments can be found there. My analysis of the evidence in Acts, *Depicting Paul*, is forthcoming (Grand Rapids: Eerdmans).

4. A charming and accurate account of the structure of Acts that emphasizes its composition in strips, or "panels" as he puts it, is provided by my doctoral supervisor, Richard Longenecker: see his "Acts," in *The Expositor's Bible Commentary with the New International Version: Acts*, ed. F. E. Gaebelein (Grand Rapids: Zondervan, 1995).

5. Paul makes five visits to Jerusalem in Acts: (1) in 9:26-30 ("many days" after his conversion); (2) 11:30 (taking money for famine relief); (3) 15:2-30 (an important meeting to discuss the terms of pagan inclusion in the community); (4) 18:22a (an innocuous and inexplicable visit as Paul has just arrived in Ephesus and seems to travel straight back there; he also takes a Nazirite vow: see v. 18b); and (5) 20:1-21:17 (Paul's final fateful visit, during which he also takes a Nazirite vow, this time more understandably: see 21:20-26).

My research suggests that visit 2 is an echo of 3; visit 3 describes the content of the meeting most thoroughly; but this meeting took place historically during visit 4. Visits 2, 3, and 4 in Acts all denote the same visit and belong together.

Paul describes visit 1 himself in Gal. 1:18-24; visit 2, 3, and 4 in 2:1-10; the events just preceding this visit, described in Acts 15:1–2, are described by Paul in Gal. 2:11–14 (so it is often unnoticed, but Acts is right on the money here); and Paul anticipates visit 5 in 1 Cor. 16:4 and Rom. 15:25–32, anticipating its danger there as well.

6. Acts describes Paul's mission in Athens in 17:15–34. He leaves Silas and Timothy behind in Berea (v. 14); and they rejoin Paul when he has left Athens and gone on to Corinth (18:5). The letters Paul wrote at this time from Athens, however—1 and 2 Thessalonians—suggest that Silas and Timothy were with him there: see esp. 1 Thess. 1:1 and 2 Thess. 1:1 (and see also 1 Thess. 3:2 and 6, which describe a journey by Timothy from Athens to Thessalonica and back again); and this is a strong implication of 2 Cor. 1:19 as well. Loveday Alexander elegantly describes the way Acts invokes an echo of Socrates in her essay "Acts and Ancient Intellectual Biography," in *Acts in Its Literary Context* (London: T & T Clark International [Continuum], 2006), 43–68, esp. 62–68.

7. The author of Acts slips into a first-person way of speaking toward the end of the book, using "I" and "we" and suggesting that he was there at the time. This way of speaking occurs first in a small section of text centered on Philippi, in 16:10–17. Then it resumes in 20:6, again at Philippi, and continues pretty much through the end of the book in chapter 28. The presence of a companion and eyewitness is not the only possible reading of this data, but I judge that, in view of the author's stated purposes (see Luke 1:1–4), and accuracy, it is the most likely. We revisit this judgment in chapter fourteen.

8. Caligula literally means "little boots," the nickname the Roman military gave him when he was a child and played in their camps dressed up as a soldier.

Notes to Chapter One

1. Scholars often question these, but I have no strong reasons for doing so.

2. The whole ancient area that is now western Turkey was dotted with Jewish emigré communities who had been drawn to its prosperous farming and trade. Alternatively, they might have been proselytizing in Cilicia after spending time back in Judea. See Matt. 23:15. The possibility that Pharisees traveled outside Judea and proselytized before the destruction of the temple in 70 CE is controversial. However, this evidence supports the hint in Matthew's Gospel that they did.

3. See 1 Cor. 15:9; Gal. 1:13; see also Acts 8:1, 3; 9:1–3.

4. Scholars sometimes debate whether to name this event a "conversion" or a "call." Conversion signifies a dramatic change and shift but has the danger of suggesting that Paul abandoned Judaism and converted to another religion altogether (i.e., to what would eventually become known as Christianity). This implication is both unnecessary and unfortunate. Paul refers to this event himself as a call (see Gal. 1:15), alluding to the prophetic calls that stud the Jewish Scriptures. He refers especially to Jeremiah's call to be a prophet to the pagan nations and there is certainly a truth here. Paul was called to an unusual constituency, the pagans. But this word may undersell the dramatic shift that took place in his life. We wouldn't normally say that someone was called when he or she

joined a sect he or she was previously persecuting. Most people would speak of this as a conversion. Consequently, I have stuck with that word for Paul but would ask my readers to bear in mind that this denotes a conversion to a distinctive religious movement but not a conversion away from Judaism. Paul converts in the sense that we might speak of someone converting from Presbyterianism to Catholicism. He or she is still a Christian.

5. The legal basis for this mission has been queried. But as a representative of the Judean hierarchy Paul would have had a degree of authority over the Jewish communities in foreign cities, which would have been highly organized and regulated internally. This is how ancient cities worked.

6. Putting things a little more technically we would say that material is introduced by people. Language (etc.) is involved. See 1 Cor. 15:1–8, esp. vv. 3–5: "For what I received I passed on to you as of first importance: that Christ died for our sins according to the Scriptures, that he was buried, that he was raised on the third day according to the Scriptures, and that he appeared to Cephas, and then to the Twelve." But the pressure of conviction comes from God as Paul acknowledges clearly in 1 Thess. 2:13: "we also thank God continually because, when you received the word of God, which you heard from us, you accepted it not as a human word, but as it actually is, the word of God, which is indeed at work in you who believe."

7. "For you have heard of my previous way of life in Judaism, how intensely I persecuted the church of God and tried to destroy it. I was advancing in Judaism beyond many of my own age among my people and was extremely zealous for the traditions of my fathers. But when God, who set me apart from my mother's womb and called me by his grace, was pleased to reveal his Son in me so that I might preach him among the Gentiles, my immediate response was not to consult any human being" (Gal. 1:13–16, NIV).

8. Doctrine, from the Latin *doctrina*, equates with the Greek *catechesis* and denotes an official body of teaching taught and learned.

9. I am referring to the "ecumenical" creeds: the Apostles' (second or third century); Nicene (325 CE); Constantinopolitan (381); and Chalcedonian creeds (451). They were called this because the entire church, through representative bishops, signed off on them unanimously.

10. I don't approve of labels for Pauline approaches because these often oversimplify and misrepresent. But they can provide a preliminary orientation provided this is not pressed too far. The approach I am urging here would be identified as "apocalyptic," an adjective drawn from the Greek words for the noun "revelation" and the verb "to reveal," *apokalypsis* and *apokalyptein* respectively. Literally these mean "unveiling" and "to unveil." Apocalyptic readers of Paul like me follow many of the views argued by the great US scholar of Paul J. Louis (Lou) Martyn. Martyn grasped and articulated this issue with great clarity. To be clear: an "apocalyptic" reading of Paul means for me that our starting point for understanding him must be the revelation to him by God of the truth concerning Jesus Christ, his Son. This was a revelation, and it revealed that Jesus was Son, Christ, and Lord. We call this apocalyptic because this is the word that Paul uses in his key text Gal. 1:15–16 that was quoted earlier when he describes this event.

11. There is a fundamental analogy here. But there is also a danger in pressing this too far. Many Christians do not retrace the specific and frequently very painful steps of the substance-abuser in recovery. So my general use of this analogy should not obscure the specifics of those particular struggles. Moreover, the moment of revelation need not be a memorable and literally single moment. It can be, but it can also be a journey with various important steps forward (and backward).

12. Krister Stendahl wrote a classic essay on how the interpretation of Paul is overly influenced by Augustine and Luther: "The Apostle Paul and the Introspective Conscience of the West," *Harvard Theological Review* 56, no. 3 (1963): 199–215. I agree with a great deal that he says in this essay, but, against him, I do still see similarities between Paul, Augustine, and Luther in this dynamic.

13. It is both fun and highly instructive to play around with ancient travel routes under different conditions with the computer program developed at Stanford under the initial supervision of Walter Scheidel. This will plot out all of Paul's probable routes, taking due account of variations in the mode of transport—foot, river, cart, etc.—time of year, and so on. See http://orbis.stanford.edu/.

14. It often cites John 3:16 and 10:10 here.

15. Rick Warren, *The Purpose Driven Life* (Grand Rapids: Zondervan, 2002).

Notes to Chapter Two

1. In Ps. 61:5 those who "revere/fear the name" are mentioned. The phrase "God-worshipers" renders *phoboumenoi ton theon* and *sebomenoi ton theon* as found in Acts, with similar phrases being attested in inscriptions in Asia Minor. I am following Paul Trebilco's recommended translation here; see his *Jewish Communities in Asia Minor* (Cambridge: Cambridge University Press, 1991). Cornelius is the stand-out example the book of Acts supplies for this person, but they crop up all over the place: see 10:1–48; also 13:26, 50; and 17:4, 17.

2. 2 Maccabees 7 details the way seven brothers endured torture at the hands of an evil Hellenistic king and his lackeys in the firm expectation of resurrection. It was probably written in the late second or first century BCE. This story was embellished into an entire book, complete with lurid details of the torture: 4 Maccabees. I date this book to just after the reign of Trajan, so in the early second century CE.

3. Alternatively, Paul's enemies in the city of Damascus were able to get the new governor to do what they wanted. The date of Paul's flight would still remain the same for this scenario.

4. More details can be found in my essay "An Anchor for Pauline Chronology: Paul's Flight from 'the Ethnarch of King Aretas' (2 Cor 11:32–33)," *Journal of Biblical Literature* 121, no. 2 (2002): 279–302.

5. It was on the cusp of the year, so it might have been in early 50 CE. Not much rides on this.

6. For a more technical discussion, see my article "Beyond the Torah at Antioch: The Probable Locus for Paul's Radical Transition," *Journal for the Study of Paul and His Letters* 4 (2014): 187–214. This can be supplemented by the evidence of Gal. 5:11. I argue the relevance of this in "Galatians 5.11: Evidence of an Early Law-Observant Mission by Paul?," *New Testament Studies* 57 (2011): 325–47.

7. Regionally Antioch/Antakya belongs to Syria. The residents of the modern city voted to join Turkey in 1939.

8. See also an insightful piece by Philip F. Esler, "Glossolalia and the Admission of Gentiles into the Early Christian Community," in *The First Christians in Their Social World: Social-Scientific Approaches to New Testament Interpretation* (London: Routledge, 1994), 37–51.

9. We must at all costs avoid introducing "Plan A–Plan B" thinking at this moment—the notion that Plan A, the Jewish plan, is supposed to fail, and that Plan B, Christianity, has always been the preferred option, and so, once it arrives, it displaces Plan A completely.

10. An important tradition of scholarship felt it had to go outside Jewish conceptual resources here. The Greco-Roman Mystery religions sometimes speak of someone being reborn by dying and rising within a god. See esp. the dramatic moment in Apuleius's *Golden Ass* when his protagonist has a mystical experience of rebirth after a key ritual, one part of which is being saturated by bull's blood. But Paul never uses the language of *rebirth*. (The fourth Gospel does.) He uses the language of death and resurrection, and of the Holy Spirit, which are all standard Jewish notions.

11. Specifically 5:12–8:13, 5:1–11, and 8:13–39 address the question of assurance on the Day of Judgment.

12. See 1 Cor. 10:14–22; 11:17–34.

13. "Then the LORD God formed a man [*adam*] from the dust of the ground [*adamah*] and breathed into his nostrils the breath of life, and the man became a living being."

14. What Paul claims has to be basically intelligible, so we need certain obvious questions answered: Do we just have a resurrected mind and not a resurrected body? Well, clearly, but how exactly does this work? We seem at present to be half resurrected. Do we ultimately need a body or not? (Paul thinks we do.) In the meantime, how does the resurrected mind from the Spirit relate to the mind he says is made of flesh? Do we have two minds at the same time? Answering these questions takes us into deep waters. I try to arrive at answers in my next book tentatively entitled *Pauline Dogmatics in Outline* (Grand Rapids: Eerdmans, forthcoming 2018).

15. This phrase is a reference back to a key motif in the previous argument in Galatians 3. It refers there primarily to Jesus's "fidelity" and not to ours. His coming has made our sonship possible.

16. Paul makes very similar claims in 1 Cor. 12:13 and Col. 3:11.

17. See here esp. T. F. Torrance's *Space, Time, and Incarnation* (Oxford: Oxford University Press, 1969).

18. Jeremy Begbie's work on the interface between theology and music is definitive: see his *Theology, Music, and Time* (Cambridge: Cambridge University Press, 2000); *Resounding Truth: Christian Wisdom in the World of Music* (Grand Rapids: Baker, 2007); and *Music, Modernity, and God: Essays in Listening* (Oxford: Oxford University Press, 2014).

19. I will supply some practical suggestions in my forthcoming *Pauline Dogmatics in Outline*.

Notes to Chapter Three

1. Rodney Stark, *The Rise of Christianity: A Sociologist Reconsiders History* (Princeton: Princeton University Press, 1996), 15.

2. A long list of names can be derived, but we don't know that much about most of the people involved—people such as Tychicus, Epaphras, Trophimus, Titus, Timothy, Sosipater, Jason, Aristarchus, Secundus, Priscilla and Aquila, Phoebe, Chloe, Evodia, Syntyche, Epaphroditus, and Luke.

Notes to Chapter Four

1. See Douglas A. Campbell, *Framing Paul: An Epistolary Biography* (Grand Rapids: Eerdmans, 2014), ch. 4, 190–253.

2. Some scholars think that the letter is pseudepigraphical or forged, and refers here to the fall of Jerusalem to the Romans in 70 CE. But at that time the temple was sacked, burned, and destroyed, not desecrated with a Roman god in the form of a statue.

3. James C. Scott, *Domination and the Arts of Resistance: Hidden Transcripts* (New Haven: Yale University Press, 1990).

4. This is not reversible. While the wealthy abandon their capital to live alongside the less wealthy, the missionary does not need to acquire capital in order to evangelize the wealthy. An arrival without wealth does not risk distorting the missionary-convert relationship because the missionary is not framing the potential convert in derogatory terms as needy and a victim. Note, a related problem can arise if the missionary accepts significant material support from the convert, which was an issue Paul faced at Corinth.

5. I have learned a lot in these respects from Jean Vanier, the founder of L'Arche, whom I had the honor of meeting once and studying at a conference at Duke. His engagements with the physically and mentally challenged members of his audiences were utterly authentic. Many of the words he spoke on this occasion are collected in a graceful volume of essays authored with Stanley Hauerwas, *Living Gently in a Violent World: The Prophetic Witness of Weakness* (Downers Grove, IL: InterVarsity, 2008).

Notes to Chapter Five

1. See only Rom. 1:3, 4, 9; 5:10; 8:3, 29, 32; 1 Cor. 1:9; 15:28; 2 Cor. 1:19; Gal. 1:6; 2:20; 4:4, 6; Eph. 4:13; Col. 1:13, 15; 1 Thess. 1:10.

2. "One Thing Remains," Jesus Culture, from the album *Come Away* (2010).

3. This is a reference to Roman imperial power, not to biological fatherhood. The emperor was *pater patriae*, which meant "the father of the country." The Roman family too was organized under the father who was the *pater familias*, "the father of the family." This title had significant legal implications. He literally possessed the power of life and death over all other family members.

4. It is a little unclear whether this is an admonition to avoid adultery or to avoid sexual relations with other men in the congregation, which would have been a possible ancient Greek interpretation of "brotherly love."

5. "As for the Jews, who had again increased so greatly that by reason of their multitude it would have been hard without raising a tumult to bar them from the city, he did not drive them out, but ordered them, while continuing their traditional mode of life, not to hold meetings. He also disbanded the clubs, which had been reintroduced by Gaius" (*Roman History* 60.6.6). See http://penelope.uchicago.edu/Thayer/e/roman/texts /cassius_dio/60*.html (accessed May 14, 2017).

6. I am assuming here that he converted in late 34 CE and his Corinthian mission ended in mid-42 after a mission there of eighteen months (Acts 18:11), an interval of seven years and some months.

Notes to Chapter Six

1. For details about the identification of this imprisonment, see my *Framing Paul: An Epistolary Biography* (Grand Rapids: Eerdmans, 2014), ch. 5, 254–338.

2. Letter 103/CIII to Sabinianus; http://www.bartleby.com/9/4/1103.html.

3. In particular, prisons are a theological crucible. They place tremendous pressure on many of our theological constructions—on our accounts of the other, of the atonement, of ethics and of church, and of surrounding society and its politics. They ask us if these constructions actually function and work in that toughest of environments, testing their coherence and strength. We should always ask the question: *Do my accounts of the gospel, or of ethics, or of the atonement, or of the church, work in prison?* If the answer is no, we need to reformulate them. But I am not going to detail that process here so much as presuppose it. Paul's authentic thinking took shape for much of the time in prison and works there. I treat the theological implications in my *Pauline Dogmatics in Outline*.

4. My *Pauline Dogmatics in Outline* presses on these questions and tries to generate some helpful solutions, staying within the parameters that Paul himself laid out.

5. *The Death of Peregrinus* 12.

6. Alternatively, they have been imprisoned themselves in the past. But if this

is the case, one might expect Paul to name both of them in these terms both times. (I endorsed this solution in my *Framing Paul*, but I tilt now toward the explanation made above.)

7. Alternatively, they might have made notes by the light of a lamp.

8. See Col. 4:18; Philem. 25; and possibly Eph. 6:23–24.

9. The story is told briefly at https://en.wikipedia.org/wiki/Letter_from_Birming ham_Jail. The text is available at http://abacus.bates.edu/admin/offices/dos/mlk/letter .html. See also Stephen B. Oates, *Let the Trumpet Sound: A Life of Martin Luther King, Jr.* (New York: HarperCollins, 1982), 222–30.

10. There is a related tradition of martyrological pieces. Christian activists facing execution pen their last wills and testaments in the manner of 2 Timothy.

11. Strictly speaking, in Paul's day the world was structured by empires and monarchies, although cities remained important political actors.

12. This is why Paul can speak of several different bodies that seem to be in different places, but assume that they all connect together—Jesus's ascended body, the body of Christ which is the church, and the body broken and shared in the Eucharist. Later theologians and scientists might speak of relational or "field" understanding of bodies here rather than a naïve and ultimately incorrect understanding of a body as a displacement of space, fixed in one place, with discrete boundaries.

Notes to Chapter Seven

1. We will talk about these shortly in chapter ten when we delve into the Jerusalem meeting and its aftermath more deeply.

2. See 1 Cor. 1:11; see also 16:17.

3. His only other major success in a synagogue was in Berea, a small town just south of Thessalonica.

4. Scholars debate the exact percentages and differences here, but this analysis, leaning very broadly on the work of Justin J. Meggitt, should convey a basic sense of the situation; see his *Paul, Poverty and Survival* (Edinburgh: T & T Clark, 1998). For those who want to investigate things further, perhaps begin with Steven J. Friesen, "Poverty in Pauline Studies: Beyond the So-called New Consensus," *Journal for the Study of the New Testament* 26 (2004): 323–61, who nuances Meggitt's description.

5. (1) Chapters 1–4 (beginning from 1:10); (2) chapters 5–7 (partly excepting 6:1–11); (3) chapters 8–10; (4) chapters 11–14; and (5) chapter 15, although this is a little shorter than the preceding discussions (fifty-eight verses). Chapter 16 is part of what scholars would call the "letter frame," functioning as the letter ending, although it resumes important issues that were flagged in block 1 (chaps. 1–4). The letter opening, with the author, address, greeting, and thanksgiving paragraph that we typically find in a letter by Paul, is 1:1–9.

6. The appointment of Christian leaders by grace or sheer benefaction would have

further exacerbated tensions. Cultural leaders were not necessarily being graced with Christian leadership, and vice versa—so Stephanas (1 Cor. 16:15–16).

7. This tendency presumably also interacted especially unhelpfully with partisanship to exacerbate existing differences. Advocating theological differences became a matter of pride and superiority.

8. Some very important but difficult issues are raised here that I process in my forthcoming *Pauline Dogmatics in Outline*.

Notes to Chapter Eight

1. See the classic study by Peter Brown, *The Body and Society: Men, Women, and Sexual Renunciation in Early Christianity*, 2nd ed. (1988; New York: Columbia University Press, 2008).

2. See his classic book *The Mysticism of Paul the Apostle*, trans. W. Montgomery (1931; Baltimore: Johns Hopkins University Press, 1998), 193.

3. A delightfully learned but accessible account of sexual activity and gender construction is Helen Fisher's *Anatomy of Love: A Natural History of Mating, Marriage, and Why We Stray*, rev. ed. (1992; New York: W. W. Norton, 2016). She suggests these figures and provides directions for further reading.

4. The question whether this is compatible with the broader thrust of his theology as a whole does need to be addressed, but it is a complex one. See my more extensive discussions in *Pauline Dogmatics in Outline*.

5. There are usually a man and a woman involved, probably because that is the most common arrangement in our essentially primate construction. But cultures develop what a "man" and a "woman" are in a thousand and one ways. There are codes of dress, of speech, of social movement, of role—of everything. In New Guinea men must be clothed with a penis sheath made out of a gourd; the women must wear a string around their waists. Others must cover the back of their necks with a hairnet—and that is all. In other words, cultures code erotic zones diversely. So in Europe today most women are quite comfortable sunbathing at a beach topless. Few people in France, for example, give it a second thought. But such behavior causes horror on beaches in the USA. Topless women can be arrested. For further details, see Fisher's *Anatomy of Love*.

6. Stanley Hauerwas and Will Willimon articulate this insightfully in slightly different terms as a colony of resident aliens: see their *Resident Aliens: Life in the Christian Colony* (Nashville: Abingdon Press, 1989). Augustine's famous image of a Christian city conveys a stronger sense that this community organizes every aspect of itself. It writes its own constitution. This is developed especially in his monumental *City of God*, trans. Henry Bettenson (New York: Penguin Classics, 1984; reprint Penguin Books, 1987).

Notes to Chapter Nine

1. Somewhat curiously, Paul describes Christian leadership in the letter in two sections. But this turns out to be quite deliberate. The first section, spreading from chapter 2 through to chapter 6, describes how his followers can take pride in someone who looks as unimpressive outwardly as Paul does. The second section, from chapter 10 through chapter 12, responds more tartly to those who despise Paul as a fool, and are almost certainly partisans of his flashier rival, Apollos. It is here that Paul develops the motif of cunning, like Odysseus.

2. I am using "economy" here in its modern, not its ancient, sense. Economy comes originally from the Greek *oikonomia*, literally, law-of-the-household, which really means household organization and management. Economics in our modern sense is related to management but is now often taken to mean "the part of something that relates to money" (Merriam-Webster online, http://www.merriam-webster.com/dictionary/economics).

3. Christian communities may also not necessarily have a lot of material resources to give. However, they will often have cultural capital to share—things like literacy and virtues like self-control.

4. Expectations yes, conditions no. There is a fundamental and critical distinction here that we will discuss shortly in chapter eleven since Paul's enemies raised it.

5. This is nicely introduced by Howard Zehr, *The Little Book of Restorative Justice* (Intercourse, PA: Good Books, 2002); and Rupert Ross, *Returning to the Teachings: Exploring Aboriginal Justice*, rev. ed. (1996; Toronto: Penguin, 2006). A powerful biblical exposition is supplied by Christopher D. Marshall, who elaborates the parables of the Good Samaritan in relation to victim reintegration, and the Prodigal Son in relation to offender reintegration in *Compassionate Justice: An Interdisciplinary Dialogue with Two Gospel Parables on Law, Crime, and Restorative Justice* (Eugene, OR: Cascade, 2012); see also his *Beyond Retribution: A New Testament Vision for Justice, Crime, and Punishment* (Grand Rapids: Eerdmans, 2001).

Notes to Chapter Ten

1. See the infamous "paroxysm" of Acts 15:37-40.

2. Phil. 3:18: "I have said to you many times and now say to you in tears that many walk [and ask you to imitate them] who are enemies of the cross of Christ . . ."

3. (1) Paul has to defend himself against an alternative account of his relationship with the Jerusalem leaders in Gal. 1:12–2:14; (2) Acts suggests that his great collection of money brought for the poor within the community at Jerusalem was rejected and had to be offered in the temple instead, being used, among other things, to pay for several Nazirite vows (21:20–26; 24:17); and (3), if the letter of James is genuine, and I have no good reasons for thinking it isn't, the Enemies were working with James's letter.

4. This letter would have been read by his congregations in Ephesus, Hierapolis,

Laodicea, and Colossae, as the messengers carrying Galatians passed through those cities on the way from Corinth to Galatia in what is now inland Turkey.

5. The Athenian Christians, Bereans, and Thessalonians would have read this as it made its way to eastern Macedonia.

6. See chapter 3 of *Framing Paul*, 127–33, for more details concerning this reading.

7. Quotations, we know now, from his previous letter to Philippi.

8. This incident also allows us to date this trial precisely. According to a beautiful but fragmentary inscription that we can now view at Delphi in Greece, Gallio's one-year tenure as governor of the province of Achaia began on July 1st, 51 CE. Ordinarily Gallio's tenure would have ended on June 30th, 52, but he felt ill and left a little early, taking a sea cruise to try to cure his discomfort. We learn this from a letter written by his fellow adopted brother, Seneca. I estimate that Paul's trial took place at some point over the winter of 51–52 CE.

9. See 1:1–15; and 15:14–16:27.

10. See 12:1–13; 13:8–10; and 14:1–15:7.

11. Romans 13:1–7 is unique and has to be handled carefully. In my view this text contains a "hidden transcript," a feature expounded by James C. Scott in his classic analysis *Domination and the Arts of Resistance: Hidden Transcripts* that we have already noted. Superficially this paragraph allows Paul deniability. He has a very bad track record and is likely to be taken to court by the Enemies if he isn't arrested directly by the Romans in relation to some civic disturbance. At this moment "anything he has written may be used in evidence against him," so this passage could have proved critical to his defense as a fundamentally nonseditious, law-abiding citizen of the empire who said that people should pay their taxes. For those in the know, however, deliberately reading between the lines, and probably listening to these lines being read in a certain way, this was an ironic, even sarcastic, passage that said in some respects the opposite of what it suggested. (In the immortal words of Monty Python: "nudge nudge wink wink.") It was also a pompous passage whose opinion could be derided. (It was probably connected in some way with the position of the Enemies.) Instead, the emphasis falls on the verses that follow headlined by the statement, "you owe nothing to anyone except the obligation of loving one another" (13:8).

12. The Greek word *nomos* that I have translated "law" here could be translated as "sacred teaching/instruction" to better reflect the underlying Hebrew *torah*. But many translators like the legal emphasis of the translation "law," so we will use that for now. See W. D. Davies, "Law in First-Century Judaism" and "Reflections on Tradition: The 'Abot Revisited," in *Jewish and Pauline Studies* (London: SPCK, 1984), 3–48.

13. See Gal. 2:15–3:26ish; Phil. 3:2–4:3; Rom. 1:16–5:1 and 9:30–10:17. Faith language occurs elsewhere in Romans, although not the entire opposition, with the possible exception of 6:7–8, in 11:22–23; 12:3–8; ch. 14, *passim*; and 15:13; see also Gal. 5:5–6, 22.

14. Fragments of this language and material occur in Rom. 6:7–8; 1 Cor. 1:30 (with faith being discussed in ch. 2); 6:11; 2 Cor. 5:21; and Eph. 2:8–10—in another eight verses then, although the full opposition is only evident in Eph. 2:8–10. The full opposition

or even two of the distinctive terms interacting together are entirely absent from 1 and 2 Thessalonians, Colossians, and Philemon. Faith occurs in these letters in isolation.

15. See Gal. 3:6–4:7; 4:21–31; 6:16; Rom. 9:3–33.

16. In particular, 1 Corinthians 10 talks about the wilderness wanderings of the Hebrews on the way to the promised land, and 2 Corinthians 3 spends some time on Moses.

17. The word Paul uses here—in Greek *ekpeptōken*—is often translated unhelpfully as "fall to the ground" or "fail." But the verb can also mean fail in the sense of deviate, and careful attention to Paul's argument in context suggests that this meaning is most likely.

Notes to Chapter Eleven

1. Two matchless accounts of these dynamics are James B. Torrance, "Covenant or Contract: A Study of the Theological Background of Worship in Seventeenth-Century Scotland," *Scottish Journal of Theology* 23, no. 1 (1970): 51–76; and "The Contribution of McLeod Campbell to Scottish Theology," *Scottish Journal of Theology* 26, no. 3 (1973): 295–311.

2. It is also overly rationalistic, that is, a false account of human thinking and behaving. But we won't go any further down this rabbit-hole for now. More information can be found in Daniel Ariely's fascinating book, written in the tradition of the new "behavioral" economics, *Predictably Irrational: The Hidden Forces That Shape Our Decisions* (New York: Harper Collins, 2008). People are anything but perfectly rational, it seems.

3. I think a limited role for self-interest or egoism in our decision-making is fine, especially when we are thinking about the consequences of sin and why it is a good idea to avoid those. But a contract sets up a comprehensively self-centered situation. There is nothing else, and this seems wrong.

4. They had a more technical reason for insisting on this. Like the ancient Jewish philosopher Philo, they thought that circumcision of the foreskin of the penis literally cut "the evil impulse" off from people as well. This was the impulse living within that prompted people to sin. (It is a male-oriented argument.) Without circumcision people had no way of resisting sinful behavior. They would spiral inevitably into deeper and deeper sins at the behest of the evil impulse, and they would be judged unrighteous on the Day of Judgment and sentenced to death and/or hell. I explain all this further in my large book on this specific issue, *The Deliverance of God: An Apocalyptic Rereading of Justification in Paul* (Grand Rapids: Eerdmans, 2009).

5. The reasoning underlying these translation decisions is complex, so I need to refer any interested readers to my more technical discussions elsewhere. See my detailed treatment *The Deliverance of God*. The argument of this book—which runs to over a thousand pages—is summarized in my essays, "Beyond Justification in Paul: The Thesis of *The Deliverance of God*," *Scottish Journal of Theology* 65, no. 1 (2012): 90–104; and "An Apocalyptic Rereading of 'Justification' in Paul: Or, an Overview of the Argument of Douglas Campbell's *The Deliverance of God*—by Douglas Campbell," *Expository Times* 123, no. 8

(2012): 382–93. A very helpful collection of essays summarizing and analyzing this argument is Chris Tilling, ed., *Beyond Old and New Perspectives on Paul: Reflections on the Work of Douglas Campbell* (Eugene, OR: Cascade, 2014). The easiest way into this whole debate is my semi-biographical piece, "Covenant or Contract in the Interpretation of Paul," *Participatio: Journal of the Thomas F. Torrance Theological Fellowship*, Supp. Vol. 3: *A Tribute to James B. Torrance* (2014): 182–200, http://www.tftorrance.org/journal /SuppVol3115.pdf. Some briefer introductory treatments can also be found in my book *The Quest for Paul's Gospel: A Suggested Strategy* (London: T & T Clark [Continuum], 2005).

6. I have written on this issue a lot, but my clearest summary essay is "The Faithfulness of Jesus Christ in Romans 3:22," in *The Faith of Jesus Christ: Exegetical, Biblical, and Theological Studies*, ed. Michael F. Bird and Preston M. Sprinkle (Carlisle, UK: Paternoster, 2009), 57–71. See also my recent "Participation and Faith in Paul," in *"In Christ" in Paul: Explorations in Paul's Theology of Union and Participation*, ed. Michael J. Thate, Kevin J. Vanhoozer, and Constantine R. Campbell (Tübingen: Mohr/Siebeck, 2015), 37–60.

7. He talks the same way with "blood" and "obedience" and "death." Technically these are metonymic moves in which the part refers to the whole.

8. But, someone might ask, how do we become a Christian? Isn't that what faith is supposed to be about? It is important to realize that Paul is not answering that question here—what we might call the how-to of salvation. He does answer it in various other places, many of which we have already discussed. In all his letters, however, he answers the questions that he had to, and here he is trying to counter a gospel that is religious. The challenge at hand is a challenge to people who are already saved.

Notes to Chapter Twelve

1. We can still use it to describe Judaism in Paul's day "phenomenologically," in terms of what various Jews at the time thought about things.

2. Another important insight from the great Pauline scholar E. P. Sanders. It is introduced in his classic study *Paul and Palestinian Judaism* (Philadelphia: Fortress, 1977).

3. See 6:13b: "And though a tenth remains in the land, it will again be laid waste. But as the terebinth and oak leave stumps when they are cut down, so the holy seed will be the stump in the land" (NIV).

4. See Col. 4:10–11, where Paul says he is comforted by the assistance in the pagan mission of fellow-Jews Aristarchus, Mark, and Jesus/Justus. Their lifestyle during this missionary work is best summarized by 1 Cor. 9:19–23, esp. verse 21: "To those not having the law I became like one not having the law (though I am not free from God's law but am under Christ's law), so as to win those not having the law" (NIV).

5. See Acts 13:14–43; 16:3; 18:18; 20:6; 21:24, 26; and 2 Cor. 11:24.

6. This phrase is ambiguous in the Greek and much debated, but I suspect that this, or something close to it, is what it means.

7. Some of these debates are usefully collected in Willard M. Swartley, "The Bible and Slavery," in *Slavery, Sabbath, War, and Women: Case Issues in Biblical Interpretation* (Scottdale, PA: Herald Press, 1983), 31–64.

8. I think he also probably reflected a lot on this dynamic as well when Jews in various synagogues quoted the Scriptures to resist his fulfilling of his divine commission to preach salvation to the pagans, and to do so without making them convert to Judaism. This was all the work of the flesh and the evil Powers, not the work of Jesus and the Spirit.

9. This is a philosophical, not a legal conditional, of the form: if it is shaped like a horse, if it has black and white stripes, and if it is wandering the plains of Africa, then it is a zebra.

Notes to Chapter Thirteen

1. Rom. 11:26 is widely debated. But the immediate context suggests that Paul is not using the word "Israel" symbolically to refer to the church. "Ethnic" Israel must be in view in some sense, meaning Jews. The opening stages of this broad sweep of argument, in 9:6–26, suggest that converts from paganism could be in view as well. Paul quotes Hos. 2:23 and 1:10 there, which speak of "those who are not my people being called my people." As noted earlier, "Israel" is the Hebrew for "God's people." There are no difficulties to the suggestion that Paul can think of future Israel in the Age to Come in these inclusive terms. Everyone who is resurrected bears the image of the resurrected Jesus, who was a Jew (8:29). But this expanded use of the word "Israel" should still be understood in continuity with ethnic Israel or the Jews who live in the world of the flesh, including any unbelievers—"enemies of the gospel"—as the immediate context of 11:26 makes clear.

2. See Benjamin D. Gordon, "On the Sanctity of Mixtures and Branches: Two Halakic Sayings in Romans 11:16–24," *Journal of Biblical Literature* 135 (2016): 355–68.

3. We all handle some texts in the Bible. Whatever position we adopt here we will have to reinterpret biblical texts. There are explicit commitments to universalism in the Bible (see esp. 1 Tim. 2:1–4, esp. v. 4): "I urge, then, first of all, that petitions, prayers, intercession and thanksgiving be made for all people—for kings and all those in authority, that we may live peaceful and quiet lives in all godliness and holiness. This is good, and pleases God our Savior, who wants all people to be saved and to come to a knowledge of the truth." In fact, everything that has just been said about universalism positively is from the Bible. My hunch is that exclusion texts that can't be handled restoratively, in terms of a judgment process that evaluates rather than punishes, should be redeployed to warn us of the terrible consequences of sin, a phenomenon we constantly trivialize. It is just that the punishment for sin will be internal to the sin and not external. Sin is destructive in and of itself. We need to face this fact squarely and not to postpone or relocate it. A reinterpretation of some of the Bible's future punishment texts will help us to be more honest about the sins we are presently involved with.

4. A covenantal approach relies for its ethical pressure on an existing relationship

of love. Good behavior flows from this. Only contractual ethics likes to induce good behavior by promising rewards and threatening punishments. So we are not weakening our ethics by rejecting the possibility of a horrific future state for those who sin. We are strengthening our ethics as we do this. Perfect love drives out this sort of fear.

5. Recall that there will be a stringent accountability. An opening might even be created here, taking into account the dignity of personhood, for some type of purgatory. C. S. Lewis explores this with typical wit in *The Great Divorce* (1946; New York: HarperCollins, 2016).

Notes to Chapter Fourteen

1. Ultimately I am not convinced that Paul wrote 1 and 2 Timothy and Titus. But I think that these questions deserve careful consideration. They are by no means open-and-shut cases, as scholars on both sides sometimes think. My reasons for these judgments are laid out in "Locating Titus and 1 and 2 Timothy," chapter 6 in my *Framing Paul: An Epistolary Biography* (Grand Rapids: Eerdmans, 2014), 339–403. I would add that I think they are incredibly helpful and interesting texts. They tell us how Paul was read in the second century, and especially as his legacy was under threat of a takeover by radical variations of his gospel. These letters basically saved Paul from Marcion and the Gnostics for the Bible and for the church.

2. A small patch of "we" data begins in 16:10 as Paul trains his sights on Philippi, and then fades away, being gone by 16:40, when Paul and Silas leave Philippi. It enters the narrative again at 20:5, when Paul returns to Philippi at the start of his final journey to Jerusalem, and continues off and on essentially through the end of the book in 28:31.

3. Another possibility is that he was a converted God-worshiper. But the author knows the Jewish Scriptures so well, it is a little easier to suppose that he was simply Jewish from the get-go. He also shows from his knowledge of God-worshipers that he is familiar with Diaspora synagogues.

4. There might be some distant resonance here with one of Jesus's sayings found in Matt. 11:29–30: "Take my yoke upon you and learn from me, for I am gentle and humble in heart, and you will find rest for your souls. For my yoke is easy and my burden is light." If Paul is referring to a fellow messianic Jew, this name or characterization would have been apt.

5. There and back was a journey of 466 kilometers or 289.5 miles. See http://orbis .stanford.edu/ (accessed May 17, 2017).

6. For example, the reliable Roman historian Tacitus says in his *Annals*, "Not equally moderate [as Pallas] was his brother, surnamed Felix, who had for some time been governor of Judaea, and thought that he could do any evil act with impunity, backed up as he was by such power" (12.54). A sorry tale of incompetence and corruption ensues.

Works Cited

Alexander, Loveday C. A. "Acts and Ancient Intellectual Biography." In *Acts in Its Literary Context*, 43–68. London: T & T Clark International (Continuum), 2006.

Ariely, Dan. *Predictably Irrational: The Hidden Forces That Shape Our Decisions*. New York: Harper Collins, 2008.

Augustine. *City of God*. Translated by Henry Bettenson. New York: Penguin Classics, 1984.

Begbie, Jeremy. *Music, Modernity, and God: Essays in Listening*. Oxford: Oxford University Press, 2014.

———. *Resounding Truth: Christian Wisdom in the World of Music*. Grand Rapids: Baker, 2007.

———. *Theology, Music, and Time*. Cambridge: Cambridge University Press, 2000.

Brown, Peter. *The Body and Society: Men, Women, and Sexual Renunciation in Early Christianity*. 2nd ed. 1988; New York: Columbia University Press, 2008.

Campbell, Douglas A. "An Anchor for Pauline Chronology: Paul's Flight from 'the Ethnarch of King Aretas' (2 Cor 11:32–33)." *Journal of Biblical Literature* 121, no. 2 (2002): 279–302.

———. "An Apocalyptic Rereading of 'Justification' in Paul: Or, an Overview of the Argument of Douglas Campbell's *The Deliverance of God*—by Douglas Campbell." *Expository Times* 123, no. 8 (2012): 382–93.

———. "Beyond Justification in Paul: The Thesis of *The Deliverance of God*." *Scottish Journal of Theology* 65, no. 1 (2012): 90–104.

———. "Beyond the Torah at Antioch: The Probable Locus for Paul's Radical Transition." *Journal for the Study of Paul and His Letters* 4 (2014): 187–214.

———. "Covenant or Contract in the Interpretation of Paul." In *Participatio: Journal of the Thomas F. Torrance Theological Fellowship*, Supp. Vol. 3: *A Tribute to James B. Torrance* (2014): 182–200. Available at: www.tftorrance.org/journal/SuppVol3115.pdf.

———. *The Deliverance of God: An Apocalyptic Rereading of Justification in Paul*. Grand Rapids: Eerdmans, 2009.

———. "The Faithfulness of Jesus Christ in Romans 3:22." In *The Faith of Jesus Christ: Exegetical, Biblical, and Theological Studies*, edited by Michael F. Bird and Preston M. Sprinkle, 57–71. Carlisle, UK: Paternoster, 2009.

———. *Framing Paul: An Epistolary Biography*. Grand Rapids: Eerdmans, 2014.

———. "Galatians 5.11: Evidence of an Early Law-Observant Mission by Paul?" *New Testament Studies* 57 (2011): 325–47.

———. "Participation and Faith in Paul." In *"In Christ" in Paul: Explorations in Paul's Theology of Union and Participation*, edited by Michael J. Thate, Kevin J. Vanhoozer, and Constantine R. Campbell, 37–60. Tübingen: Mohr/Siebeck, 2015.

———. *Pauline Dogmatics in Outline*. Grand Rapids: Eerdmans, forthcoming 2018.

———. *The Quest for Paul's Gospel: A Suggested Strategy*. London: T & T Clark International (Continuum), 2005.

Davies, W. D. "Law in First-Century Judaism" and "Reflections on Tradition: The 'Abot Revisited." In *Jewish and Pauline Studies*, 3–48. London: SPCK, 1984.

Esler, Philip F. "Glossolalia and the Admission of Gentiles into the Early Christian Community." In *The First Christians in Their Social World: Social-scientific Approaches to New Testament Interpretation*, 37–51. London: Routledge, 1994.

Fisher, Helen. *Anatomy of Love: A Natural History of Mating, Marriage, and Why We Stray*. Rev. ed. New York: W. W. Norton, 2016 (1992).

Friesen, Steven J. "Poverty in Pauline Studies: Beyond the So-called New Consensus." *Journal for the Study of the New Testament* 26 (2004): 323–61.

Gordon, Benjamin D. "On the Sanctity of Mixtures and Branches: Two Halakic Sayings in Romans 11:16–24." *Journal of Biblical Literature* 135 (2016): 355–68.

Hauerwas, Stanley. *Hannah's Child: A Theologian's Memoir*. Grand Rapids: Eerdmans, 2012.

Hauerwas, Stanley, and Jean Vanier. *Living Gently in a Violent World: The Prophetic Witness of Weakness*. Downers Grove, IL: InterVarsity, 2008.

Hauerwas, Stanley, and Will Willimon. *Resident Aliens: Life in the Christian Colony*. Nashville: Abingdon Press, 1989.

Lewis, C. S. *The Great Divorce*. 1946; New York: HarperCollins, 2016.

Longenecker, Richard. *The Expositor's Bible Commentary with the New International Version: Acts*. General editor, Frank E. Gaebelein. Grand Rapids: Zondervan, 1995.

Marshall, Christopher D. *Beyond Retribution: A New Testament Vision for Justice, Crime, and Punishment*. Grand Rapids: Eerdmans, 2001.

———. *Compassionate Justice: An Interdisciplinary Dialogue with Two Gospel Parables on Law, Crime and Restorative Justice*. Eugene, OR: Cascade, 2012.

Meggitt, Justin J. *Paul, Poverty and Survival*. Edinburgh: T & T Clark, 1998.

Oates, Stephen B. *Let the Trumpet Sound: A Life of Martin Luther King, Jr.* New York: HarperCollins, 1982.

Ross, Rupert. *Returning to the Teachings: Exploring Aboriginal Justice.* Rev. ed. Toronto: Penguin, 2006.

Sanders, E. P. *Paul and Palestinian Judaism.* Philadelphia: Fortress, 1977.

Schweitzer, Albert. *The Mysticism of Paul the Apostle.* Translated by W. Montgomery. 1931; Baltimore: Johns Hopkins University Press, 1998.

Scott, James C. *Domination and the Arts of Resistance: Hidden Transcripts.* New Haven: Yale University Press, 1990.

Stark, Rodney. *The Rise of Christianity: A Sociologist Reconsiders History.* Princeton: Princeton University Press, 1996.

Stendahl, Krister. "The Apostle Paul and the Introspective Conscience of the West." *Harvard Theological Review* 56, no. 3 (1963): 199–215.

Swartley, Willard M. *Slavery, Sabbath, War, and Women: Case Issues in Biblical Interpretation.* Scottdale, PA: Herald Press, 1983.

Tilling, C., ed. *Beyond Old and New Perspectives on Paul: Reflections on the Work of Douglas Campbell.* Eugene, OR: Cascade, 2014.

Torrance, James B. "Covenant or Contract: A Study of the Theological Background of Worship in Seventeenth-Century Scotland." *Scottish Journal of Theology* 23, no. 1 (1970): 51–76.

———. "The Contribution of McLeod Campbell to Scottish Theology." *Scottish Journal of Theology* 26, no. 3 (1973): 295–311.

Torrance, T. F. *Space, Time, and Incarnation.* Oxford: Oxford University Press, 1969.

Trebilco, Paul. *Jewish Communities in Asia Minor.* Cambridge: Cambridge University Press, 1991.

Warren, Rick. *The Purpose Driven Life.* Grand Rapids: Zondervan, 2002.

Zehr, Howard. *The Little Book of Restorative Justice.* Intercourse, PA: Good Books, 2002.

Index of Persons, Places, and Topics

Index of Scripture References